AN
IMPROBABLE
PIONEER

THE LETTERS OF

EDITH S. HOLDEN HEALY 1911-1950

COMMENTARY BY

Cathy Healy

Washakie Museum & Cultural Center
Legacy Collection

WORLAND, WYOMING

Book design: Marty Ittner
Cover design: Marty Ittner
Map art: Meagan Healy
Family tree art: Leah Stabenow and Marty Ittner

Library of Congress Cataloging-in-Publication Data

Healy, Cathy
An Improbable Pioneer: The Letters of Edith Holden Healy 1911-1950
Includes Index

ISBN 978-0-9897453-0-7 (paperback)
ISBN 978-0-9897453-1-4 (ebook)

Washakie Museum Legacy Collection
An imprint of Washakie Museum and Cultural Center

Washakie Museum and Cultural Center
2200 Big Horn Ave
Worland, WY 82401
Phone (307) 347-4102
www.washakiemuseum.org

Printed in the United States of America

"Most folks are about as happy as they want to be."

–Quote by Abraham Lincoln found in
Edith's collection in her handwriting

CONTENTS

Top: Edith's graduation picture from Boston Girls Latin School, 1897.
Above: Together with Alec, upper right, their two sons and their families in 1948:
Top row: Lorraine (Mrs. Alec, Jr.), Dan, Alec, Jr., Alec, Sr. and Martha (Mrs. Dan).
Children: Cathy, Tim, Diana, Alex III, and Mike.

PREFACE

"You'll be lucky to get Edith out of bed in the morning," her mother warned my grandfather before he married her.

My grandfather quickly learned that his wife enjoyed mornings in bed writing letters—mornings when she was the nexus of her world. My grandmother often signed her letters "Affec. Edith," or "Affectionately," sometimes "Love," "Lovingly," or "Love to All," and sometimes "Hastily." Her loops and dashed dots over the i's sprawled across pages and pages of small, plain white notepaper—big, fat letters dispatched from a small town in northern Wyoming called Worland.

By the time I started first grade, I was allowed to walk the two blocks down Culbertson Avenue alone to my grandparents' home. I can remember mornings sitting in the rocker while Edith sat propped up against the headboard writing letters on a white, wooden bed table. Her hair was swept up in elegant style, her makeup was in place, and her ruffled, dusty rose Neiman-Marcus bed jacket was as citified as the wardrobe she purchased for an amazing, career-girl doll kept handy for visiting granddaughters. Edith wasn't sick. She liked writing in bed until at least 10, sipping tea and cheered by the sun coming through the eastern and southern windows.

Edith Sampson Holden Healy wrote to friends and family about the weather, people she knew, local encounters, household frivolity, and trips around the United States, Europe, and Latin America. She also shared recipes. I remember a little pile cut out from magazines sitting within reach on her bed stand. She used letters as a vehicle for organizing projects with Wyoming and national women's groups she worked with, such as Colonial Dames, the Daughters of the American

Revolution (DAR), and the Philanthropic Educational Organization (PEO). Edith's management skills and enthusiasm landed her on the Girl Scouts' National Board of Directors.

Only a small portion of my grandmother's letters survives. Most important among them are Edith's letters from Buffalo, Wyoming, written to her widowed mother in 1911. That was the year Edith left her Beacon Street, Boston, home as the bride of Alexander Healy, following an eight-year courtship. Alexander Healy was a wealthy, Massachusetts Institute of Technology (MIT)-educated sheepman. In the American West, *sheepmen* are the sheep-raising counterpart of cattle ranchers.

They married one stormy Boston evening about a hundred years ago, and then honeymooned across a developing South still recovering from its own Civil War and on the cusp of World War I. These letters give a glimpse of everyday life during that era. They show a woman rare for her time and a couple who fashioned a loving and unusual marriage. Edith and Alec made remarkable choices together about what they wanted, how they wanted to achieve it, and what they thought and believed. Theirs was a life not commonly found among their contemporaries. Edith, in particular, whose decisions to become serious about her practice of the violin, to leave a sophisticated Boston for the untamed West, to travel the less traveled routes in Latin America, to adopt older children, and to become a major force in the Girl Scouts of America, led an extraordinary life.

Editorial Decisions

My impetus for this book was the desire to share the letters my grandmother wrote to her mother and friends. Almost no one read them because some were stored at her grandson Mike's in Worland, Wyoming, and others at her granddaughter Kay's in Bartlesville, Oklahoma. If anyone did access the letters, they soon abandoned the idea of reading them given the struggle to decipher her hurried handwriting on mouldering one hundred-year-old paper. After my father, Dan, and I transcribed the letters, I first wanted to see them available to the rest of Edith's family as an archive and then realized the zest of the writing along with the historical interest might give them a wider audience. Others agreed with that assessment, so here we are today.

Expanding to a wider audience required a greater degree of editorial explanation, fact-checking, and sometimes what amounted to information-based conjecture to produce a reasonably satisfying narrative. Discerning people's reasons for their decisions without their input combines research and art. I have indicated any swaying into art by using "maybe" and "probably" and the occasional "I think."

One of my more difficult decisions was whether to publish all of Edith's letters or to cull the letters based on interest. I sought advice from family and independent readers and was baffled to find that some readers most appreciated the very parts of letters others would cut and vice versa. In deciding to include all of Edith's letters, I have remained true to my original intent to produce a family archive. I also worked to make the book useful to historical researchers while still creating an enjoyable read for everyone.

When preparing a book of letters written in another century, the writer of course cannot provide context or answer questions or edit content and style for publication. So decisions that should be the letter writer's purview end up in the editor's lap. Let me explain what I did and why.

First is the issue of privacy. These letters were never meant for anyone but family and friends. Edith was an Edwardian lady and sensitive to the feelings of others. She would have cut her frank observations about people if editing the book herself. And Alec, a dignified, somewhat shy gentleman, would have been mortified that others (including his children and grandchildren) could see the letters he wrote to Edith's mother asking for her daughter's hand in marriage. Fortunately for Alec, his love letters to Edith must have been destroyed.

Second are issues of letters written early in life that tend to freeze the reader's perception of the writer on that subject and cannot show growth and change over a lifetime. Connected to that issue is recognizing that these letters were written in the context of another time. Edith's early observations about "Southern Negroes" make us grandchildren cringe, and we talked about editing them out. I decided that this book is in part a historical archive and that Edith needs to be understood in the context of her times. My own sense is that her thinking—she thought segregation contemptible—was ahead of her time, but she was still a product of her culture and her language sometimes bears this out.

There were other questions for the editor. Should I make alterations in Edith and Alec's writing for readability? Edith exuberantly filled her pages, leaving only a narrow margin on the left side, and when she ran out of paper but not words, she turned the paper sideways and filled up the remaining margin. She did not indent paragraphs or leave space between them. Instead, Edith left a longer space than usual after sentences that ended a paragraph. My editor argued for the addition of paragraphing, and I concurred.

Grammar was not a problem. Edith's English was impeccable, but sometimes her pen raced faster than time to put apostrophes in contractions. She didn't use periods after abbreviations, like Wyo., Mr., Mrs., Jr., as we do today. That was not an uncommon style from an earlier era in England, so Edith was likely comfortable with it. The first sometimes made reading difficult whereas the second never did. Contractions in; abbreviation periods out.

Occasionally Edith scratched out a word or phrase. If she'd been on a laptop, no one would ever have known, but with a pen, a change of mind is permanent. Because none of her scratched-out passages added information, I decided not to keep them.

Alec's letters were written deliberately, with well-defined margins, indented paragraphs, and all apostrophes in place. Nice.

Names

Patrick Healy, Sr., the patriarch of the Healy family, pronounced his last name, HAY-lee, which is the Old Irish pronunciation—he was from County Kerry in southwestern Ireland where the Old Irish language persisted the longest. Patrick, Jr., began to pronounce it HEAL-Lee, which is the English pronunciation.[1] Alec continued with Old Irish, as did Edith and their children. As their grandchildren moved to cities, they usually settled for the English pronunciation.

Do I call Alexander, "Alex," as he was known and as he signed his letters to Edith's mother, or do I call him by his nickname "Alec," as Edith did? (Alec is a Scottish nickname for Alexander.) I decided on "Alec."

No one in our family called the couple "Edith" and "Alec." Their four children called them "Mother" and "Father." Their two oldest grandchildren, Kay and Dick Bonine, called them "Gramma" and "Grandfather," but the Bonines moved to Miles City, Montana, and when they came back to visit, Edith had been renamed "Grammy." As one of the middle grandchildren in the pack of eight, Edith was

YOUNG EDITH

Edith and her violin, c. 1890, taken in celebration
of her performance with a symphony.

Edith's parents, CW and Elizabeth, were well-established 41-year-olds when she was born. They delighted in formal portraits of their youngest, who was adored by her parents, sister Mabel, nine years older, and Grandmother Harriet Harmon, whose other two grandchildren were older.

Grammy to me. Grandfather was always called Grandfather, as befits the tallest, most esteemed man in any gathering.

Another decision: What do I call Alexander Healy, Jr.? Friends and strangers called him simply "Alex." Edith refers to him both as "Alec, Jr." and "Alex, Jr." Within the family, he was called "Ike," reportedly because that's how his baby brother, Dan, mispronounced his name. His sister Helen says that he didn't like being called Ike, but likely that was when he was a teen. His son Tim doesn't remember a dislike of "Ike" and recalls people around Worland calling him Ike. I always called him Uncle Alec, so I settled on Alec, Jr.[2]

Mostly I call Dan by his given name, but sometimes I use "my father," especially when the account reaches the years when I was part of the events. At that point, I include myself more in the history.

Stories for Family Website

Alec was not a storyteller, and he confessed as much to Edward N. Wentworth in 1940, when Wentworth was researching his definitive history, *America's Sheep Trails: History, Personalities*. Alec told Wentworth, "I am sorry that I can't color up a good story to make it readable, but I have no gift in that direction."

Edith did have a gift for storytelling, as do others in the family. Many of the stories, facts, and photos that did not make it into *An Improbable Pioneer* can be seen on the website—www.improbable-pioneer.org—created in conjunction with the book's publisher, Washakie Museum and Cultural Center. The website includes recorded oral histories and video interviews, such as one with Aunt Helen. The website will be maintained as a living archive of the Edith and Alec Healy family.

Every one says that's a fine ride while the roads are in ordinary condition so Lynn will dare that when we come out later unless the elevator stops running but I can't imagine we should have gotten off at evening and driven over you now tho I only wonder I could think of could have stood it without yelling "I could cry again."

12th letter and end of journey.

My dear Mother,—

Well I am actually in Buffalo at last and I know you are anxious to hear all about it from the very beginning so I'll start there.

My last letter was from Sheridan saying it looked like rain and we didn't know whether we would be stuck there or not. Well it rained all night quite hard but it cleared in the morning so we started—

Six of us. Another girl and her husband two other fellows and Alec. and the chauffeur— It is, in ordinary weather and with ordinary roads a two hour and a quarter ride.

Mother, never in my whole life have I had any

April 25, 1911: Edith's exuberant recounting
of her hair-raising arrival in Buffalo.

Sweethearts: Alec, a reserved mining engineer, and Edith,
a serious violinist and lively leader of her friendship circles.

INTRODUCTION

"Theirs was an improbable marriage," Professor Holden Furber[3] always began when talking about his aunt and uncle. Educated at Harvard and Oxford, his deep, precise voice with its distinctive Bostonian accent charted the personal story of Edith Sampson Holden and Alexander Healy, weaving their tale into the broad sweep of American experience.

Edith and Alexander's forebears sacrificed to come to the New World and create better lives for themselves and their families—Edith was nine generations removed from immigrants who endured grim work and hunger in this foreign world, while Alec's father was an immigrant and his mother was the daughter of immigrants. The American story is woven by newcomers eventually marrying into the ranks of the longer-established families.

The Holdens were in the latter category. Edith lived at 876 Beacon Street, Boston, in a stately, four-story townhouse, the younger of two daughters of *Mayflower* descendant Charles William (CW) Holden and his wife Elizabeth Harmon Holden. The Holdens were not original Bostonians. They had moved to the city from Portland, Maine, where the Holdens and the Harmons had lived for generations—the Harmons since before 1679. When they died they were transported home to Portland to be buried with their families. These were the most Yankee of Yankees. All forebearers on both sides of the family sailed from England to Massachusetts (which then included Maine) within twenty-five years after the arrival of the *Mayflower* in 1620.

Besides having Maine[4] in common, the Holdens and the Harmons were craftsmen by occupation and exercised restraint by temperament. CW's grandfather, William Holden, was a soap boiler who made candle tallow and soap in his home—a dangerous, smelly occupation, with vats of boiling animal fats mixed with lye.

CW's father, Charles Holden, rose from printer's apprentice at fourteen to prominence as the editor and publisher of the *Eastern Argus*, a daily that was known as an outspoken politically liberal newspaper since its founding. An abolitionist and a member of the Maine legislature (intermittent terms in House and Senate, 1839–1871), who once served as acting governor, Charles was equally active in local affairs. For more than fifty years he was on Portland's School Committee. Charles also dedicated himself to arranging apprenticeships for craftsmen through the Maine Charitable Mechanic Association (founded in 1815) and to managing the Widows Wood Fund, a private charity that distributed fuel to widows in need. In later years, Charles was a director of two Portland banks, trustee and treasurer of the Gas Company, and treasurer of the Portland Railroad Company. Moreover, he continued to write and publish literary pieces, essays, and histories.

Back when he was a journeyman printer slotting up to two thousand wooden letters in the presses per hour, the *Eastern Argus* sent Charles to Boston to learn from the inventor how to add gears and power to the traditional wood-framed press, thus printing pages four times faster. Charles spent seven months in the big city and there fell in love. In the fall of 1830, he married Elizabeth Sampson, the eldest daughter of a bricklayer whose ambitious sons already were making their marks as traders in China and Alabama.

In Portland, the artistic Harmons specialized in the design and decoration of useful objects. Elizabeth's grandfather, Dominicus Harmon, originally a saddlemaker, expanded his skills and business by transforming unfinished sleighs and one-horse carriages into more

Harmon Family

Edith's grandfather, James Harmon, probably painted in his 30s,
and grandmother, Harriet, in studio portrait shot at about age 73 on a trip to
San Francisco. Harmons arrived in Maine before 1679.

Edith's mother, Elizabeth, at about 55, and her Uncle George, about 54.
Missing is Aunt Caroline, about 52 then.

refined vehicles. The Harmons dominated the carriage trade from Portland west to the southern border of the state.

Elizabeth's handsome father, James, started as a printer like Charles Holden, but practiced a more aesthetic brand of printing. James and a business partner printed, bound, and sold books, pamphlets, flyers, and newspapers in their shop downtown. In time, Elizabeth's younger brother became a watchmaker and opened a jewelry store in Portland with their brother-in-law, an optician. The families also shared a home.

CW Holden, the younger son, started on the same path as his father and older brother, George, joining the *Eastern Argus* as an apprentice printer in his early teens soon after his mother died in 1851. However, his father soon moved CW to the business office.

In 1854, when abolitionists formed the Republican Party and when the widowed Charles turned fifty, he sold his interest in the *Eastern Argus* and became increasingly involved in politics. Although George remained with the daily, eventually becoming editor and publisher of its weekly, *The Argus*, CW struck out for Boston in early 1857, soon after his nineteenth birthday.

The socially adept young man arrived with the advantage of family connections. CW's grandfather, Zephaniah Sampson, still lived in his home on Charter Street and his Uncle George R. Sampson possessed a worldwide reputation for his clipper ships, topping the Sampson male tradition of being shipbuilders and ship carpenters.

Uncle George's first born, Augustus N. Sampson, was only a few months younger than CW and was to marry the same year as CW, to a woman named Georgiana. The couples remained lifelong friends.

CW set to work. With entrepreneurial drive, natural sales ability, and tireless effort, CW advanced from clerking for a life insurance company to opening his own office, The Holden Agency, in 1868. The climb took him eleven years with a hiatus during the Civil War spent mastering sales dexterity in the sugar refining business.[5]

Despite CW's reputation of always being in a hurry, CW and Elizabeth, known as Charley and Lizzie when Portland schoolmates, didn't marry until they were twenty-six,[6] seven years after he moved to Boston.

As the eldest child, and a girl, in a family of five children—the last two died when they were babies—Elizabeth must have had many responsibilities, among them, the charge and care of the younger ones. Conceivably, she developed a capacity to both anchor and encourage the ones she loved.

Was Elizabeth's steadiness the characteristic that held jaunty CW's heart despite the temptations of the city girls in Boston? Was he captivated by Elizabeth's eyes, her thick, dark hair, and her diminutive frame? Was CW eager to marry and Elizabeth the one who hesitated, not wanting to leave her family and friends?

In sifting through records, a family marriage pattern begins to emerge. Edith and Alec would marry on April 3, 1911, forty-eight years plus one day from the day CW and Elizabeth wed in Portland on April 2, 1863. Coincidentally, Elizabeth died the night of her fifty-third wedding anniversary, with Edith by her side. The next day, the mourning daughter marked her sixth wedding anniversary alone.

A year after the Civil War ended, while CW was still in sugar, a transformational event occurred back home in Portland. The first Independence Day celebration after the war was set to be a glorious one. Perhaps the Holdens traveled home to Portland to be with their families for the big event. A fire, which started when a boy tossed a firecracker into a pile of wood shavings at a boat yard, destroyed all the shops, churches, newspapers, and manufacturing in downtown Portland and also many nearby homes. CW's father's home was one

Holden Family

HON. CHARLES HOLDEN.

Above: Edith's grandfather, Charles Holden, perhaps during his years in the Maine legislature. This photo accompanied his obituary in 1875. Right: The following year, Charles's two sons posed together, CW, 38, on the left, with Edith's Uncle George, 45. Missing is their sister, Ann Holden, then 34. George and Ann lived in Portland, Maine.

Elizabeth Holden, 32, with her first born, Mabel in 1870.
About ten years later, Mabel models with her with her little sister, Edith.

Elizabeth Holden and her daughters, c. 1891. Edith Sampson and
Mabel Harriet were given popular first names, while their middle
names were for family: Sampson was the maiden name of CW's
mother and Harriet was Elizabeth's mother's name.

Above: The Holden Agency occupied the entire Merchants Building with classic arches at 30 Congress Street in this c. 1900 photo. "Aways pushing CW" was known for his staff of 30 "young, zealous and never-tiring agents." Below: Elegant Beacon Street at its zenith, two miles from the Holdens' newer townhouse at 876 Beacon Street. Credit: The Bostonian Society.

San Francisco, 1892: CW took Elizabeth, Mabel, and Edith (not pictured)
to California for his first vacation in 35 years. The bearded man and seated woman
on the right are yet unknown.

of them. The flames missed the Harmon's home as the fire stopped a few blocks away. Fifteen hours later, ten thousand people—a third of the city population—were homeless. Close to 1,500 buildings were destroyed, and the fire went down in history as the United States' worst until the Great Chicago Fire five years later.

Portlanders assumed that all insurance offices would fail, but "within a few days, it was demonstrated by actual payments, that all but two of our insurance offices[7] were perfectly safe, and would meet every loss without quibble or delay," wrote John Neal later that year in a pamphlet, *Account of the Great Conflagration in Portland, July 4th & 5th, 1866*.

Portland was rebuilding "to larger enhancement than ever," reported Neal. Much of the restoration, however, took place without insurance monies as "very few of our people had more than a third or half [of the] insurance [they needed], while others, by hundreds, had no insurance at all."

CW became a believer. When he opened The Holden Agency two years later, he specialized in fire insurance, while also selling life insurance. Ultimately, his agency grew to become the largest miscellaneous insurance company in New England with spacious offices occupying a building in the financial district at the corner of Congress and Exchange streets. Along the way, CW helped found the New England Insurance Exchange and served as its president.

CW was also an inventor and co-filed for two mechanical inventions. A third patent, issued soon after his death, was co-filed under Edith's name.

The Holdens wanted the best for their two daughters and could afford to spoil them, which they did, but to a purpose. The girls were well educated, both academically and artistically. After thousands of hours of education, the girls internalized the disciplines of study and practice.

Mabel, nine years older than Edith, learned decorative arts with a bent toward delicate, meticulously-drawn and painted flowers that are clearly the result of diligent work with outstanding instructors. Mabel was slight and serious with the strikingly large dark and round Harmon eyes. In her photographs, Mabel looks as delicate as her flowers.

Dainty (5′ 2″), beautiful with lively hazel eyes and popular, Edith graduated from the most rigorous high school for women in the country, Boston Girls Latin. A serious violinist, Edith's parents gave her the means and will to succeed in a city attuned to music. CW and Elizabeth purchased two violins for Edith—an 1864 German-made violin and a 1740s French performance violin—and arranged lessons with the best instructors. A photo of Edith when she was eleven years old shows a wide-eyed child standing with her violin tucked under her chin.

Edith once told her son, Alec, Jr., about nervously auditioning as a child with a well-known violin teacher. The teacher listened to her and then said, "Your tone quality is no good, your approach is not very polished, and your lesson is Tuesday." It took the frightened girl a few minutes to realize that she had passed the test. In later years, Edith told her best friend, Cornelia Metz,[8] that shortly before her marriage, she had been offered a position as a violinist with a woman's symphony.

It was probably expected that Edith, like her sister Mabel, would marry a well-educated, financially successful Yankee. At thirty-one, Mabel wed William Harry Furber, a Bostonian and Harvard graduate whose mother was from Maine. Harry Furber maintained his family ties as a timber merchant by contracting logs from the far northern forests of Maine through Boston companies.

Unexpectedly, Edith married Alexander Healy and moved to his home in Buffalo, Wyoming, population seven hundred. Alexander Healy was enticingly exotic and, although he denied being a storyteller,

Patterson Family

Alec's Patterson grandparents, Alexander and Mary Fife, came from Clackmannan, Scotland, as did almost everyone on both sides. Because of the LDS churche's excellent genealogical records, the Patterson family is traced back to 1545.

Alec's mother, Mary Ann Patterson, about 15, perhaps five years before her marriage in 1876. Called simply, "Mary," she was the sixth of eleven children, all but two born in Utah.

he may have captivated Edith with precarious accounts of the time he hid under a bed in an Idaho cabin with his mother, brother, and sister while an Indian war party rode by or when his brother grabbed a rifle and rode out to end a standoff between cowboys and sheepmen during a time when cowboys were killing Healy sheep and menacing their sheepherders out on the open range.

In many ways, Alec was a proper catch. He was a tall (6'), erect, and handsome MIT graduate (Mining Engineering and Metallurgy, Class of 1903) with a father who was a financially successful entrepreneur and a mother who was socially prominent. Alec Healy was an eligible, marriageable commodity for any old-line New England family save for a double deal-breaker—he was the son of Irish Catholic and Scottish Mormon immigrants from Ogden, Utah.

Alec's mother was a Patterson, whose parents spoke with the rolled rrrrr's and soft vowels of the Highlands. It was there, to the dismay of her father's parents—a fisherman father and a coal mining mother—that Alexander Patterson, a coal miner himself, had accepted the Mormon religion in Clackmannan, across the firth from Edinburgh. Patterson's wife, Mary Fife, and her family also converted and the families immigrated together to Utah in 1851, just four years after Brigham Young led the first Mormons into the Salt Lake Valley.

It was an exhausting journey and a difficult life afterwards. Their oldest child died in St. Louis; another child was born on the wagon train, which arrived in Salt Lake in the middle of winter. Alec's mother, Mary Ann Patterson, was a middle child in a family of thirteen.[9] A brunette beauty who came to elegance naturally, Mary Ann refused to talk in later years about her early life, once telling her grandson, Dan, "All I can remember is always being hungry and always being cold."

Mary Ann's father mined limestone for the Temple and then

turned to farming. He was an inventive man, introducing alfalfa to the Ogden area and buying the first thresher for his farm.

Alec's father, Patrick ("Patsy") Healy, was a dark-haired Irish Catholic, the son of peasants from Kenmare Bay on the famously beautiful Ring of Kerry, a peninsula in the semi-tropical southwestern corner of Ireland, where tree ferns, palms, and purple rhododendron parade across emerald hillsides that plunge to the Atlantic surf below. This is the most Gaelic region of Ireland and one of the poorest.

Patsy's parents, Maytor and Eleanor (Nellie), survived the Irish potato famine, the blight that reached its greatest devastation in 1848. Patsy had been born the previous year in February, their third child, but only their first, Mary Bridget, b. 1844) had survived.

Sometime between 1858 and 1862 Maytor arrived in Michigan's Upper Peninsula via the cheaper route from Ireland through Canada and went to work in the Quincy copper mine. The Upper Peninsula dominated United States copper mining at the time. By the 1850s, the Quincy mine was actively recruiting experienced European miners. Maytor may have gained experience in an Allihies copper mine, only thirty-five miles from their home in Kenmare. In *Michigan's Copper Country*, Ellis W. Courter reports that the Irish were uncomfortable working underground, so they handled the surface work and the Cornish worked below. Wilderness life was rough. Fights were common and whiskey lubricated the restless, single men as they endured primitive, dangerous working conditions and winters in a snow belt that averaged 220 inches a year.

The demand for copper during the American Civil War (1861–1865) raised low prices so that by 1862, Maytor could send for Nellie and their six children to join him. They traveled via the pricier steerage route through New York and settled into the Quincy mine's new company town of Hancock.[10]

HEALY FAMILY

Alec's parents: Patrick and Mary Ann, c. 1880, when Patrick was 33 and Mary was 24. Patrick, along with Mary Ann's brother, Adam Patterson, built a fortune trailing sheep from mountain pastures to markets on the West Coast.

Ogden, Utah

Above: The Healy Hotel in Ogden on the left, opened in 1901.
It is photographed from Union Station, the most important junction
on the transcontinental railroad. Below: Lobby of the New Healy Hotel,
remodelled in 1911. Credit: Weber State University Stewart
Library Special Collections.

Lobby New Healy Hotel
Ogden, Utah.

Alec's parents purchased this "classic high Victorian" home at 2529 Jefferson Avenue, when Alec was in high school. His mother lived here until her death in 1934; his sister Helen's painting studio was in the front tower. Credit: Weber State University Stewart Library Special Collections.

Surprisingly, Alec, right, looks like a blond version of his father, left, in his Ogden High School graduation photo.

Like many young Irish, fifteen-year-old Patsy worked the mines, and perhaps in the smelter, then traveled west for more opportunity, moving from a laborer building the transcontinental railroad to locomotive engineer[11] to becoming one of the major sheepmen in the country. Patsy and his brother-in-law, Adam Patterson, ran about 100,000 sheep, separated into bands of 8,000 to 10,000 with three men and their horses and dogs, trailing them from Utah, Wyoming and Idaho into Oregon and California. Eventually, Patsy became a banker specializing in lending money to sheep herders to buy their own herds as well as loaning funds to sheepmen who wanted to expand their business. To top it off, Patsy built the luxurious Healy Hotel directly across the street from Ogden's train depot, where for many years, all passengers going east or west had to stop and change trains.

The hotel's backstory, according to family lore, is that Patsy wagered fifty thousand dollars that William McKinley, who supported continuing the monetary gold standard, would beat William Jennings Bryan, who wanted to change to a silver standard, for the U.S. presidency in 1896. When he collected his winnings, he told the Bryan man, "I'm going to build a monument to your folly." Was it true? Patsy, with a reputation for Mark Twain drollness, related grand stories. Western humorist Bill Nye, founder of the Laramie *Boomerang* and a syndicated columnist, related two Patsy Healy stories in the Detroit *Free Press* in 1882. When it was Patsy telling the tale, truth was apt to be a might skittish.

The contrast between Alec's and Edith's families could not be more striking. CW Holden kept meticulous records while selling insurance policies for eight competing companies, all of them praising his honesty and loyalty. On the other hand, Patsy Healy didn't keep any books in his partnership with his brother-in-law, which "operated in quite a big way," according to *America's Sheep Trails:*

History, Personalities.[12] Patsy concocted a system to divide up real estate that was a calculated gamble and required its own level of honesty and loyalty. As Alec explained, "Parcels were agreeably grouped in two groups and the partners played a game of cards to determine who would get which group."

Such high-spirited behavior sounds—stereotypically—more Irish than Scottish. Patsy's gregarious first-born, Patsy, Jr., was more Irish in character and the next son, Alec, more prudently Scottish, just as their names imply. Both, though, were Healys. That's Irish.

By the turn-of-the-century when Edith and Alec met, the worst of the anti-Irish prejudice in Boston (the most ferocious in the United States) had abated. Although the formerly ubiquitous No Irish Need Apply signs for housing and jobs had disappeared, descendants of the famine still earned their bread as laborers and housemaids, still lived in Irish neighborhoods, and still faced the persistent negative image that all Irish were brawling drunks who were more loyal to the Pope than to their new country.

Meanwhile, the Holden family followed Unitarianism, the faith of the John Adams family, Ralph Waldo Emerson, and Henry David Thoreau. The most analytical of Protestant denominations, a tenet of Unitarianism is to respect other religions. For CW and Elizabeth Holden, this probably meant respect from afar. Having a Roman Catholic son-in-law would have required their daughter Edith to convert. Having a Mormon son-in-law would have been unthinkable in their society. Even though Alec's grandfather, Alexander Patterson, had but one wife, the Mormons did not outlaw polygamy until 1890, a step required so Utah could join the United States. That was less than a dozen years before Edith Holden and Alec Healy met. Mormonism was still highly stigmatized in most of the country.

Actually, religion was a nonissue for Alec. He left the Catholic Church after his confirmation at age twelve and may not have received family pressure to become a Mormon—his mother didn't practice her faith until after her husband died. Opting out of a family religion or two was not as radical a move for an Ogden boy as it might have seemed to an Easterner. The tracks for the transcontinental railroad, built by competing companies, didn't quite meet. It was in Ogden that every passenger going east or west had to disembark and cross the tracks to continue on their journey. Many stayed for a few days. As a result, Ogden, like a port city, became a wide-open city with a wicked reputation. Mormons and *gentiles* rubbed shoulders. After four years at Boston Tech, as MIT was then known, Alec fit comfortably with the Unitarians.

Moreover, Edith was not an effete Easterner. She was a strong canoe paddler and thrived on summer trips to Maine where she and her sister and mother stayed at the extravagant Poland Spring Resort with room for 450 guests and quarters for their servants. Edith may have been a counselor at the first camp for girls in this country, Camp Wyonegonic.[13] Located in a forested lake district in Maine, about thirty miles from Poland Spring, Wyonegonic opened in 1902, when Edith was in her early twenties. At 28, she copyrighted the words and music to *Wyonegonic Song*.

Although for the most part Edith's parents seemed to enjoy being anchored by routine, a six-week train trip to California with her parents and sister when she was thirteen fired up her traveler's spirit.[14] Edith clearly carried the family's adventuresome gene. Her ancestor, Henry Sampson, was the youngest Pilgrim on the *Mayflower*.[15] Another forebear, Deborah Sampson, was a pensioned Revolutionary War solider, who fought as a man until a chest wound ended the deception. George R. Sampson, co-founder of the famed clipper ship company, Sampson

& Tappan of Boston, astonished the world with his daring and surely captivated his sister Elizabeth's three children, among them her oldest son, George Holden, presumably named after her brother.

Uncle George, as he was to the Holden children, launched *Stag Hound* with his partners just days after CW's thirteenth birthday and a few weeks before his mother died. *Stag Hound* for a time was the largest merchant ship in the world with nearly eleven thousand square yards of canvas under full sail.[16] Four months later in June 1851, Sampson & Tappan debuted *Nightingale*, the most luxurious and fastest clipper to date. After racing and losing a bet equivalent to five million in today's dollars to the owners of a British clipper on the Shanghai–London run, Uncle George and company laughed off the loss, rechallenged the British for the same prize with *Nightingale*, and won the new race by more than a week. Treasured gifts from George to his sisters (Miss Ann Sampson lived with the Holdens) included an embossed, deep rose-colored silk shawl, which was later packed into one of George R. Sampson's trunks from China and traveled with Edith and Alec to Buffalo in 1911.[17]

Edith and Mabel's Gilded-Age lives began to lose their luster as the nineteenth century drew to a close. The Holden Agency experienced reverses and warning sign probably increased.

Nonetheless, Mabel's wedding on March 27, 1901, to Harry Furber looks lavish in the photograph that his sister, Miss Jennie Furber,[18] kept by her bedside for decades before giving it to the Furbers' son Holden. Mabel's high-necked white wedding dress is draped with extravagant tulle overlays and cascades of ruffles rising a couple of feet from the hem. Her five attendants, including Edith and Jennie, wear scoop-necked gowns with ruffles at the shoulders and arms and hems. The men are in white tie. Harry, of slim build with a dark handlebar mustache, stares directly at the camera. Mabel looks fragile in her crown and train. Edith, 22, standing at an angle next to her thin father, appears luminescent and lovely, with her dark hair piled in a pompadour topped with an artificial camellia. The senior Holdens seem frozen, waiting for the camera to flash. CW's prosperous paunch was gone.

Alec wasn't part of Edith's life yet at the time of Mabel's wedding. He was a sophomore at Tech studying gold mining, enjoying life in the Sigma Alpha Epsilon fraternity and friendly with the charismatic Douglas Fairbanks, a young man from Denver with similar interests. Fairbanks had spent a term at the Colorado School of Mines, may have been a student at Harvard, and was certainly trying to break into acting in New York City. Dan said that his father and Fairbanks were roommates and planned to take a cattle boat to Europe, a dream only Fairbanks fulfilled, traveling across the Atlantic in May 1901 with two pals and fifty dollars each in their pockets.[19] Fairbanks went on to become the swashbuckling icon of silent movies and a founding owner of United Artists.[20] Alec traveled north to Nova Scotia with sixteen classmates and professors for MIT's summer mining camp. He was secretary of Tech's Mining Engineering Society and then elected president in his senior year. Inspired, Alec and his fraternity brother, Lawrence Underwood, wrote a joint senior thesis on gold mining techniques in Nova Scotia.

The story of how, when, and where Edith and Alec met is lost, but they fell in love quickly, according to their wedding announcement in the Ogden *Evening Standard*, which reported that "cupid became active within a very short time after first acquaintance." Their daughters, Eileen and Helen, thought they may have met at a musical event, which seems reasonable. Likely they met during Alec's junior year, late in 1901 or early 1902, while Edith was open to love and before the Holdens' world collapsed.

Edith relaxed giving casual performances and vacationing in Maine at either the exclusive Poland Springs resort or Camp Wyonegonic, the first U.S. camp for girls. Below: Edith's picture that Alec carried in his wallet and his 1903 MIT graduation photo.

March 27, 1901. Mabel Harriet Holden marries William Harry Furber.
Relevant photo identification: 1–Lillian Harmon Stone; 2–Edith; 3–CW Holden;
4–Elizabeth Holden (CW's great-niece); 5– Elizbeth Holden
(mother of the bride); 6–Harry Furber; 7– Mabel; 8–Jennie Furber;
9–Maria Louisa Furber; 10–George E. Furber

It's easy to imagine petite Edith being happy that spring of 1902, smiling up, up, up at the lanky, reserved Westerner from a world away. When Mabel announced her pregnancy with a due date near Edith's twenty-fourth birthday, Edith was surely looking forward to sharing birthdays with her first niece or nephew.

Separated for the summer, time must have passed slowly, even though they were busy—perhaps Alec was with his older brother Patsy, Jr., at Healy & Patterson headquarters in Buffalo, Wyoming, and Edith playing her violin with trips to the shore and to Maine for respite from the heat. Maybe by then Alec had tucked into his dark brown leather billfold the simple photo of Edith cut into an oval and signed "Sweetheart—I love you." The billfold is now rusty brown and the edges smooth with wear.

Alec returned for his senior year lean, tan, and eager to see Edith. He arrived as Edith and her family were grappling with their shocking news. In late summer, Mabel's doctor had discovered that she had diabetes, which was a death sentence in those days. When Mabel delivered her baby, the prognosis was that she would bleed to death.

Childbirth, babies, and death held personal suffering for Alec, whose parents had seven more children after Patrick, Jr., Helen, and Alec. Several of his brothers and sisters died shortly after birth and several lived two or three years, long enough to become well-loved members of the family, but one after another, they died. Patsy, Sr., and Mary Ann named their last baby Agnes. She was born in 1895 and lived seven months, old enough to sit up by herself and chortle as Alec enjoyed his fifteenth birthday. One week later, Agnes died, leaving Alec forever the youngest.

When he returned to Boston in the fall of 1902 for his last year in college, only six years had passed since Agnes's death. Surely Alec had ample cause to believe that Mabel's baby might not live either.

Alec was in love but what are the rules for courting a woman whose sister is marked for imminent death? The demands on Alec must have been enormous as he faced an intense academic year at Tech with the pressures of keeping up his grades, completing his senior thesis, and making vital career decisions.

Urban early-twentieth-century courtship was just beginning to shift from invited parlor sitting under the watchful eyes of the parents to attending concerts and neighborhood events under the watchful eyes of the community. The Holden household, which included Mabel and Harry, was already grieving. Alec loved a woman in need of hope, which was probably difficult for the realistic engineer to give considering his early life experiences with death. Alec could give Edith support, share her moments of premature mourning, and perhaps give her some much needed attention and activity to lift her spirits.

Mabel delivered a healthy son, Holden Furber, in her family's home on Beacon Street on February 13, 1903. She passed away that same afternoon.

Generations later, Edith's family still referred to this time as The Tragedy. The Holdens' problems multiplied. CW's health never recovered. His February 5, 1905, death certificate gave cause of death as arteriosclerosis, stating that he had developed the disease three years before. Dan always said, "My grandfather died from a broken heart." Edith and Alec's oldest child, Alec, Jr., said that he heard that one of CW's trusted business associates had betrayed him at this time, as well, and caused severe financial problems for The Holden Agency.

Alec graduated on June 9, 1903, and said good-bye to Edith. Shearing was over, snow was melting on the high mountain pastures, and herders were moving their sheep up into the Big Horns.[21] Alec's brother, Patsy, Jr., needed his younger brother to help manage the

MABEL

One of the exquisitely detailed
plates painted by Mabel.

Fri. 1903 Went to inquire for Mrs Holden & found that Mabel's baby had come. After Evelyn's lesson went back to Harry, but left soon for home Edith soon telephoned for us, but Mabel had died before we got there.

190

Diary entry by Jennie Furber: "March 13. Friday, 1903. Fri. Home. Went to inquire for Mrs. Holden & found that Mabel's baby had come. After Evelyn's lesson went back to Harry, but left soon for home. Edith soon telephoned for us, but Mabel had died before we got there." Jennie, a Wellesley College graduate was a part-time piano teacher and Harry lived with Mabel at the Holdens.

Readng Jennie's terse diary, you can watch the families cope with Mabel's impending death with daily routine. Only once did Jennie confess her sadness.

operation because Patsy, Jr., was traveling to Grinnell, Iowa, to marry Marie Violet ("Mary") Sedwick on July 29. A Grinnell graduate, Mary was a Pennsylvania native who had moved to Buffalo to teach English and Latin to the children of the civilizing frontier, and she and Patsy, Jr., would raise their children accordingly.[22] Within a year, Patsy, Jr., would buy out his Uncle Adam Patterson's share of the sheep business and the outfit was renamed Healy & Healy.

Back on Beacon Street, Baby Holden moved to the Furber's residence to live under his father's care. Since his father traveled back and forth to Maine for business, the three women of the household—maiden aunt, grandmother, and Irish servant who spent most of her life with the family—took charge of the rearing of the baby. Every Sunday afternoon, the Furbers brought Holden to visit his mother's side of the family and everyone sat in the parlor and watched him play.

Elizabeth and Edith coped. Probably after CW died, mother and daughter turned their expansive home into a boarding house. The 1910 census notes that six boarders, ages thirty-four to sixty-eight, and two female servants lived with Elizabeth and Edith at 876 Beacon Street. Two of the boarders were men. The census reports Edith's profession as a musician. Years later, Edith advised her sons and his college friends who had bands that musicians need to play what their audience wants to hear. Edith's shift at this time from playing for her own pleasure to playing to earn a living must have taught her this lesson.[23]

When CW died in 1905, the mining engineer who loved his daughter was still struggling to find good work. Alec probably was eager to leave Buffalo; sheep ranching was his brother's realm. The younger son dreamed of striking it rich in mining. This seems ironic given that both of Alec's grandfathers as well as his father had at least for a time been snared in the back-breaking, low-wage work of mining. But Alec came of age in Utah when silver and gold discoveries in Tonopah, Nevada, launched one of the richest booms in the West. Up in Oregon in a mountain valley near Sumpter, close to the Idaho border, new gold fields generated millions of dollars, and a railroad line financed by Ogden businessmen hauled out the ore.

Digging for millions proved a million miles out of Alec's reach, nor could he find an engineering job. For three years, the only work he found in Nevada and Oregon was pick-and-shovel.

By December 1905, Alec's father was seriously ill. Helen was engaged and still living with her parents in their turreted Victorian home at 2529 Jefferson, the avenue of Ogden's elites. Patsy, Jr., and Mary arrived by train from Buffalo to be with his parents, and Alec probably hurried home, too.

Patsy, Sr., would live for another dozen years, but his slow recovery in the winter of 1906 altered Alec's life. His father offered to start the younger son in the sheep business, as he had his firstborn. It was one thing to begin your own business with the wisdom and backing of an experienced father available. If Alec waited and Patsy, Sr., died soon, he might find himself in the complicated position of starting a new enterprise from an estate and without his father's advice.

Alec stepped into his future. He took over the 30,000 sheep that Healy & Healy were wintering in the Red Desert of southern Wyoming, which was about equidistant from Ogden (about 250 miles southwest) and Buffalo (about 300 miles northeast).

Did Alec make it home for the February 5, 1906, wedding of his sister, Helen? Probably. The two were so close that years later, Helen named Alec the guardian of her child. In fact, Alec may have introduced Helen to her future husband, John Connor Lynch, who was "heavily invested in the lumber and mining business" in Tonopah, Nevada, where Alec probably once worked. The Ogden *Standard* reported, "Owing to her father's illness, the wedding was a quiet one, only relatives and a few intimate friends of the contracting couple being present." A priest from Salt Lake City officiated.

Watching Helen marry into all that gold–silver rush optimism, did Alec still hanker to strike a mother lode? Possibly not. His children later teased that when ranching times got tough their dad would start making plans to sell out and buy a peach farm in Oregon. Alec said nothing about Oregon gold.

Running livestock puts you at the mercy of nature, a gamble that could be benevolent or malicious. Alec's first disaster struck that fall on October 23, 1906, when one of Wyoming's vicious autumn blizzards hit southern Wyoming. It was one of the freak storms that roar in from the northeast, not the usual snowstorm from the west. The early storm likely trapped Alec's sheep and herders in the relatively flat Red Desert while they still were trailing down to the sheltered gulches near the Union Pacific tracks for the winter. Alec told my father that he lost 10,000 sheep, one-third of his livestock. Newspapers reported it was the "worst storm since 1886, or maybe even 1871." Eight sheepherders across the state died.

Alec recovered from his losses, and in 1908, he bought out his father's share of the business and moved his sheep to Buffalo. The enterprise became the Healy Brothers.

Alec must have felt confident this change meant he could afford to create a home for Edith and conveyed this idea to her. That summer Elizabeth Holden took Edith to Europe, some say with the hope of changing Edith's mind about marrying Alec.

Serendipitously, mother and daughter sailed on the steamship *Romantic* to the Mediterranean. Elizabeth kept a journal of their trip, thick with her impressions and postcards. Other than scattered clues, this journal is the only record of Elizabeth's thoughts. The intriguing opening and closing to her journal tell of an internal journey begun with fear and disgust of the new and ending with a transformation.

Elizabeth's tale of their tour begins from the Boston neighborhood port of Charlestown.

> Sailed May 30th 1908 from Charlestown, a hot day but lots of friends were there to see us off. Holden was the last person we saw as we sailed away and I wished I was on the wharf with him – a very pleasant voyage – no storms. Edith not very sick, able to be on deck every day but two. I was not sick at all. We arrived at the Azores' Ponta del Garda [sic] on the 7th of June at five o'clock and left at 9 o'clock. We went ashore and I was scared to death for fear of being left there in the dark with those gibbering Idiots. I was glad to get back to the steamer.

Four months later, home again in Boston, Elizabeth reflected:

> A most delightful voyage I wish it were longer, and I wish I could have seen one big wave, but they said they were big enough to wash over the bow and the steerage passengers had to stay inside, so perhaps it was better it was no worse.
>
> I am glad I went and I am glad I am at home. I think if I had realized the many things that might have happened to us I never would have gone. People can go alone to Europe for the first time and get along all right but it is not easy, especially to travel all the time, so many moneys and languages and customs. I had nothing to do with the traveling part. I paid no bills or had anything to say.
>
> Edith was a wonder to me and I feel after last summer's experience she can go anywhere and get along all right.

Edith and Alec had entered into their fifth year of separation. Two family theories explain why their courtship lasted so long. One

Elizabeth, 71, and Edith, 29, sailed on the steamship *Romantic* for a summer in Europe in 1908. Although nervous at first, Elizabeth was disappointed she didn't see even one big wave.

explanation has it that not only did Alec have to establish himself so that he could afford to care generously for Edith, but also that he was not considered suitable. Another theory is that Edith did not want to leave her widowed mother alone, that she felt the love and protectiveness that would be natural for an only surviving child. If Edith left with Alec, she would be separated from her mother by days of travel. They could never speak—no telephones could carry voices that long a distance—and mail took longer than a train ride to such a remote place.

Most likely both suppositions are true, ebbing and re-emerging at different times. When Elizabeth wrote the final sentence in her European journal, she was seventy-one years old. Elizabeth's conclusion seems to signal her acceptance of the courtship. Still, in the end Edith and Alec's courtship lasted eight years. Nearly two more years passed after the European trip before Alec wrote to Elizabeth in the spring of 1910, asking for Edith's hand in marriage. That fall he came to present a ring, and another six months passed before the wedding. The family story is that Elizabeth finally countered her daughter's excuses, saying, "I've lived my life and you have yours to live, Edith, so go ahead and marry Alec."

Buffalo, Wyoming

One more "leading character" dominates Edith's letters—the movie set village of Buffalo, Wyoming. The eastern slope of the Big Horn Mountains—a verdant land of everlasting water—needs no introduction, only a reminder. This is the land of cowboys and Indians and the U.S. Cavalry riding to the rescue (or defeat) that has filled the coffers of Hollywood and the imaginations of people around the world.

From the Custer battlefield at the north end of the Big Horns in

Montana to the outlaw hideout, Hole-in-the-Wall, near the southern end—a 160-mile drive—this is The Wild West of our collective fascination. Think of *Battle of the Little Bighorn, Lonesome Dove, Sitting Bull, Little Big Man, Butch Cassidy and the Sundance Kid, Shane, The Sheepman, Son of the Morning Star, Bury My Heart at Wounded Knee, Last Stand at Little Big Horn, Brokeback Mountain,* and *Heaven's Gate.* As of this writing, sixteen movies, television segments, and miniseries alone have been filmed about the battle lost by General George Armstrong Custer and his men to a combined force of Sioux and Northern Cheyenne in 1876. Only thirty-six years had passed since that battle when Edith married Alec and moved to Buffalo, 104 miles southeast of the Custer battlefield. The first of the many movies to come, *Custer's Last Fight,* a silent film, was released in 1912, the year after Edith and Alec's wedding.

Stories become mythic when they involve high stakes and struggles that transform character. Nowhere were the stakes higher in the thirsty West than the wet side of the Big Horns where water flows generously and winters often are milder than elsewhere in the Rockies. Shaped like a bear claw scratching across the plains toward the Black Hills of Dakota, the Big Horns are older than other ranges in the Rockies. Geologists describe the Big Horns as "fault block mountains," meaning that as tectonic plates stress vertically, the uplifted blocks of rock and down-dropped blocks form multitudes of canyons, with snow-fed creeks bearing names that hint at the mountain's geography and history: Ten Sleep, Crazy Woman, Piney, and the Powder River are a few of them.

For at least 11,200 years, maybe for more than 15,000 years, humans have known that even in the driest of times, grass and animals thrive where the high plains abut the Big Horns. Paleo-Indians hunted mammoth with Clovis-tipped spears here. One important archaeological dig, the Colby Site, lies near the outskirts of Worland. Rock drawings in the lower elevations of Big Horn Basin to the west date back at least 10,500 years. Mike Bies, who spent decades as the Bureau of Land Management's staff archaeologist in the Worland district, said that when Indians, regardless of tribe, go with him to see the art, they point out many familiar symbols.

Who painted the art? No one is quite sure. Much of it appears on limestone overhangs in cave-like shelters. Archaeologists do know that at least ten thousand years ago, Sheep Eaters were driving Bighorn sheep into traps and killing them for meat and pelts. These prehistoric bands of indigenous people were named after the food they ate, but were considered Mountain Shoshone. As tools improved, the Shoshone hunted deer, elk, bear, and buffalo with bows and arrow, all on foot. Theirs was a balanced diet, says Mike. "They also feasted on berries, Sago lilies, Biscuit root, Bitter root, and small animals."

When the Great Drought parched the grasslands in the Mountain West at the end of the Ice Age, between six thousand and nine thousand years ago, more humans moved to the foothills and stayed. Naturally, an oasis like the Big Horns with green foothills nestled in rounded (not sawtoothed) mountains with meadows and abundant wildlife attracts envy.

Initially the Shoshone dominated the area, but they were pushed out by the Crow. The Arapaho then fought the Crow and the Northern Cheyenne joined in the battles. Then the Shoshone traded buffalo hides for guns and horses with Indians in the southwest who had been trading with the Spanish for hundreds of years. Advantage Shoshone. They pushed the Crow out of the Big Horn region. Then the Crow got horses and guns from the Mandan in North Dakota and pushed the Shoshone back out.

Intertribal warfare intensified as the U.S. population moved westward. The Chippewa drove the horseless Sioux from their traditional lands at the headwaters of the Mississippi circa 1700. The Sioux walked into the northern plains, eventually acquiring horses and guns and a predatory reputation. Within seventy or eighty years, the Sioux had conquered their way to the Big Horns and wanted it all.

These tribal wars did not yet include fights with land-hungry settlers because the U.S. government had forbidden non-Indians from encroaching on a large area of the northern Rockies. The law was more or less obeyed until gold was discovered in Virginia City, Montana, in 1863, during the Civil War. The swiftest route to the excavations was an illegal shortcut north to Montana from the Oregon Trail which arced from Fort Laramie in the far south of Wyoming, north along the well-watered eastern Big Horns, and turned west to the gold fields. Miners ignored the law, and Texas cattlemen followed the forbidden route with their Longhorns. The Indians pushed back ferociously causing the U.S. Cavalry to safeguard the miners' nonexistent rights. The prohibited shortcut became known as The Bloody Bozeman Trail.

When the Civil War ended in 1865 and the U.S. Army could increase its troops and funds for the western battles, the attacks intensified. Indian forces of Sioux, Northern Cheyenne, and Arapaho led by Red Cloud, a sinewy Oglala Lakota with the ability to gather some-time-enemies and direct them toward a common purpose, defeated the U.S. Army. The peace treaty of 1868 gave the Indians legal control of Powder River County, including the Big Horn Mountains. Specifically, no non-Indian could settle there.

The treaty of 1868 lasted eight years, ending when gold was discovered in the Black Hills, the next (and last) mountain range east of the Big Horn Mountains. Americans exerted relentless pressure on the U.S. government and on tribes for land and gold, for grazing land, timber, rich soil to till, and for the freedom to recreate their lives in the frontier. After the Great Sioux War of 1876, which included Custer's Battle of the Little Bighorn, the U.S. Army pushed American Indians onto reservations and opened the countryside.

Crow, who had helped the U.S. Army to save themselves from the Sioux, were to receive nearly all of the Big Horn Mountains. In the end, they only obtained the northern tip mountain land, with the rest of their reservation prairie, all in Montana, on the other side of the Wyoming border.

Custer's defeat provoked a deep reaction in Washington then under the presidency of Civil War General Ulysses Grant. Congress was compelled to open Indian lands and protect the settlers. By 1878, Fort McKinney was built on Clear Creek, a few miles from where the creek dropped out of the mountains. Tradesmen, merchants, and saloon owners quickly followed the soldiers, establishing the nearby town of Buffalo to supply the troops. (To the surprise of visitors, Buffalo was named after Buffalo, New York, not for the buffalo herds roaming the plains, a not unreasonable belief considering the town's winding main street looked like a buffalo trail should look.)

With plenty of business from the fort and desirable land to home-stead—160 acres for free if you could manage the start-up farming costs and hard physical labor—Buffalo boomed. It quickly became the seat of government for Johnson County, a huge territory that at the time extended north to the Montana border and included Sheridan, thirty-five miles north, and ranged west to the Big Horn River in the Basin. By the time Wyoming became a state in 1890, Buffalo boasted a population of about 1,100 young, ambitious pioneers, who built good schools, churches, banks, stores, and a hotel. The Occidental Hotel is where in 1902 Owen Wister wrote portions of *The Virginian: Horseman of the Plains*. Many of Edith's 1911 letters were written in the Occidental, where she and Alec stayed when she first moved to Buffalo.

Clear Creek surges through Buffalo as it drops from the
Big Horn Mountains (on the horizon) in 1910, a year before Edith arrived.
Credit: Johnson County Library.

Lust for the land continued to incite battles. Buffalo imploded for several days in April 1892 when the long-simmering anger between cattlemen and small farmers, who were fencing off the open range, ignited like a lightning fire. Still known as the Johnson County War or as locals call it, The Invasion, the war pitched a consortium of wealthy, well-connected Wyoming cattle ranchers and their gang of twenty-five hired guns from Texas (in fiction, ruffians like Rooster Cogburn in *True Grit*) against small ranchers—allegedly rustlers—until finally President Benjamin Harrison ordered the U.S. Cavalry at Fort McKinney to restore order.

The bad conflict was good luck for the risk-taking Patsy Healy, Sr. That spring, cattle were not driven up to northern Wyoming from Texas as usual and the lapse opened up relatively vacant grasslands to sheep. Patsy and his brother-in-law, Adam Patterson, had been looking for a place to relocate their southern Idaho headquarters that had become too settled and fenced. Less than six weeks after the Johnson County episode, Healy & Patterson moved some of their herds that had wintered in the Red Desert of southern Wyoming nearly 300 miles north into the Big Horn Mountains for summer grazing on the open range. Those herds were trailed down to the lower altitudes outside Buffalo to winter rather than returning to the Red Desert and soon after, the Utah partners relocated their headquarters to Buffalo from Soda Springs, Idaho.

Patsy Healy, Sr., didn't believe in investing his money in land. As Alec said, "Father never took kindly to the ownership of real estate. When a locality got crowded, he moved into a new territory." But the open range was shrinking, and Healy & Patterson changed its tactics. They acquired considerable rangeland, including a small headquarters ranch for shearing and wintering operations on Clear Creek, about eight miles east of Buffalo, and land in the Big Horns centering around the luxuriant meadows at Billy's Flat.

Although Patsy, Sr., may have bought land, settled in, and settled down, maybe mellowing to the new ways, he remained a force to be reckoned with. Longtime Washakie County Commissioner Bob Swander tells a story he heard about Patsy, Sr. A new, ambitious family moved their sheep into the Big Horns and began trespassing on the range of some "educated, nice people" who couldn't defend their grass. The head of the family who owned the ranchland handled the situation by leasing his property to someone tougher than the newcomers— Patsy, Sr. As the story goes, one day the head of the encroaching family was sitting on a rock holding the reins of his white mule when "a rifle cracked and cut the reins off right out of his hands." The tale doesn't implicate Patsy, Sr., specifically, but ends with Bob musing, "That Patsy Healy was a pretty tough guy." So legends are made.

Meanwhile, Buffalo's residents suffered setbacks in their ambitions. In 1893, the year after The Invasion, the Burlington & Missouri Railroad arrived in Sheridan, attracted in part by the large coal fields nearby and per- haps influenced by the tensions to the south. Although Buffalo remained the county seat, Sheridan County to the north split from Johnson County and soon Johnson County was subdivided into three more counties when the semi-arid basin on the dry western side of the Big Horns was trans- formed by large-scale irrigation projects that turned sagebrush steppes into great green fields of alfalfa and sugar beets. This was the Big Horn Basin, encircled by the Big Horns, Bridgers, Owl Creeks, and Absarokas, with the Big Horn River flowing north through the center, a life-giving gift of water when it touched the parched Basin soil.

The arrival of farmers brought law and order to the frontier where previously might equaled right. Not everyone was happy with the change, as every moviegoer knows. The arrival of sheep in cattle country outraged the cattlemen and this didn't end when Shane got on his horse and trotted off toward the mountains. Even in the 1950s when I was a kid going up to our ranch with my dad, Dan, I watched how bitter feelings ran deep between the sheep foreman and the cattle foreman—even though the sheep grazed the high hills ("Sheep love to climb," my dad said) and the cattle grazed the valleys and lower sides of the high slopes. To protect against overgrazing, herders kept moving the sheep and cowboys punched the cows forward. To ensure harmony between sheepherders and cowboys, Dad fired both stubborn foremen.

With fenced land, grass is finite and good grass is necessary to get good gain on the livestock. Destroying grass is foolish to the point of stupidity. In the time of the open range when Healy & Patterson were trailing tens of thousands of sheep from Wyoming–Utah–Idaho to the Pacific Coast, if herders didn't keep their bands walking, they easily grazed down to the roots. Driving Longhorns from Texas to Montana and back to market beat up the range, too.

I asked John W. Davis, an award-winning author of Western history, about the animosity.

> First, if sheep got to the grass first, cattle couldn't graze it. Second, racial prejudice. A lot of people who ran sheep were not of Anglo-Saxon origin.[24] And third, religious prejudice. Many of the sheepmen were Mormons. [Fourth,] I don't know why, but cattlemen and cowboys are assertive physically, they are very aggressive people.
>
> In the writing I've done about the change from the Frontier to the mature society, it happens when farmers come in. They are a very different kind of people. They insist on law and order. Sheepmen are closer to farmers in the way they handle life.

While the bias against sheep was less savage in the Buffalo area, it occasionally exploded on the other side of the mountains. John's first book, *A Vast Amount of Trouble: A History of the Spring Creek Raid*, details the first time in the conflicts that the law did anything about the brutality. In April 1909, three sheepherders were killed, two wagons burned, and a couple dozen sheep were killed. Five cattlemen were arrested in May, tried in November in Basin, a town thirty miles north of Worland, and convicted by a jury mostly composed of farmers.[25]

Although the Healy Brothers—Patsy, Jr., and Alec—ran sheep on both sides of the Big Horns, and Spring Creek was close to their summer pastures, Alec must not have been afraid. Within five months after the sentencing, he wrote to Edith's mother proposing marriage to her daughter.

As it turned out, the successful court resolution to the Spring Creek Raid marked the end of coordinated murderous violence against sheepmen in Wyoming. It was safe for Edith to move to Buffalo.

Reflection

In her early married years, Edith lived a small-town variation of a prosperous Bostonian woman's life, with babies, hired help, and ladies' afternoon bridge games. She was sought after to play the violin at church on Sunday mornings, and she organized and led women's clubs livened with cultural and intellectual programs.

Edith loved Buffalo which, along with Sheridan, was a sophisticated pocket in Wyoming where cattle-ranching younger sons of British lords and trust funders played polo, which preceded the advent of rodeo to the area. The move to Worland, a farming center on the dry side of the mountains, challenged her optimism. And yet in Worland, Edith stepped into her father's footsteps and discovered a cause that was worth selling.

She dedicated herself to the Girl Scouts, an international network of girls learning to confidently slip outside society's corrals, a broadening experience that offered girls in isolated places like Wyoming a chance to widen their vistas. Likewise, the Girl Scouts opened the world to Edith, who was eventually appointed to its National Board of Directors, an entrée she used when she traveled internationally.

In the saga of American history, Edith and Alec were figures in the tapestry. But Edith's letters give us far more than a slice-of-life report about a colorful quasi-frontier experience in 1911. Edith writes to understand how to live and how to die, how to adopt older children, and how teens can find a welcome in high school. Edith shows how even an adventurous spirit like hers needs to face down fears, as when in January 1946, five months after the end of World War II, she wrote farewells to each of her four sons and daughters and their spouses with instructions on each sealed envelope, "To Be Opened After My Death." Then she sailed off on a freighter to Rìo de Janeiro with Alec, his 16mm movie camera at the ready and her blue ink pen and empty journals in her handbag.

They safely returned home to Worland and took the high school students traveling with them by way of the Kerby Theater on Big Horn Avenue, Worland's main street. Alec ran the projector, and Edith handled the reporting in her elegant Boston accent.

Yet in the final analysis, *An Improbable Pioneer* remains a love story. When I read my grandmother's letters, I discovered that my sometimes scarily formal grandfather was tender and that he thrilled to exploration, too.

A family story goes that when Edith and Alec went to see *Gone with the Wind*, she raved about the acting, the scenery, the story, the filming.

"Four hours of sitting," said Alec.

Thanks to Edith's letters, I now know he was teasing. Or, maybe he wasn't, but now I know that he was brave and romantic and handsome and curious, that he was ready to jump on a horse or his 1911 motorcycle or a train or a plane and go find out for himself, like Edith.

Despite the long courtship that kept them mostly apart for eight years, Edith and Alec spent thirty-nine years together. They raised four children—Alec, Jr., Dan, Eileen, and Helen, in that birth order. Helen Healy Bonine, 95, is still with us.

Edith wrote to Alec in his "To Be Opened After My Death" letter, "I've had a glorious and interesting life and enjoyed it to the utmost." I hope you enjoy a glimpse into their lives, too.

Cathy
Edith Catherine Healy
Occidental Hotel, Buffalo, Wyoming
April 28, 2013

Married at 32, Edith retained her youthful looks. The eye-catching flower on her hair is reminiscent of the gauzy "blossom" she wore for Mabel's wedding.

CHAPTER 1

PROPOSAL AND WEDDING

MAY 1910

BOSTON

In 1910, Marie Curie published her treatise on radioactivity, Frank Lloyd Wright's influence on architecture spread to Europe, W. E. B. Du Bois founded the National Association for the Advancement of Colored People (NAACP), and Mark Twain died. The country was prospering under the self-styled progressive Republican president, William Howard Taft, who worked to bust corporate monopolies, reform the civil service, and increase the speed of mail delivery.

Healy Brothers was prospering, too. With about 45,000 sheep, Alec and Patsy, Jr., ranked as one of the largest, if not the largest sheep operation in northern Wyoming. Earlier, probably in the fall of 1909, Alec's older brother, Patsy, Jr., had moved Mary and Patricia, 5, into Buffalo from the ranch house to be close to schools and social life. Mary settled in briefly before traveling to Los Angeles to take advantage of better medical care for the delivery of Patrick Healy III, on April 30, 1910.

Minding the ranch alone in Wyoming must have left Alec eager for his long-distance courtship to end. Less than a month passed before the twenty-nine-year-old bachelor mailed this precisely penned letter to Edith's mother.

Buffalo, Wyo
May 25 [1910]
Mrs C W Holden
Boston, Mass.

My dear Mrs Holden,

I have loved your daughter for a number of years. Now she may consent to marry me. I therefore write you to ask you for your consent to the marriage, provided Edith is willing when I see her in September.

I fully realize the sacrifice that you must necessarily make in having your only daughter married to a man who lives so far away. Perhaps I am too selfish, nevertheless I do ask you to make such a sacrifice. Edith & I will do all that we can to make it as light as possible. I should like to have you spend at least part of each year with us. If you should long for Boston Edith would spend the rest of the year there with you.

I know that I am asking you for the one who is dearer to you than anything else in the world. She is that to me also. I trust that you will look at this in the light that I do and say yes.

Sincerely yours
Alexander Healy
Buffalo, Wyoming

This undated letter below was written after Alec's September proposal visit to Boston in 1910. Likely then Alec presented Edith with an Old European cut, 1.5 carat diamond engagement ring.

The Aunt Georgia he refers to in his follow-up letter was Georgiana Sampson, the widow of CW Holden's cousin, Augustus Sampson. Aunt Celia may have been a family friend.

Dear Mrs Holden,

I send the enclosed pictures to give you some idea of the looks of our town. I am not sure whether they will make you think more or less of the town than before.

I am not in the habit of handing out compliments but I have to say that Edith has one of the finest & noblest mothers in the world. I appreciate fully the sacrifice that I have asked you to make & which you have consented to make. Your willingness makes it so much easier for Edith & for myself.

Things look some better on the range but there is so much room for improvement.

My mother & sister are very much pleased with the prospect of a new daughter & sister-in-law. My father hasn't expressed himself but he is naturally undemonstrative. I told him before I went to Boston what might happen & he was glad.

Affectionately
Alex.

I have thought many times that while in Boston I met some of the finest elderly ladies. Remember me in particular to Aunt Georgia & Aunt Celia.

———

On April 3, 1911, Edith Sampson Holden married Alexander Healy in her mother's home. Freezing cold rain—some reports say snow was expected—chilled the city that Monday, but inside the Holden's stately brick townhouse with large bay windows, lights glowed as the couple walked through an aisle of fourteen bridal attendants wearing white gowns with blue chiffon scarves. Several newspapers from both Boston and Ogden covered the ceremony. The Ogden *Standard* referred to Edith as "a Boston Heiress," which though no longer true showed Western enthusiasm and dutiful pride for the achievement of a native son.

"Wedding with Notable Features," announced the Boston *Evening Transcript*, the newspaper that the Holdens read, and described a ceremony with no maid of honor and no best man. Edith and her mother created a ceremony that in some ways foretold Edith and Alec's lifetime together. One of those ways was by being inclusive of Edith's many women friends. She must have found it difficult to narrow her list down to only fourteen attendants—including Alec's sister, Helen—and only six musical friends to play for the service and the reception. Breaking with tradition, another omen of things to come, some of her friends in the wedding were married.

As Edith's letters unfold, they reveal her friendships and networks of friends growing and growing, with Alec happily roped into the gaiety, but occasionally bolting for the ranch to regroup from too much socializing. Reserved by temperament, Alec suffered through small talk but benefited greatly from Edith's talent of nurturing friendships.

Boston Evening Transcript – April 4, 1911
WEDDING WITH NOTABLE FEATURES

———

Miss Edith Sampson Holden to Be Married
to Alexander Healy of Ogden, Utah

A home wedding, which is to have some unusual features, will be that of Miss Edith Sampson Holden, daughter of Mrs. Charles W. Holden, of 876 Beacon Street, who is to be married at eight o'clock this evening to Alexander Healy, of Ogden, Utah, a graduate of the Massachusetts Institute of Technology, 1903. He is the son of Mr. and Mrs. P. Healy of Ogden, and his father is a prominent wool grower of the West. The late father of Miss Holden was well known in Boston insurance circles.

At the wedding tonight at the resident of the bride's mother, Rev. Arthur W. Littlefield, minister of the Second Unitarian Church in Brookline, is to officiate. The bride and bridegroom are to dispense with bridesmaids and the usual best man, but fourteen friends of the bride are to serve as at attendants, forming an aisle through which the bridal pair will walk. These attendants are the Misses Constance and Elizabeth Holden, cousins of the bride; Marion Cushing, Julia Sampson, May Young, Grace Dunning, Ethel Towle, Ellen King, Jessie Douglass, Marion Clapp, Mrs. John Lynch, a sister of the bridegroom; Mrs. Hartley W. Thayer, Mrs. Leslie W. Millar and Mrs. Ralph Haskell.

The bride is to wear white satin, veiled with marquisette and made with a square train and an overdress of Chantilly lace. Her veil of tulle will be fastened with conventional orange blossoms and the bridal bouquet will be of lilies of the valley combined with orchids. Her fourteen attendants are to be gowned alike in white, with which pale blue chiffon scarfs will be worn. They will carry large clusters of daybreak carnations. The bride will be given in marriage by her mother, and at the reception which follows the ceremony, the group of ushers will include Dr. William W. Wolcott, Dr. Hartley W. Thayer, Lester W. Millar, Frederick H. Cook, Arthur B. Emmes and W. Harry Furber.[26]

The bride is an accomplished violinist and six of her intimate musical friends are to play the music incidental to the ceremony and for the reception. They are Miss Estella Davis, Miss Gertrude Sands and Miss Susanne Cawley, violin; Miss Beatrice Pray, viola; Mrs. Frank Piper, cello, and Miss Helena Soren, piano. Mr. Healy takes his bride South for an extended wedding trip, after which they will go to their future home at Buffalo, Wyo.

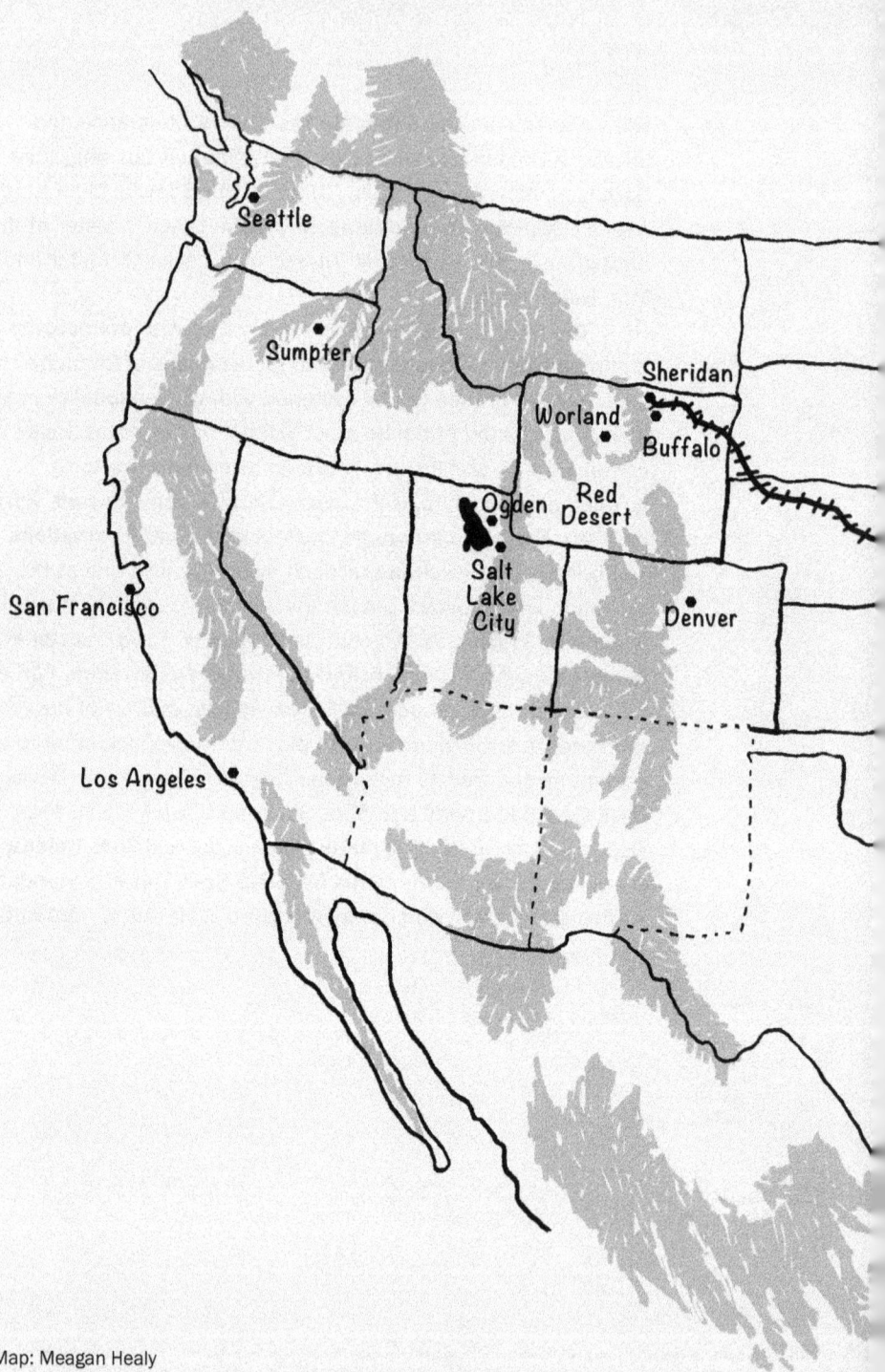

HONEYMOON TRIP, 1911

Seattle

Sumpter

Sheridan

Worland

Buffalo

Ogden

Red Desert

San Francisco

Salt Lake City

Denver

Los Angeles

Map: Meagan Healy

Boston

Chicago

Lincoln

St. Jose ph

Washington, DC

Fortress Monroe

Chattanooga

Charlotte

Memphis

Atlanta

New Orleans

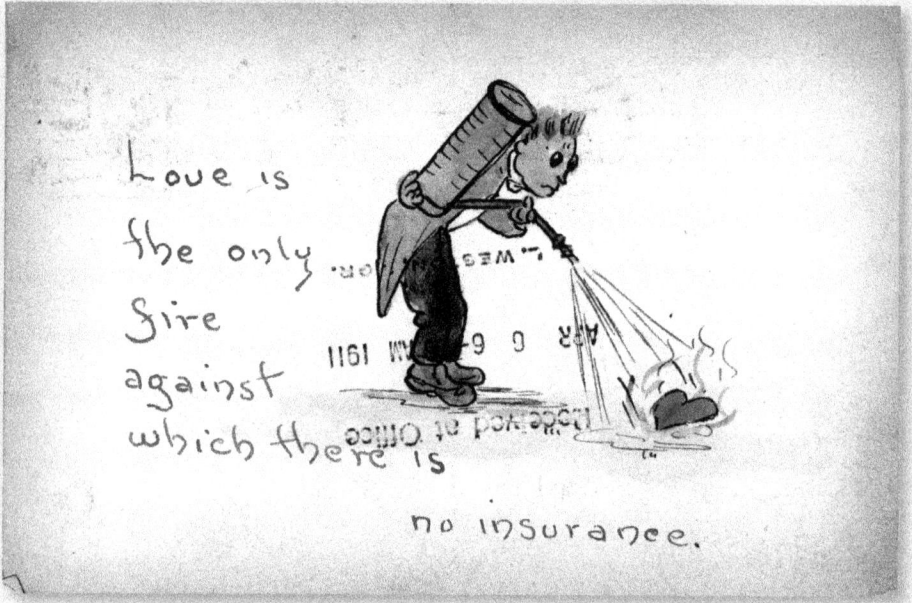

This unsigned postcard was waiting for the newlyweds when they arrived at the Raleigh Hotel. Since CW Holden was well-known for fire insurance in New England, the card probably was sent by Edith's mother, knowing it would charm Edith and Alec.

CHAPTER 2

HONEYMOON TRIP

APRIL 3 TO APRIL 23, 1911

WASHINGTON DC – FORTRESS MONROE – CHARLOTTE
ATLANTA – CHATTANOOGA – MEMPHIS

The day after their elaborate wedding, Edith and Alec took the train to Washington DC, arriving late that night. Edith mentions in this letter that she didn't feel well at lunchtime. A note by Dan Healy in February 1988 says that riding a passenger train pulled by a coal-fired steam locomotive in those days could be sickening. Not only did the train jerk and sway, but the locomotive sent "coal smoke along the length of the train, filling the cars with smoke and soot, which substantially added to nausea." Edith was inclined toward motion sickness and this coal smoke added to her discomfort.

> The Raleigh
> Washington, D.C.
> April 6th, 1911
>
> Dear Mother:
>   Look what we just found at the office. That's from Miss Todd, isn't she the limit!
>   I'll commence way back and tell you as much as I can in half an hour, for that is all the time I have at present.
>   First before I forget it. That box arrived this morning with all the things I needed in it. I had been hunting for that black scarf. My, but it's hot here. This is the first pleasant day for three days.
>   Alec bought an electric stove and flat iron and forgot to tell you about them. If they come too late to put in the trunk, and if you forgot to put in the chafing dish and some of those

pretty table cloths, do them all up together and ship to us. If it doesn't cost too much send by express.

Well, wasn't it an awful evening, that of the wedding. That is a dandy limousine. We stopped and made the man get out to see if anything conspicuous was on it, but there wasn't anything.

That was fine confetti, for with the exception of some which stayed in my pockets, nothing stuck.

We had a suite at the Victoria. A parlor, one large bedroom, a small bedroom, and bath. We stayed a while in the parlor and telephoned you, then talked.

Alec used the small room for a dressing room and the large bed room, so we got along remarkably well.

We were called the next morning at six. Such a day. We had a fine breakfast at seven and took a taxi to the train. We got the Post and the Herald. They were pretty near right in what they said.

It was great to have that drawing room, for I rested most all day. We read those two papers then, and that's all we did all day up to nine o'clock last night. The porter was on to us all right, and kept popping in on us so frequently that we took to locking the door after he went out.

I didn't feel very good at lunch time and didn't eat much. My hair was a sight and I had to stand up and balance myself in that little stuffy place and do it over. I won't do that again, raise my hands over my head, before eating.

They took the dining car off at New York, so we had dinner served in our little private room, and it was fine. Alec had raw oysters and soup, then a delicious steak, etc. We were quite late in arriving. Such a beautiful station! It comes up to the St. Louis one, and that's saying a great deal.

We took a taxi up to this hotel which is a stunner! Looks something like the Lorraine only much bigger. We have a nice room and bath. Also a balcony and long French window. This morning I didn't get up until nine. We have just had our breakfast and been down to the market. I saw a woman pick out a live chicken and grabbing it by the legs, put it on the scales to weigh it. She kept on till she got one the right weight and then walked off with him squawking in her basket.

We are going down to get some lunch now and take a sight-seeing auto at one o'clock to see and go through things till one. It is twelve and I must stop.

I am having the time of my life!!!!!!!!

Affec.
E.S.H.
So am I. A Healy.

———

The Raleigh
Washington, D.C.
April 7, 1911

Dear Mother Holden.

I am sorry that those cooking appliances were not delivered until the trunks had gone. I think you had better express them to Buffalo. I forgot to leave some money with you for packing, freight, etc. I spoke to Edith about sending it to you but she said that you would make those payments and I was to pay you.

We had a delightful day yesterday. Edith is surprising me with her endurance. She hasn't been tired yet & we ran around a great deal.

We must go now.
Affectionately, Alex

———

The Raleigh
Washington, D.C.

Dear Mother.

We had a fine time yesterday afternoon. Took the sight-seeing auto and did the same way we did in London. They took us to the buildings and we got out and walked through. Saw the Treasury first, then the White House. Just the lower floor sort of a wing, and the East room. It reminded me of the ballroom in

Queen Wilhelmina's palace only it's a little larger, I think. From there to the Engraving Dept. where we saw them making bills. Then Smithsonian, then Nat. Museum, Congressional Library, and finally the Capitol. Of course we didn't half see the two last ones and we are going to spend half a day in each, but now we have some idea of the way the city is laid out and how to find our way around in the buildings.

In the Capitol I couldn't help thinking of what that man said to me about our conductor, "Wouldn't he be happy if he had us on roller skates!" Both houses have adjourned until Monday. And by the way, after all my forethought, I forgot my ticket from Senator Lodge. Alec has written to his Senator and Congressman, so we'll be all right if we want to stay until Tuesday.

It's cold, damp, and raw today. We wanted to go to Mt. Vernon, but it isn't any day for that or Arlington either. We wrote the Commander of Ft. Meyer but haven't heard yet and the drill is today, so I guess we don't go. It isn't good enough anyway. I am about to put on Aunt Lizzie's white sweater, my ermine, and my long fur coat and take the auto that takes you through the residential district, and the foreign embassies.

We aren't doing much each day but getting good and rested. Nothing yesterday morning and took a nap after the ride, had late dinner & a walk around town.

We'll take this ride today and perhaps the theatre tonight. So glad to hear the house is cleared up and you slept well. Wish you were here too. We're having such a fine time.

E.S.H.

———

The next letter was written April 8 and mentions Alec ordering "gape Raleigh." This may refer to a gaper, which is a type of crab with a permanent opening at its back hinge. Also, Wyoming's territorial legislature decreed that women could vote in 1869; it entered the union as the first state to allow women's suffrage, so Edith could vote for the first time when she moved to Wyoming, as well as serve on a jury.

By 1911, three other states allowed women to vote. It took nine more years before the Nineteenth Amendment was ratified, when Edith was forty-one years old.

> The Raleigh
> Washington, D.C.
>
> My dear Mother.
>   This is Saturday night, and just about as cold and damp as it was the night we were married. It has been snowing and just turned to rain. We wanted to go to Mt. Vernon today, but it was out of the question. We spent most of our time in the Corcoran Art Gallery, then went to the D.A.R. building which is near it. Were informed we couldn't enter as Saturday was a half holiday and it closed at noon. It seems to me a building like that ought to be open all the time.
>   We then went to the Bureau of Republics.[27] A beautiful building with a large court made to represent a Spanish American house. It had a fountain playing and all sorts of tropical plants, including banana tree, coffee, chocolate, and bread fruit.
>   That's about all we've done today besides going in for a while this evening to the New Willard [Hotel].
>   Yesterday we took the auto ride around the city. A fine trip. Then at four we took another auto ride in just such a machine as you and Aunt Lizzie went in to Concord, and went to Arlington Cemetery. A splendid ride. We waited until sunset at the conductor's suggestion and stopped at Ft. Meyer and saw all the troops line up to take down the flag. The band played, cannon were fired etc. A most impressive sight.
>   In the evening we went to see Lillian Russell. Very pretty theatre but so small. Pretty poor show. Lillian's gowns were about all there was of interest.
>   Another event of the day was our luncheon. We were neither of us hungry (which was lucky as it turned out later) so I said I was going to have something I'd often read on menus

and heard about, fresh mushrooms cooked under glass. Alec had a gape Raleigh, also an experiment. Talk about rich, well, I could eat about three mouthfuls of mine. They are cooked under glass in the oven and are really cooked by their own steam. Alec's turned out to be chopped up crabs, with other things and a big mushroom in the center. He could eat about four mouthfuls of his. We called it an educational luncheon and now we know what not to order again.

Last night we had planked roe shad. I never tasted such shad in my life. They served oysters done up in bacon with it and the roe was brown and crisp. It seems that shad roe and bacon is a great dish around here. You are constantly seeing it advertised.

Tomorrow if pleasant, we are going to Mt. Vernon. If not, to church to hear Mr Pierce.

Do you know I left that ticket I wrote to Lodge for, at home. So Alec wrote his Senator and Congressman. Had a fine letter from the Senator with a ticket and telling us to look him up, and just where to find him at certain times, and Congressman Mondell[28] called on us, if you please and left his card and a note with a ticket.

So Monday, we shall go to both houses. You certainly are much more important in a State that doesn't have so many people, and next year, my vote will count.

There's one thing about Washington that's fine for a honeymoon trip. You are only one of many. You see brides and grooms everywhere. There are several sets in this hotel. One couple we can't lose. They are always eating when we are, and today they were in the Art Gallery at the same time.

Yesterday the man on the auto pointed out a building and said it was one of the most important in Washington. The place where the marriage licenses were issued. Everybody laughed, and so did we. The honors were shared by another couple, so it wasn't so bad. Glad to get your nice long letter and know how things were going. Miss Elizabeth Walker was at the wedding

Love to all.
E.S.H.

Am feeling fine. Have never had such good color for months. Alec wants you to send him the bill of lading to Buffalo later. E.S.H.

———

The Raleigh
Washington, D.C.
April 9th

Dear Mother.

Such a nice day, so we planned to go to Mt. Vernon. Just as we were starting, I happened to think and asked if Mt. Vernon was open on Sunday and they said it was not. Stung! Wouldn't we have been mad if we had go way out there.

So we went to church, at least we tried to. I never saw a Unitarian church so crowded. When we got there the street and sidewalk was lined with people all waiting for the President to come. We tried to get in but only succeeded in standing jammed up against the wall, so heard them sing the Palms, then departed, as I should have fainted if I had to stand long with so many people. The Pres. didn't come after all.

Then, we went to the zoo. Such a wonderful place. I never saw such a collection of queer animals. Queer peacocks walking all around the grounds. They looked so pretty with their bright plumage among the trees and rocks.

We didn't get home until two. Had a good dinner and rested all the afternoon. Called up Rachel Sewall, but she was out of town. Tonight we have been to the Congressional Library again to see it lighted. It is far more beautiful at night.

Now about the clock. I don't think we need it as we have Mr Spiller's, and I should think it would be time enough if you sent it with the other things some time later. What do you think?

When you write again, direct to Piedmont Hotel, Atlanta. We are planning to get there. We can only stay two days at Old Point. Leaving here Tues. at 6:45 PM on boat arriving at 7 AM.

Affect,
E.S.H.

———

Hotel Chamberlin
Geo. F. Adams, Manager
Fortress Monroe, Va.
April 11, 1911

Dear Mother Holden.

Edith wrote seventeen letters this morning & was going to write seventeen more this afternoon while I was writing to you, but her plans for the afternoon miscarried. It is now nearly six o'clock & I am just beginning this. It is awfully hard for us to do anything useful.

The night before last we went to the Congressional Library. It was beautiful by electric light. The room seems to need electric light to show it off.

Yesterday we went to Mount Vernon by trolley. While there we met a Mr Wing who is connected with the wool firm of Dewey Bould & Co. of Boston. He is the only person that we knew that we have met so far.

We left Mount Vernon by boat & had a delightful ride up the river. Yesterday afternoon we called on Senator Warren of Wyoming in his committee room. He is Chairman of the committee on military affairs. He invited us to call, but when we called he was so busy we only had a minute or so with him. He sent a clerk with us to show us around the Capitol & into the Supreme Court.

We then called upon Congressman Mondell who had the fight in Congress some weeks ago. Mr Mondell was quite pleasant. He says he is coming to Buffalo next summer. Mr Mondell is the man who called on us at the Raleigh.

In the meantime (at 3:40 to be exact) we decided to change our plans about staying in Washington another day & leave that same evening at 6:45. Well it took some hustling to get trunks packed, make reservations, etc. We didn't get excited but we just worked using our heads. We made the boat all right. The ride down here was delightful. The moon was bright, the night warm, etc. Edith & I paced the deck for a long time. This morning the boat rocked a little & Edith was afraid she might get sick, but the rough water only lasted a short time & she did not get sick. We arrived at this hotel at 7 this morning.

I called Fred Cooke on the telephone & asked him to come over across the water to dine with us. Since starting this, Fred has come & gone.

We had dinner & now Edith is getting ready for bed. This hotel is a delightful place. We don't want to leave. It is right on the water. We can see Norfolk, Newport News, Hampton Roads, Fortress Monroe, & the Exposition town of Jamestown from this hotel. There were at least 400 people in the huge dining room at one time this noon. 5 battleships steamed up & anchored right off the hotel just for our benefit. Tonight we watched them give signals to each other.

I enclose our invitation to tea. We intended to go but as I said before we can't do anything useful. We will probably accept tomorrow.

I must stop now.

Affectionately,
Alex & Edith
P.S. What did you do with the bill of lading for the freight? Don't send any mail to Denver. We may not go there. We will keep you posted.

———

The Selwyn
Modern and Luxurious
Charlotte, N.C.
April 15th

Dear Mother.

Just a line to tell you we are all right. Got here last night after travelling from eight in the morning until nine at night. Great trip straight across the State of Virginia. One of these small local trains that stop everywhere. Such fun the people were. Everyone talked to everyone else, up and down the car and told them their whole family history.

The conductor, brakeman, and train candy boy[29] seemed to be engaged by the company to entertain the passengers. They came and talked with us, and asked us to come again. At one time all the people were divided into different groups talking, for all the world like an afternoon tea.

At noon the train stopped in front of a house and the conductor and Alec and I got out and had dinner. Meanwhile the train went to the station to leave passengers and then came back to wait for us. We didn't feel hurried at dinner because he was with us and we knew the train wouldn't go without him. He asked me where I was from and I said Mass. Then he said, I suppose you'll be going back there soon and I said, Oh no. Then he roared and said Honeymoon Eh! The woman that had cooked the dinner instantly became interested and when we left, hoped we'd come again.

Of course he spread the fact through the car when we got back, but we have reached the state where a little thing like that doesn't bother us. In fact Alec gets quite cross if people don't seem to think we are. The dinner was good and we had a fine time. That train boy was a caution. He called out oranges, bananas, and apples until he was tired, then for a change he yelled oysters, lobsters, and crabs! When he came through with coca-cola at last he said, "What you afraid of. Perfectly harmless. Lizzie drinks it!"[30]

Must stop now. We are going to take an auto round this town, then train for Atlanta.

Hastily,
E.S.H.

———

Edith's next few letters from the South include both her surprise and recoil at segregation and her observations about Blacks that reflect now-embarrassing stereotypes about life in the former slave states.

The "line drawn between the colored and white people" from her April 20, 1911, letter from Memphis, Tennessee, refers to local and state Jim Crow laws enacted by southern states between 1876 and 1965. They imposed segregation between the races in all public facilities. Given Edith's contempt for segregation, she would have favored civil rights and looked for ways to diversify her own experience and that of others in her circles of influence. Choosing not to delete or alter Edith's language in several of her letters, like the reference to "Southern Negroes" in the April 16 Piedmont letter, was not an easy choice to make. Edith and Alec did not live to see the end of segregation in their lifetimes. The U.S. Supreme Court ruled segregation legal in *Plessy v. Ferguson* in 1896. Segregation did not officially end until the Civil Rights Act of 1964 and the Voting Rights Act of 1965. By then, Edith had been gone for fifteen years.

At the end of the next letter dated April 16, Edith mentions that she had received a letter from Ethelyn Coolidge Haskell. Ethelyn was Edith's close friend and related to Calvin Coolidge, who would become the U.S. president (1923–1929). Later in the year this letter was written, Coolidge, the popular mayor of Northampton, Massachusetts, was elected to the State Senate.

> **The Piedmont**
> **Atlanta, Ga.**
> **April 16**
>
> **Dear Mother.**
>   I am sitting at the table waiting for dinner to be brought and as they take forever to serve anything here, I think I shall have plenty of time to write a long letter.
>   We had a long ride in the train yesterday, from Charlotte to Atlanta. Left at ten five and arrived at six o'clock (five o'clock by Atlanta time). First we have had to change our watches.

It was an easier ride than the day before because we had a fine train with diner and parlor car seats. The last of the trip from Danville to Charlotte we were discovered by a group of three girls. They spent most of their time walking up and down the aisle and giggling. I don't know why.

Passed by lots of tobacco fields where they were starting the young plants under sheets. Peach orchards too. Fine looking ones with all the leaves on. That is a great industry in Georgia they tell me. Lots of Carolina pine too. I thought all the pine trees were in the State of Maine, but I am living & learning.

We had a fine dinner last night of broiled chicken etc. We are trying to eat things that are specialties of the country. Crabs & oysters and shad in Washington, Old Point, & Norfolk. By the way, I am mailing you today a series of the menus of this place. They are the craziest things I ever saw. The English is all off and so absurd. Just have a look at them. We had a fine luncheon dish at the Raleigh which would be good for you. Take a thick slice of round bread, hollow it out a little and toast it. Put a dropped egg inside and cover with cream sauce with a little ham grated on the top. It was fine.

This morning I had sausage in buckwheat cakes. It is a Southern dish and is fine. The sausage is rolled up in a cake. You put syrup on it and cut it down through. Mighty good for a change. Be sure and show those menus to Jane. I think she would enjoy them. We are now waiting for George Washington campfire chicken stew ("a gastronomic dream of Old Virginia").

Last night we went out for a little walk after dinner but soon came back as we were tired. This morning we went to church. The waiters are so slow in the dining room (Southern Negroes who move like snails) we got later and later so didn't have time to hunt up the Unitarian church. I asked two people, but they didn't know where it was so we went to a big church near here and it proved to be a Baptist. It is on Peachtree Street. Isn't that a funny name for a street. Music fine, but mighty poor sermon. (Alec proved to me he hadn't been to church often for he put a dollar bill on the plate.)

After dinner we started out in quest of my unknown cousin with Aunt Georgie's letter for guide.[31] 196 Ivy Street. Well we found it. It was an apartment house and new. No one at home so we put our cards in the box and I wrote on the back of mine who I was and how sorry we were they weren't at home and that we were stopping here and leaving tomorrow afternoon and hoped we could see them. Then I went back to the hotel to write letters. I didn't get far, for Alec it seems had engaged a carriage for a drive and I wish you could have seen the swellness. Victoria and a span of dandy horses. Colored coachman in livery, etc. We had a splendid ride all through Atlanta's best residence streets and parks.

Didn't get back until quarter of seven. When we did we found cards in our box from Mr & Mrs John Murrell, with phone number.

As soon as we got upstairs we telephoned them, and found she had had a letter from Aunt Georgie saying we would be here the first of the week. She thought it was the first of last week but she has called up the hotel each day, and last night found we were here and so came over this afternoon. Didn't get my cards at all as she lives at 195 Ivy Street across the street from where we went. Was home at the time. Isn't that just like Aunt Georgie. I laughed so over it. To get the number wrong. She is coming over tomorrow morning at eleven thirty, so it didn't matter about the wrong number. We are to meet just the same.

This morning before I was up, a knock came on the door and a big box of pink roses was handed in. Isn't Alec the thoughtful boy. He went out last night after he had been in the barber shop and hunted up a florist and ordered them to be delivered this morning.

I thought it took him an awfully long time to get a shave and haircut, but I thought perhaps as this hotel is so crowded he had to wait his turn, so I was completely surprised. We got some lovely flowers out in the country today while we were driving. White ones and some purple and lavender ones.

I must go back now to Old Point. It was a wonderful place and we had a great time. There were five warships in the harbor and lots of men in uniform around the hotel. I never was in a hotel so large and crowded. I'll bet there were fully six hundred people there. We had a fine auto ride all around Hampton. We telephoned over to Fred Cooke and asked him to dinner and he accepted. He thought as long as he had come so far to the wedding, we ought to. They dressed a good deal for dinner so I put on my pink party dress and Alec his dress suit. Fred had to leave early on account of the way the boats ran but made us promise to go south from Norfolk and come over, take dinner with him, go to theatre, then to a Rathskeller, and start the next morning for Charlotte.

We didn't realize we were running into Race Week at Norfolk and we had an awful time getting a room. I was afraid I would be seasick on the boat going across so I made Alec get some brandy. He put it in his hip pocket. Half way over (dinner has just arrived so must pause).

(Just finished dinner and will tell you about it after finishing my other story.) Half way over he put his hand behind him and jumped up quick. The stopper had come out and half the contents gone. It had soaked his coat and overcoat and wet him clear through to the skin. How I laughed! He smelled like a regular bar room. He stood up and let his coats fly back and finally dried off. It did stain a little but the cloth is a mixed one and you can't hardly see it.

Now about the dinner. It was worth waiting for. First they brought in a metal tray, then a brazier of burning charcoal on little legs. On that was put an iron pot in which the stew had been made. I never tasted anything so good and it kept so piping hot over the coals.

If George Washington had invited me out to Mt. Vernon to have that stew, I certainly should not have had a previous engagement. I can just picture it being cooked in that big brick fireplace in the kitchen at Mt. Vernon.

I must stop now and write my letters that I still must finish.

I forgot to say how fine it was to get three letters from you last night when we got here, also one from Aunt Georgie and Ethelyn. Got your letter from Mrs Treadwell. Shall write when we are coming. Hope to see them.

Shan't hear from you again till Buffalo, as we don't
go to Denver.

Lovingly,
E.S.H.

———

The "Jennie" mentioned in this letter is Jennie Furber, Edith's
unmarried sister-in-law, who was instrumental in raising Edith's nephew,
Baby Holden, after his mother died. Holden once asked his Aunt
Jennie, "Why don't the other children call their mothers, "Auntie?"

Hotel Patten
Chattanooga, Tenn.
Tues April 18th

Dear Mother.
Alec mailed a postal I wrote you yesterday but can't
remember putting a stamp on it, so it probably won't arrive.
Well Mrs Murrill and Mrs Savage came to call. They both
were very pleasant. Mrs M. very attractive and pretty and her
mother pleasant and cordial. They stayed about an hour and
asked all about you and Aunt Georgie and Celia and Julia. They
also asked after Miss M. Harnett but I don't know anything
about her. I remember Aunt Georgie speaking of her but it is
very vague. Mr Murrill came in also for a few minutes. His office
was right across the street. We left Atlanta at five o'clock and
got to Chattanooga at 9:35. Came to this hotel. Isn't the paper
and envelope awful.
This is a corking hotel. The central room is all white
marble with frescoes painted all around for a frieze. They
represent the battles which took place around here and really
are very well done.
I wonder what Jennie meant by saying we would not like the
south, the hotels were so poor. The hotel in Atlanta was a fine big
one too, and Norfolk too. We haven't struck a poor one yet.

This morning it was sort of drizzly and the sight-seeing auto that is advertised to leave at ten didn't leave on account of the rain. What did Alec do but engage a private auto and chauffeur to take us around the battlefields. I shan't tell you how much it cost, you'd have a fit. Anyone would know he was on his wedding trip all right. I don't know when I've had such an interesting ride. We were gone three hours and a half and went about fifty miles. With the glass up in front you weren't conscious it was raining at all.

We went to the battlefield of Chickamauga. There are tablets and stones all along showing where each Northern regiment stood and opposite where the Southern ones were. The battle lasted two days. It shows how the Northern men were pushed back over the fields. You could see just how each regiment was forced back. Just think of it, thousands of men were killed in that two day battle. One field he showed us, very good sized too, he said when the battle was over you could walk the length of it on the dead.[32]

The city of Chattanooga was where the Union Army retreated. They were cut off for sixty days from supplies. The town is in a valley surrounded by mountains. The first relief they had was when Gen. Hooker came across way up at the top of Look Out Mountain, which is the highest one here, and fought the "Battle above the Clouds". You can see the ledges that his men came across. At the same time at the other end of the valley, Sherman crossed the river at night with his men.

Then came the battle of Missionary Ridge. He took us up on that ridge. Showed us where Grant's headquarters were and where Bragg, the Confederate General's, were. The Confederates were on the top of the ridge and the Unions charged up. The monuments scattered about in the trees show which regiments got the farthest up. Sheridan's was right on top. If the Confederates hadn't feared Sherman was coming around on the other side of the ridge, they probably would have held it. As it was, when they saw the Union men coming running up the hill, they held it a while, then retreated and went to Atlanta, in fact left this part of the country, so it was a Union victory.

Gen. Rosecrans commanded the Union army at Chickamauga where they lost so many men, and if they hadn't got Grant in here they might have lost their army. At Chic. the battle line when drawn up ready for fighting was three and a half miles long. It certainly was about the most interesting morning I ever spent.

We leave here tonight at 10:25 and arrive in Memphis at 8:45. The first night travel we have made. The other day trains were locals and no parlor or diner, so we have to go this way.

I have written the Treadwells we expect to arrive in Kansas City Friday morning. Wasn't it lucky you happened to send me that letter with the address. Haven't time to write more.

Affec.
Edith

———

Peabody Hotel
Memphis,
Thursday, April 20, 1911

Dear Mother.

Just remembered I didn't drop you a line yesterday. I meant to but we decided suddenly to go to the theatre and I forgot.

We arrived at 7:50 yesterday morning after the first night spent in the train. I didn't take my hair down, so I could put my hat on and not have to go in the dressing room, as we got breakfast at the hotel. I didn't feel nearly so bad as I thought I was going to. This is a big place. Larger than Atlanta. But what surprises me is that the foliage is much further advanced than in Atlanta and this is so much farther north. I wore my fur coat on that ride in Atlanta and was perfectly comfortable.

Well yesterday at about eleven Alec ordered an auto to come for us to show us the town. Fine easy riding machine with a southerner who talked so southern we could hardly understand him. Fine big parks and residences here. Signs all around "Make Memphis Mighty".

The town has grown from 120,000 in 1907 to 135,000 now. There was a fine park all along beside the Mississippi river, which by the way is rising rapidly. We can see it from our window, and this morning it has completely covered a point of land we could see yesterday, and there is a house over on the other side with no land around it at all. Such dirty brown water. Out in the park it has eaten great hunks out of the banking. I shouldn't want to live side of such a treacherous river. We got back from our drive about quarter of two having seen everything worth seeing.

What surprises me is the line drawn between the colored and white people. Separate cars, separate decks, and sides, on the boats, and here separate amusement parks.

The chauffeur we had in Chattanooga said he had been on a car where they had stopped it in the middle of the city and taken off the bell rope and "hung a nigger" with it. They treat them with such contempt.

The largest cotton warehouse in the world is in this city and we are going to hunt for it this morning.

We leave tonight for Kansas City tonight at eight. I wish I had told you to send some mail there to the Treadles. I can stand not hearing for a few days, then I get uneasy.

Tell Mr Stone to send by mail some more pills like Miss Lothropic. We are both well and having the time of our lives!!!

E.S.H.
Finished all my notes before I left Atlanta, about 62 in all. Will send you the list later so you can check them off. E.S.H.

———

Memphis
April 20, 1911

Dear Mother.

Have just looked over the list and am enclosing it. I am sitting in the station now waiting to start for Kansas City.

We didn't look up that warehouse after all, but took a trip of two hours on a Mississippi River boat. The water is rising rapidly and we saw where it is flooding the country bordering on the river. Great trunks of trees are coming down stream, and this afternoon, green trees which means danger. The water was surrounding some farm houses, and others had only a strip of land left. There were lots of Negroes on board playing the banjo and singing. I'm so glad we went, for it was a typical Southern scene.

Train is late. Hope I don't mind sleeping in the train tonight. I'm so glad to have those letters off my mind. You didn't tell me what Alice Ropes sent.

Love to all.
E.S.H.
Check these names off in the book, then look through to see if I have forgotten anyone.

_____

Saturday, April 23, 1911

Dear Mother.

I didn't get a chance to write you yesterday. We were an hour and a half late so we didn't get in until twelve o'clock.

I didn't feel awfully good when I began to get up. I laughed to myself when Alec was buttoning my shoes and handing me things. It certainly did seem funny to have a man doing it. He certainly is a dear. I thought it would be fatal to go in the dining car, and I also thought we were going to get in early and I wouldn't need any breakfast. Alec had some hot coffee and a couple of oranges sent in from the dining car, so I was all right. I was the way I am on the steamer. All right if I sit still.

The Treadwells called up at 12:30 and we were invited to go out to their house to dinner. Alec went to the stockyards in the afternoon and I stayed at home, slept and read the Ladies Home Journal. At five thirty Helen & Marguerite came with Paul Campbell their brother-in-law. He had a touring car and took us for a ride about the city first, then to the house. I forgot to say at five o'clock, the loveliest bunch of sweet peas and lilies of the valley arrived for me to wear (from Mr Alexander Healy).

Mrs Treadwell was just as cordial and kind as ever. The dinner delicious. Grapefruit, soup, broiled chicken, potatoes, asparagus, tomato & lettuce salad, ice cream & coffee. The ices were individual ones in different shapes. Mine a bunch of purple grapes. Prettiest thing I ever saw. After dinner (Paul Campbell was there) we went over to Emily's house. She has grown quite stout but it is extremely becoming. Paul C. has an Amati violin and Emily's husband plays piano so I played to them most of the evening.

I am writing this on the train, so I can't write very well.

Mrs T. looks well but the girls look worn out, especially M. Guess they have had too good a time.

I guess there may be something doing between Paul C. & M. (don't tell anyone else this). If there isn't, I will say I don't like the way they acted. Too free and easy to suit me. The other brother Herbert (Helen's man) was not mentioned. We were brought home in the auto. I was afraid I had taken cold, so I took a hot bath, and we got a hot lemonade and I took some rhitertis, so this morning I feel better. I haven't wholly got rid of it yet in my head, but it is broken up all right.

We stop this noon at St. Joseph, Missouri for luncheon. That is where the McKinneys came from. We arrive in Sheridan tomorrow at 2:45. Left K.C. at 10:30 AM.

This is the longest stretch we have had to travel at a time. It has been a fine trip. We have had everything the very best and the easiest and most comfortable.

When we arrive in a city a porter meets the train, takes us to a carriage. We go to the best hotel, always have had a room with bath. If we get in in the evening, we go out and take a walk down the principal business streets. If in the day time, leave an order at the hotel desk for an auto or a carriage to see the city.

If we stay overnight, generally we have been to the theatre. I discovered when we were in Memphis that it would take only the same time it took to go to Kansas City, to go to New Orleans. If we only had the time we would go, as Alec says, he still has plenty of money. So we will land in Buffalo not broke. Isn't it too bad we haven't the time to go.

These night journeys are what use me up though and I guess I've had enough of a trip for covering so much ground.

People have spotted us as bride & groom in this train all right, on account of those flowers. I put them away last night and they look perfectly fresh, and girls don't generally travel with a bunch of flowers in the morning when the man is with them.

I never had anything so convenient as that long black silk scarf. I don't see how I ever lived without it.

I have been traveling in my blue check skirt, crepe waist and black silk coat. I washed the crepe waist with the dots on it and it dried in three hours. I washed it about eleven o'clock and when I came back from lunch it was ready to wear. Looked finely too. My brown suit I had to put in the suitcase as we couldn't have our trunks on such a short stop. We got to the hotel at 12:30 PM and Alec called for the hotel valet at once, and he took my suit and waist and pressed it and I got it back at three o'clock.

We have certainly had all the luxuries the city and modern hotel can give. Now for the wilderness and only absolute necessities.

The thought doesn't bother me at all.

Affec.
Edith

Edith and Alec sloshed and slid through the muddy ruts that traversed the foothills of the Big Horns between Sheridan and Buffalo. This 2013 shot was taken from Massacre Hill above the old road. Credit: Jerry D. Sanders.

CHAPTER 3

WILD WEST

Edith and Alec's train trip ended in Sheridan, thirty-five miles north of Buffalo. From there, the Chicago, Burlington & Quincy turned north to Montana to meet the transcontinental Northern Pacific. The Healys, however, were headed south to Buffalo so made the last leg of their honeymoon in a canvas-topped taxi after a heavy spring rain that resulted in a frightening five-hour skid up and down the steep foothills of the mountains. Today, even in a rainstorm, the trip only takes about twenty-five minutes on I-90.

Edith mentions that Alec got off the train at Clearmont to talk to the station master about whether trunks and packages they mailed had arrived. Buffalo and Clearmont were both established on Clear Creek and small ranches were built along the creek between Buffalo and Clearmont and beyond. Although the Healy Brothers Ranch was closer to Buffalo, they shipped by rail from Clearmont, not Sheridan. In the spring, the brothers sent wool east to the mills in Rhode Island and Massachusetts; in the fall they separated the mountain-fattened lambs, some to go to the markets in the Midwest, usually Omaha, the rest to be wintered in the lower-elevation rangelands by the ranch.

The Sheridan Inn
Warner & Canfield, Proprietors
Sheridan, Wyo.
April 23, 1911

Dear Mother.

Well here we are so far. Arrived at three o'clock this afternoon.

I felt pretty well when I wrote that letter to you that I mailed at St. Joseph Mo., but after that I felt sort of horrid. We had our lunch there at St. J. but they put on a diner at night. Alec could see I didn't feel very well, so instead of asking me every few minutes how I felt (you know how mad that makes me) suggested that as we had a fifty minute wait in Lincoln, Nebraska (Bryan's town[33]) we take a cab at the station and drive up to the Lincoln Hotel and get something to eat and I wouldn't have to eat in the diner.

The cab to the hotel was a joke for as soon as we turned the corner at the station we saw the hotel, about two blocks from the station. We told the waiter how much time we had and he hustled and we had a fine meal which I could enjoy.

When we got back to the station we ran across a man Alec knew named Meyers. He used to have a Drug store in Buffalo. I sent him an invitation. He and his wife went fifty miles up the road on our train. Both about our age and very pleasant. She said she knew I'd like Buffalo. This morning I felt absolutely the limit. I got dressed while the train waited at the station. Alec had grapefruit and coffee sent in but it was all I could do to swallow it. Sleeping cars do finish me. Later in the morning I began to revive, and by noon, when I could get out on the platform at each station for some air I was all right. Had a good dinner and felt real well when we landed here.

I came right up to the room and got off my clothes and took a nap while Alec called up his brother to see if he could do anything for him here, and tried to fix up our trunks to go over tomorrow. He got off at Clearmont and saw the station agent, who said no trunks had arrived yet but two express packages,

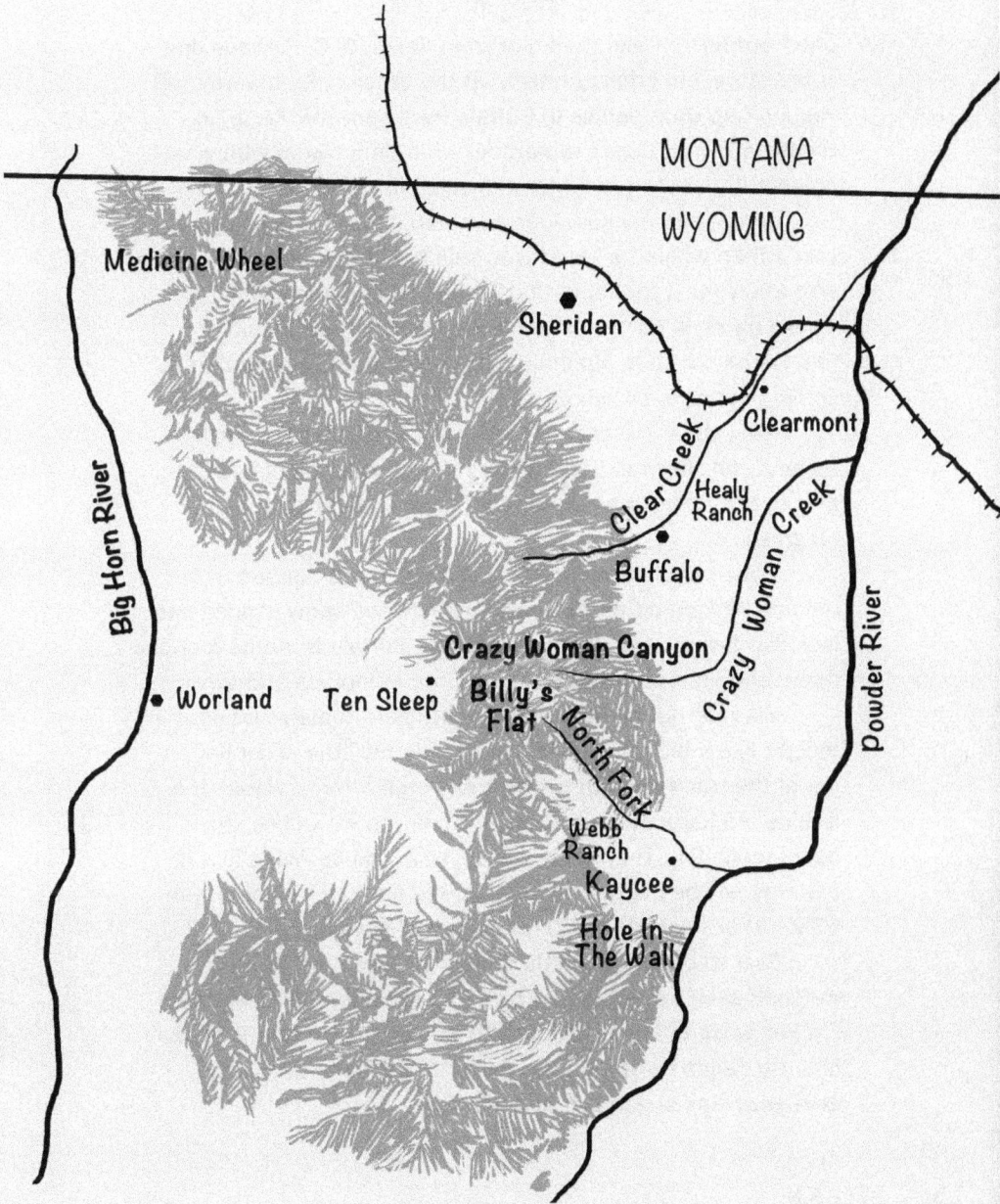

MONTANA

WYOMING

Medicine Wheel

Sheridan

Clearmont

Clear Creek

Healy
Ranch

Big Horn River

Crazy Woman Creek

Buffalo

Crazy Woman Canyon

Worland

Ten Sleep

Billy's
Flat

North Fork

Powder River

Webb
Ranch

Kaycee

Hole In
The Wall

Map: Meagan Healy

one from Boston and the other from Wash. D. C. Perhaps that is the stove, but I don't know what the other is. By the way, will you look up what people in Buffalo have sent me. I tore up the list and now I can't remember what name went with what present and when I meet them I would like to know.

After I had my nap, Alec came up and said he had just met a man whom he knew, who said his Mother knew a lady who knew me. I met him after dinner. Fine looking chap, whose name is Turnbull and his Mother is a great friend of Mrs Fairbanks up to our church. Isn't that funny. His mother is coming out here this summer.

Now about the country. If I hadn't seen Utah[34] it might be an awful shock to me. I know you will have a large sized fit over it. Stretches of sandy hills with just sagebrush and dried up grass.

However when we struck this town, those blessed mountains loomed up. They are magnificent, snow capped and look like Switzerland. We are, or rather Buffalo is, at the foot of them, and I know I shall never get tired of looking at them.

We may not be able to get out of here tomorrow. Looks tonight like a big rain storm. I shall take my little black hat out of the trunk and put my best one on if it rains. However if it rains too hard, the autos refuse to run, so we will be stuck here indefinitely. They need rain so, what will be Alec's loss in one way, will be his gain in another. We have come home with $350.00 besides the $200.00 his father gave him.

Ever since we struck the border of Wyoming he has watched each expression on my face. The poor boy is so afraid I'm not going to like his country. It was actually pathetic to see him. He needn't worry for I'm perfectly willing to take what goes with him, sagebrush and all.

Affec.

E.S.H.

The Occidental Hotel
Warren & Co., Props.
Buffalo, Wyo.,
April 25, 1911

My dear Mother.
    Well I am actually in Buffalo at last and I know you are anxious to hear all about it from the very beginning, so I'll start there.
    My last letter was from Sheridan saying it looked like rain and we didn't know whether we would be stuck there or not. Well it rained all night quite hard but it cleared in the morning so we started.
    Six of us. Another girl and her husband, two other fellows, Alec and the chauffeur. It is, in ordinary weather and with ordinary roads, a two hour and a quarter ride.
    Mother, never in my whole life have I had anything that could touch it. It certainly was a red letter day in my existence. In my wildest dreams I never imagined anything like it.
    In other words I think if I thought I was going to have another like it, I'd lay right down and cheerfully die (provided Alec did the same) rather than go through that experience a second time.
    To begin with, and end with, the roads were a mire of slippery mud and up and down curved and hilly places. The way that car skidded was enough to make your hair stand on end. By skidding, I mean slewing around in the mud when the brake has no hold on it. We ploughed through mud, up sides of hills, slipped and slid across bridges that had no side rails. In fact did everything but upset and that is what we (I anyway) expected any moment. When two hours of this had passed I thought to myself, well I don't believe I can stand much more and I asked how far we were from Sheridan. Twelve Miles!!!! was the answer. Forty miles between Sheridan and Buffalo and we had come twelve in two hours. Six miles an hour in an auto and we hadn't stopped once. Well I said to myself, I'm in the hands of Providence and I've got to take what's coming

to me and if I am in need of training in Western nerve, here's
where I get it good and plenty.

There were two places where I thought we were gone
sure. The first was where we were in a deep ditch like place.
We tried to go ahead but the machine stuck so the driver
backed and in backing the car skidded and went along
backwards at an angle of forty-five degrees. One more degree
and we would have gone over. Why we didn't I don't know but
the car righted itself. The other place was when we were nearly
in to Buffalo. You climb a long succession of hills and as we
were almost at the top of the last one, it struck a slippery place
and began to slide backwards across the road toward a ravine.
It was there the other girl let out a scream. I think I should
have, had I been on the side of the ravine. As it was I had all
the sensations I wanted. The brakes caught and stopped us just
a foot from the edge!! I said in a firm decided voice, I am going
to get out and walk up this hill even if I get covered with mud.
You should have seen those men jump. They were all dying to
do it but each one didn't want the other to think him a coward
so they didn't suggest it themselves but I never saw men so
eager "to oblige a lady."

It took us five hours to make the trip, and when I
happened to look down from the windows of the hotel on to the
top of the canvas cover over the machine, I found it was thick
with mud, so you can imagine what we went through to throw
mud that height. That was the worst trip the driver ever had
and he has been making trips every day this winter.

I think we girls behaved remarkably well. She only
screamed once and I not at all. I never spoke from the time we
started until we landed, so when Edith is silent five hours you
may know there is something doing.

Lame and sore! My gracious when we weren't being flung
from side to side we were being tossed up in the air, hitting our
heads constantly against the canvas covering! Alec says in all
his life he has never had such a strain on the nerves.

This is the day after and all the effect it has left on me is that I am tired. I am going to bed now and will mail this, writing you the rest tomorrow.

Affectionately,
Edith

Alec has gone to the ranch and out on the range tonight and I am alone. He hated to go but it was necessary. This is what I have to get used to so I might as well begin.

Everyone says that's a fine ride when the roads are in ordinary condition, so don't imagine you will have to go through anything like that when you come out here, unless you choose the rainy season as I did. We should have gotten off at Clearmont and driven over.

You were the only woman I could think of who could have stood it without yelling. I don't think I could again.

Freighters haul goods and barrels of water up Buffalo's Main Street.
This photograph, probably taken from the bridge over Clear Creek, dates
to the 1905-1910 era. Credit: Johnson County Library.

CHAPTER 4

FIRST IMPRESSIONS

APRIL 26, 1911

BUFFALO – MEETING BROTHER AND SISTER-IN-LAW

Patrick, Jr., often called Patsy, like his father, and his wife, Mary, welcomed the newlyweds with dinner at their home on Wednesday evening, Edith and Alec's second night in Buffalo. Edith mentions the couple's two children, Patricia, 6, and Patrick Healy III, whose first birthday was the next Sunday. A son born in Buffalo on December 18, 1906, had died shortly after birth. Consequently, in 1910 Mary had traveled to Los Angeles to deliver Patrick, III, and returned to Los Angeles later in 1911 to deliver their last child, Stuart Sedwick Healy, on December 26.

In telling her mother about the welcome dinner, Edith mentions the bouillon cups and plates that Mary used, "like the ones that Helen did for me." Helen Healy Lynch's wedding gift to the couple was a set of white *Hulschenreulher Selb* Bavaria porcelain that she hand painted with gold bands. She initialed an "H" in gold on the serving dishes. Helen and her husband, John, manager of the Healy Hotel in Ogden, lived near her parents' ornate Victorian home. Helen kept a studio for her work in the third-floor turret with light from three directions. Her oil paintings, water colors, fancy needlework, and painted china were displayed throughout the nearly six thousand square foot, four-bedroom, gabled house.

Occidental Hotel
Buffalo, Wyoming
April 26, 1911

Dear Mother,

This is the next morning and I am sitting under a cottonwood tree on the bank of Clear Creek, which is rushing by me, and straight in front of me are the most wonderful mountains, all snow capped. I haven't gotten over the surprise in their beauty yet. Do you remember our ride into Chamonix, the last part of it, with that range of snow capped mountains ending in Mt. Blanc. Those with the glaciers down the sides. Well, this reminds me of them. These mountains are just as beautiful, leaving out Mt. Blanc. No, I won't say that either, for over to the right I have just discovered a new high peak. There are foothills in front of them, so you don't see such an expanse of snow as Mt. Blanc. They say here they are snow capped even in summer. Imagine what it will be to be up among them this summer.

Well, my last letter was telling you of the ride over, but I only told you the disagreeable part. I didn't tell you how beautiful the scenery was. Hill after hill without a tree and some of the hills were bright red in color, just like those pictures you see of the Grand Canyon or the Colorado. Such interesting scenery. Nothing like the southern part of the state that we struck first.

I certainly am pleasantly surprised with it all. I don't want to say too much, because I don't want you to be disappointed when you see it. All the trees there are, are cottonwoods and grow along the edge of the creek and into the town. The town was put here on account of the creek, as water is so scarce in this country. Well, we landed here at 1 o'clock, had dinner, and I went directly upstairs for a nap. The hotel is a nice clean looking place on the main street, right beside the creek. It seems to be run by a couple of men who look like college boys. I should say one is about 28, the other 26. O yes, there's another older one who doesn't look so like a college man, and he is about 35, I guess. He told me this morning he came from Omaha, had only been here a year, but wouldn't go back for the world. Going upstairs that day after dinner, Alec introduced me to a mighty nice looking fellow named Allen who informed me he came from Gloucester. The next morning a young fellow stopped and spoke to Alec, who asked him to sit down and have breakfast with us. I don't know whether it was intentional on Alec's part, but I certainly was nonplussed when this one said he came from Providence. There certainly are a lot of Easterners in this country. The Gloucester man said he never was going back to stay. That fellow Turnbull, whom I met in Sheridan, who came from Boston, said the same thing. I guess it's in the air.

I told Alec one good thing that that ride did for me, was to make me contented to stay put for awhile and not try to get back home while the roads are like this.

Just after I started to lie down, a knock on the door, and a lovely lavender primrose in a brass jardiniere was handed in with a card from Mrs Patrick Healy, Jr. Alec wanted to call up his brother, so I told him to go down and do it, and thank Mary for the plant and find out what time they would like us to come over. I didn't know whether she had forgotten or not, that she had invited us to dinner the day we arrived. I got the letter in Boston and answered it in Atlanta.

He came back and said we were expected at 6 o'clock. He then went and got the mail. I had two nice fat letters from you and a D.A.R. one, and the pictures. I had my brown suit in the suitcase, so Alec took it across the street and they had it pressed and brought back by 4 o'clock. He went to the Express Office and saw your package there, but didn't take it, as we have no place to put it, but brought another one. It was a beautiful tall dish or vase-like thing, with a silver ladle. It is all open work silver and on a silver standard, and inside, with a half-an-inch edge showing, is an etched glass bowl. It would be lovely for berries, or you could use it for flowers. Really, it is a stunner. It was sent from Omaha to 1876 Beacon Street, returned to Omaha, and sent here. It came from a Mrs H. G. Cook. Alec nearly dropped dead when he saw it. It is from a man who has sheep and they are constantly having fights, he says, over the range. It is (Cook's) sheep that are always butting into theirs, etc.

Mary was extremely pleasant. Looks just about like her picture. I don't think Alec's brother looks like him at all, and yet when I saw him in the street yesterday, I could see the family resemblance in the way he stood and walked, and something too, in the general build. But nothing alike in features. We had a very nice dinner. Soup in bouillon cups like those Helen did for me, also plates like them. I admired them, and she told me Mrs Healy gave them to her.

The children are healthy and bright looking. We left at 8:30 as I was rather tired. Came home in the pouring rain.

The next morning Alec took me to the bank, and I deposited my check and he gave me power of attorney over his account there. It is a national bank, so you can draw checks on it. Then he had to get into his ranch clothes and start out for the sheep with his brother.

When he was dressed, he came in my room, and when he walked over toward me, and knelt down by my chair to say good-bye, I felt as if I were in some kind of a play with costumes and that I ought to have some lines to say. (It's lucky I didn't have them to say, as it would have been a physical impossibility.) He looked just great in his gray flannel shirt, leather belt, dark blue trousers tucked into high, tan riding boots, with his blue coat over his arm and broad-brimmed hat in his hand. I don't see how the girls out here ever let him get away.

Mary, the other night, said, "I know one young lady here, our music teacher, who is wild to see you. She intended to marry Alec herself, so I guess she won't love you an awful lot." If looks would kill, Mary would have been dead on the spot from the one Alec gave her.

I have seen this wonderful music teacher, and she's very attractive, and a hundred times better looking than I have ever thought of being. She was on the ground too. I wonder how I ever won out.

After Alec went, I tried to pick up things a little, and sat down for awhile to read the new Ladies Home Journal, when a knock came on the door, and there stood Mary and Patricia. I was in my kimono, but thank goodness I had fixed the room up, so I asked them in. It was about half past eleven, and she said, she wondered if I didn't want to come up and have lunch with her, and eat up what was left of the dinner we had last night. I said yes, if she would be willing for me to leave right afterwards, as I had to write a long letter to you.

So they waited until I got dressed, and then they had several errands to do, so it was after one when we sat down to lunch. I stayed till about 2:30 and then came back and started my letter. I wanted to lie on the bed and write, so took off my skirt, and slipped on my kimono. A knock on the door, I opened it to find two ladies dressed in their best with their cards in their hands and me in a kimono! I laughed and said, "If you'll just step in the parlor (it was next door to this room) I'll slip on my skirt and be in in just a second."

Apparently they don't have bellboys here. If you want anything, you ring, and the clerk at the desk runs upstairs, three steps at a time, leaving the safe open, etc. and goes and gets what you want. These ladies were Mrs Mather and Mrs Kube, both about my age. Very pleasant and cordial. Wanted me to come right over and see them soon, especially when they found Alec was away, they were very urgent. They made quite a call. When they had gone, I came back, but in slipping off my skirt again, I put it where I could grab it on my way to the door. It is my brown suit and that skirt wrinkles awfully. I don't understand why.

Well, another knock on the door, and I took my time answering, getting properly clothed. This time it was the clerk, and he handed me a card, saying the lady was in the parlor. I wonder if those ladies spoke to him about their predicament when they went downstairs. This was Mrs Langworthy. Alex had said a lot about her, and said she wasn't young nor pretty, but he liked her best of anybody here in town. I had pictured her about 55, rather stout, etc. She's about 35 or 38 and slender. Not pretty, but sweet, and extremely pleasant. She came here as a bride from Buffalo, New York, about eight years ago.

She told me some funny experiences she had. One of them was when they were in the hotel. The old one before this

BUFFALO, WYOMING

Inside Adams & Young grocery store, a gathering place
for men to solve the problems of the world, c. 1905-1910.
Credit: Johnson County Library.

Left: Adams & Young Grocery's delivery buggy waits to be loaded, while a crowd of men seems to have nothing to do but stand and observe at W. H. Zindel's bar and hotel next door. The hotel also had an entrance from the alley for discretion, a herd of elk in a backyard pen, and a reputation for exceptional cleanliness.

Below: Edith wrote several letters from the balcony of the Occidental Hotel. The gathering outside was the 1912 Good Roads Convention, held the weekend before a flash flood in Clear Creek destroyed a large part of downtown. Edith was still in Boston with baby Alec, Jr. during the disaster. All photos credit: Johnson County Library.

new one was built. She had hung her husband's dress suit up against the wall, way in the back of the closet, which was an outside wall. He didn't need to use it for some time, and when she went to get it down, it was frozen solid to the wall! She had to get a lamp and thaw it out and pry it off the wall. It seems that there was a big snow bank on the other side, so that accounts for it some.

As I have been sitting here (I am now back in the hotel again and have had my dinner at noon!) I have seen cowboys dash past and just now, three carts lashed together passed, drawn by six pairs of horses. The first two carts looked like farm wagons, but a prairie schooner brought up the rear. Every man in sight has on either a black or brown sombrero.

After Mrs Langworthy went, I remembered the mail comes in at 4 each day, so I hurried downtown to see if I had any from you. I got stung, only an announcement of Sidney Garrigues' wedding. As I was coming back, met Mary on the street, and then we saw brother-in-law in auto, just in from the ranch. So we got in and sat there while he did his errands, and then he took us for a short spin, bringing me back to the hotel. After supper, I wrote that letter to you, and one to Mary, and then went to bed. I'm so sleepy all the time. They say it's change of air.[35] I guess it is. I feel just as I do at the beach the first few days.

This morning after breakfast, I strolled out and found that dandy place I described in the beginning of this letter, then came back for my writing materials. Found a package awaiting me. A present from Mr and Mrs Peter Balden. You know planked steak and fish are quite popular. You cook them, then put them in the oven on a certain kind of wood and finish cooking them. Well, this is a plank with grooves for the gravy to run in so you can get it easily. It has little silver knobs, one on each end (guess they are nickel though, silver might melt.) Then there is a filigree silver open work dish to set it in for the table. Mighty pretty. Has two handles, one on each end. I never saw one before. It came from the jewelry store here. And tied with this up-to-date cotton ribbon like we saw first in Europe.

I have written the three notes of thanks, to Mr Cook, Mr and Mrs Martin Hibbard, and Mr and Mrs Peter Balden. Will you enter these in the book.

It is now 3:30, and I think I have told you everything up to date.

I never saw so many young people in a town. I could count the fingers of one hand, any people over 50. More good looking young men between 20 and 30. When I was passing a stable, there was a fellow there harnessing a couple of horses into a farm wagon. Alec spoke to him. He said after we passed, that's one of our ranch hands. Graduated from the University of Minnesota, I believe. That Mrs Langworthy said during our talk she and her husband had planned a trip around the world in the spring. He is the president of one of the banks here, but a banker in a town of so few people, you wouldn't think could make such a lot of money. She was awfully nice and invited me to come anytime, if only to sit on the piazza and read a book. She's fond of bridge, and as soon as Alec gets back, wants us to come up for a game in the evening. Here I've been here only two days, yet I don't feel lonesome at all. People are so kind.

Before I forget it, I wish you'd send me those fancy cutters for potatoes and vegetables that we got Christmas time at the Mechanic's building and didn't give to the cook. They would be just the thing to dress up a plank steak with.

Mary has lots of dandy books, and I have borrowed one already. The Ordeal of Richard Federal by George Meredith. Alec subscribed for the Thursday and Saturday Transcripts, so I can keep track of what you are doing in Boston. What a long run that play at the Castle Square is having. Hope you go, and also that the girl who wrote it gets something more substantial than praise out of it.

Love to all,
Affect.
E.S.H.

There isn't a house in this town more than one story above the street. I can't get used to it. Everyone stares at me, and whispers to the person with them who I am. Hope they like the looks.

Sheepwagons were the original camper-trailers that many in Wyoming enjoy today. These undated photos are from the Basque collection at the Johnson County Library.

CHAPTER 5

TWO FIRSTS

MAY 2 TO MAY 9, 1911

FIRST TRIP TO HEALY RANCH – FIRST TRIP TO
A MOUNTAIN SHEEP CAMP

Edith wrote this undated note on an envelope sometime around May 2, 1911.

Dear Mother,

Spent my first night in a sheep wagon. Slept from 8 in the eve. to 8 in the morning. Guess I'll do. Used the grey worsted socks in my sweater suit for my feet and they were fine. Alec is now out catching his two horses for we are going to drive to the ranch and get the saddle horses. It will take all day, so we have put soup in the thermos bottle, and with fruit, and crackers, and sweet chocolate, expect to live through the day. I'll mail this at the ranch.

Affec.
E.S.H.

———

Sheep Camp
Dry Creek
May 5, 1911

My dear Mother.

At last I've settled down to writing you a good long letter. I've been here four days now, and I've seen such new people and things that I don't know just where to begin to tell you about them. The reason I have such a fine chance for writing you is that Alex had to go to the camps on Antelope Spring and Rattlesnake Spring, and fascinating as the latter place sounded, as it was a long trip, I decided to stay at home.

As soon as he went, I did some washing. Among other things I washed out the crepe waist Julia did for me. I put it on a hanger to stretch it right, then went out on my front lawn to see where to hang it. I tried the front door knob, but the wind blew it against the wagon and got it all dirty and I had to come back in and rinse it again. Finally I decided I guessed my favorite clothes horse, the cactus, was the best place. It was grand. I just laughed out loud when I looked at that waist on a coat hanger, fluttering from a cactus. With a crepe waist you have to pull it every now and then to have it dry in shape, but with this, I just pulled it, then punched one of the cactus needles through the place and held it there. So I never went near it at all, and it looks great.

I looked out the front door, and it certainly did look funny to see each cactus holding up a piece of my underwear, and although the wind was blowing a gale, nothing got away. Then I came in and swept my house and made the bed. I was going to start and write then, but a brand new copy of the Transcript tempted me, and I fell (on the bed). Alec has the Thursday Transcript for the wool sales, and subscribes to the Saturday one for me.

A freighter came from town last night bringing the papers and also a letter from you. I was so glad to get it. I will write Aunt Emma Williams about the Dinah.[36] It wasn't in the book, that's why I forgot it. I asked Lillian[37] to enter those Portland things Uncle George brought and she must have forgotten it. After I read the Transcript, every word, I went and took in my clothes, which were fine and white and dry.

Then it was dinner time, and now that I've had my dinner, I'm sleepy, but I know if I don't write today, I'll put it off too long. I'm so glad you had such a nice time in Providence. Grace Calvert's wedding must have been lovely.

Well now, I'll begin at the beginning, and that was last Monday.

I repacked the trunks, as we left them in the hotel, and

the new wedding presents we've had since we came to Buffalo. Mr and Mrs Langworthy gave us a lovely little silver basket. The trunks and my best suit and Alec's good clothes are all in a closet of the hotel, locked up. We brought out here a suitcase, Alex's grip, my Mexican satchel, and my violin. It had had to be my good one, and the other one, which I had fixed for this occasion (how do you spell that word anyway) is in the trunk that hasn't come.

Oh, by the way, we got the bill of lading all right, and the agent in Clearmont is to call us when they arrive. (That express bundle was from Omaha from Mrs R. G. Cook, a very massive silver dish, not Washington, D.C. as he said.)

Where was I? O yes, well we bought a large army bag like one of those sailor bags we used to have. Made of heavy cloth and drawn up at the top. By the way, in this country, the only thing that is a bag is a grip or satchel, everything else is a sack. I have been laughed at a good many times for speaking of a paper bag. It's a paper sack, or just a sack. It sounds so funny to me. Well we had that army sack full of things. My perfect riding habit had to go in it, and the riding boots, and the high brown boots, another suit of clothes for Alec, bag full of holey stockings for Edith, books, etc. All these things, including a big barrel of water, were piled on the buggy. The water out here is too alkaline to drink.

It took us until after dinner to get started for we had so many things to collect. We bought a lot of things at the grocery store Saturday night, and they were brought out on a freight wagon.

Things like fruit, and soups, coffee, cocoa, dates, figs, cheese, peanut butter, olives, chow chow[38], catsup, baked beans, shredded wheat, pineapple, shredded cod fish, bacon, etc. Lots of those things they have here in camp, but we got the best grade, whereas they have a medium grade.

It's lucky we didn't have to bring those things on the wagon with us. We got started at about 2 o'clock. I wish you could have seen us on the main street of the town, filling our water barrel. A crowd collected on the sidewalk (a crowd for

that size of a town, about 10 people) as they always do when
anything interesting is going on. All sorts of costumes on the
people. Two ladies stopped and Alec introduced me. A Mrs
McRae and Mrs Anderson. Both live on ranches and were in
town doing some shopping. They heartily approved of my going
out to the camp and said I was the right sort.

It was a cold, disagreeable day, and in the morning,
snowed a little. Alec said if it wasn't pleasant and didn't warm
up, perhaps I'd better not go, but anything I hate is to get all
ready to go anywhere and then give it up. And I knew he had
to go anyway, so we started. I had on my old green dress, black
fur coat, with a grey scarf and long grey mittens, so I was fine
and comfortable. We got out here about 5. I never saw such
country in my life. Such brilliant coloring. Bright red hills, all
sprinkled in with green hills, and with a deep blue sky, it looks
like the picture postals that always make things look more vivid
then they really are. It doesn't take an impressionist's eye to
see color in this country. On the whole of that drive we never
passed one single house.

This landscape can never get tiresome, even if there are
no trees, because the horizon is so broken. A lot of the hills
look like extinct volcanoes they are so pointed. As I look out the
front door of the wagon, the skyline looks like this.

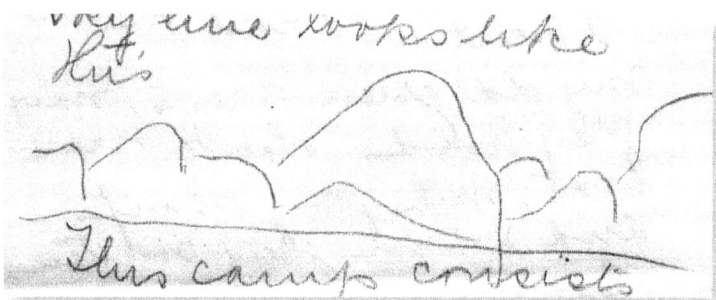

This camp consists of one cabin and one sheep wagon.
The cabin is of logs plastered with mud and has two windows
and a door, and a sort of a shed behind. In the cabin there is a

stove, a long table covered with oil cloth, and several shelves around, which hold supplies. Four soap boxes are chairs. When we arrived, the cook, who was the only person around, had a nice hot cup of coffee ready for me. It tasted mighty good for I was just beginning to realize I was pretty cold.

Meanwhile, Alec had gone to work with a broom and scrubbing brush to get that sheep wagon in some kind of order. He had had so much on his mind he had forgotten to tell one of the herders to do it before we came. I can easily see where he might forget most anything, for it's no joke to be one of the heads of an outfit the size of this one. By the time we got our things in the wagon, it was suppertime. The wagon was right side of the cabin and Alec wanted it moved, but it is quite heavy and his team of horses couldn't pull it any distance, as they aren't large horses. So when a freighter from the ranch appeared with his four-horse team, we got moved all right. We are about as far from the cabin as Hitchcock's Drug Store is from 876.[39] There is quite a rise of ground between so you can't see the cabin at all. O, I forgot. There is quite a large corral back of the cabin that they use for the sheep when they want to sort them out. Different little yards opening out of each other, with gates that swing.

This is not a new sheep wagon. You see Alex didn't want to buy a new one until we saw whether I could stand the life, because they cost $240 apiece and they have 14 in the outfit now. They are the same shape as a prairie schooner, only not such a high or curved top.

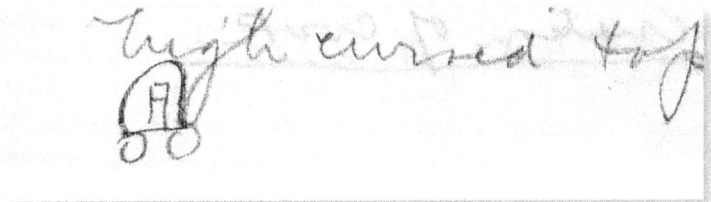

Isn't that artistic. The wheels are going wrong. There's a front door with a good-sized pane of glass in it. The door is

divided so you can have half open at a time if it is too cold.
In back are three little windows. Just as you enter the door on
one side is the stove, with a funnel going through the canvas
roof. By the way, the body of the wagon is wood, and from side
to side are curved pieces of wood. This frame is covered with
white canvas.

To go back to the stove. It is a very large one, it seems
to me for the size of the wagon. It has four holes and a
good-sized oven. In fact, the stove in the cabin is exactly
the same thing, and the cook served dinner to ten men
the other noon. In back of the stove, fastened on the wall of
the wagon, is a good-sized cabinet with doors. That's where
we put our provisions.

The bed is the next thing, for it takes up the most room.
Over the bed is a revolver stuck in the wall, just for local color,
I guess. It[40] is really a shelf that goes from side to side of the
wagon. It is quite broad and so high up you have to climb into
it. No springs!!!!!! You are supposed to work so hard during the
daytime you won't feel the lack of springs at night. A mattress
comes first, then a couple of grey cotton blankets for sheets,
and then all the blankets and puffs you can beg, borrow, or
steal. That night I wore a union suit, flannelette nightgown and
Alec's heavy blanket wrapper. I was fine and warm and I slept
like a top as I have every other night, so I guess springs aren't
necessary for me.

Under this shelf bed is a fine big, clapboarded place to
put things. Our army bag is there and the suitcase, two bags
and sundry boots and sweaters that we may want to grab at
a moment's notice. Running along the sides of the wagon
are seats, that is, a long shelf to sit on. Where it isn't over the
wheel, it lifts up and you can put things in there. Outside in the
back, there's a large place for provisions too. It really goes in
under the bed, for that place where the bags are only takes up
half the room. There are two drawers, too, where the bed shelf
goes over the seats that run along the side. The floor and the
top of the seats on each side are covered with oil cloth, and
under the stove is a piece of tin.

Top: Sketch of the old Healy Ranch House by Dollie Iberlin, who lived there from first grade through high school. Most likely the first house in Johnson County with smooth, finished wood, it was a gracious home with high ceilings and large airy rooms, each with its own outside door.

Above: Edith wrote to her mother: "This is our good Jimmy. Looks horrid and so do I."

There is a place for a lamp, and several hooks around.
One big one over the bed holds my violin, another holds my
little black hat in a black silk bag. It certainly is cozy in the
evening with a fire in the stove and the lamp lit. It's hard to
keep it cleaned up because there's so little space that you
seem to need it all to move around in. When I come again,
I'll bring some sofa pillows. You certainly need them.

The next morning after we got here, Alex wanted to go
to the ranch. So we heated some soup and put it in a thermos
bottle, took Uneeda biscuits,[41] and oranges, apples, bananas,
and figs, and sweet chocolate, and started. It's only about eight
or nine miles from here, but driving in this country is not exactly
like on the Newton Boulevard. I thought I'd seen steep hills for
driving in Maine, but I've got over the idea. No dwellings, exactly
one lone sheep wagon, did we pass on our drive to the ranch.

The ranch is in a valley, or rather on the flat place between
hills, and is a fine location. In itself it is just a group of farm
buildings with a good sized white house. Alec's brother happened
to be there, and took me inside the house. It has stood empty
ever since they moved into town in the fall. All the rooms on one
floor. A good-sized living room with fireplace, dining room, two
bedrooms, and bathroom with modern plumbing. It would need
a good deal of fixing up, but it could be made quite attractive.
However, I don't think I want to live out there when both men say
they can run the business as well from town as from there, as
the sheep are seldom near there except at shearing time.

They have big shearing sheds and a wool warehouse. They
have two men and their families living there who have leased it.
I don't quite understand it, but they seem to be superintending
the ploughing of the ground, etc. They raise alfalfa and oats,
wheat and potatoes. In the shearing shed is a gasoline engine
for shearing sheep. At shearing time they have 20 shearers
working at once. About May 20 they begin.

We went to the ranch to get a couple of saddle horses.
One that Alec had been keeping especially for me, and one he
wanted for himself. So Alec departed on a horse to drive them in.
This is when brother-in-law and I had our trip through the house

and talked. I asked him how many horses they had in the outfit, and he thought for a moment, then said counting everything, they had about 150. Think of it. They have to have a man come up every year to break the young ones in for riding and driving.

Alec was gone quite awhile, but by and by I saw a cloud of dust and eight horses tearing along the road with him in back of them.

I said what on earth is he bringing so many for. Does he think we need four apiece? How Patsy roared at me. He said Do you think he could go out in the hills, and pick out your two and drive them in. He would never be able to get them that way. He has to drive in a whole bunch that is feeding together and get them into the corral. Then get a halter over the head of the one he wants, put it in the barn, go after the other, put a halter over his head, and after getting him into the barn, let out the others again onto the range.

When they came dashing up the road together, Patsy called to me and said, you stand on one side of the gate and I'll stand on the other, and perhaps I can dodge the two he wants into the little corral. To which I replied firmly, "If you think I'm going to be tramped to jelly, you've got another think." Me for the buggy.

I thought he'd die laughing. He couldn't get over it. He said "How do you ever expect to get on a horse if you feel like that. My but I'd like to see your first try at it." Then he would howl with joy at the thought.

It began to look like rain so we hurried into the house for our lunch, and then started for home.

We had a pair of the horses on the buggy anyway, so he tied my saddle horse by the bridle beside the span, and put the other on behind, as the road is sometimes narrow. So feeling like a circus parade, we hurried for home.

O by the way, I forgot to say they use coal to cook by here at the camp. There's a small ledge of it right below us on the creek. They have a good coal bank on the ranch land,[42] and Patsy told me each fall they would get out 20 tons and put it in the cellar for the furnace and that would last them all winter.

On our way home, Alec said he guessed he'd stop at that coal bank and get some. It was easier to get at than ours. So the circus parade went up the side of a hill, and he took the pick that was there and got out a few hunks which he put in the back of the wagon. He said it is not the best grade of coal. It has to be used soon after it is taken out or it crumbles to pieces. If you put it in the house for the winter, by spring it begins to crumble.

We got a little wet, but not enough to amount to anything. Alex had just got back and I have read this to him, so the corrections are his fault.

He said he's got to go to town tomorrow for the sheriff, so I am going too and will mail this and write the rest later.

Affec.
E.S.H.

———

Edith's letters show a love of horseback riding, but she must have given it up fairly early as her son, Dan, didn't remember ever seeing her ride. Alec continued to ride horses out to his camps, but liked moving faster. By the end of 1911 he owned a motorcycle and by 1919 he owned a stripped down Model-T Ford that you had to sit on the gas tank to drive.

While the Healys were on the mountains thinking about horses in 1911, the first Indianapolis 500-Mile Race took place and Louis Chevrolet was a few months away from releasing his first Chevy, which General Motors would acquire in 1918 to compete with the Model T.

Dry Creek
Sheep Camp
May 9, 1911

Dear Mother.
Well this is the second installment of my long letter. I believe I left off where we were coming home from the ranch.

O, by the way, I do know now about leasing the ranch to those two men. They run the ranch on shares. It is quite a common thing in this country. You see they (those two men) don't have to have any capital to do it. Everything is provided, land, seed, horses, and machinery to work with and they supply the work and take as pay a certain proportion of the crops. It is a good thing for Alec & Patsy as they haven't the time to see to it and yet have to have the alfalfa and oats for the feed for the horses. The horses that are working have to be fed. Those who are not working can get along on the grass on the range with an occasional meal of oats.

Well when we got back from the ranch that night and had our supper, Alec wanted to know if I didn't want to try my horse. I wasn't so crazy about it but I thought it was as good a time as any. After he had had that trip from the ranch he wouldn't feel very lively. So I got into my clothes and got on. I rode much better than I expected I could, but I haven't got on to that "lope" yet. I can trot as I'm used to that but I do bump awfully when he tries that rocking horse effect. It looks so easy when Alec is doing it. I have been riding several times now and have made some improvement but mighty little.

It's great though, riding in this country. You don't stick to the road but go across country. The horses are all so sure footed and climb like cats. You go down into these gullies and up again without thinking much about it. The bank is steep but the earth is soft and I am using Mary's saddle which is a Mexican one and has a high knob sticking up in front. You aren't supposed to touch that but I hang on to it when I'm going down and up a steep place. Riding in this country is certainly worthwhile.

The next day we didn't go anywhere and I stayed in bed late. Alec generally gets up at six and has his breakfast with the men, and talks over with them what they are planning to do, and often rides out with one to help him if there is anything important to do. He gets back about eight when I have my breakfast.

After that day off, the next one we started for Crazy Woman. So at last I've seen that wonderful place. Side of it, Sedgwick[43] is a howling metropolis. In Crazy Woman district are two houses, five miles apart with a school house between and two sheep camps that move all the time. O, there is one log cabin they use as a sheep camp in winter. That's all! The drive over was lovely. We took my saddle horse along too with the span, as now and then Alec would see a bunch of sheep up on the hills and he'd get on the saddle horse and gallop up to see the herder in charge. I never am afraid because in all the drives I've taken about here I've never met a person and you can see all around you for miles and miles, and could see a person half an hour before he would get to you.

We ate our dinner in a lovely little grassy place under some trees, about the only group of trees I've seen since I've been here. We had a nice lunch. Tomato soup, hot out of the Thermos bottle, Uneedas to eat with that. A bottle of olives, crackers and cream cheese. An orange, banana, and apple apiece and for desert sweet chocolate with nuts in it. After lunch Alec smoked his pipe awhile and then, as everything was so peaceful and quiet, we both found ourselves sound asleep before we knew it. When we woke up we were struck with the same idea at the same moment. We would go wading in the creek. I felt I had to make that creek live up to its name of Crazy Woman, so I added another to it. We started for home at half past four getting here at seven.

That was on May 4th, hardly the way we spent April 14th. I tell you what would have been a fine present for someone to have given us and that is one of those automobile lunch baskets. We have to take so many all day trips. Next time you go downtown will you look at them in Jordan's and see what they have in them and the cost.

Saturday, as I wrote you, we went in town stayed to dinner, and I got some clean clothes from the wash woman's and we came back in the afternoon. I got your letter written Monday night when I arrived in town and we waited for the mail which is open at four and your letter, 2 in one envelope, mailed Tuesday morning came on that mail.

Yesterday we made an all day trip to Antelope Spring. That was Monday. On Sunday we didn't go anywhere for we were sort of tired from our trip to town. In the afternoon we had just finished dinner. We had it in the wagon for a change instead of at the cabin with the men. We had just got it cleared up too and Alec was smoking and I reading out loud one of your letters which I got in town and he hadn't heard, when he gave a jump and said, Callers! Quick! I jumped too, because I had taken off my dress while we were clearing up, and was sitting in my white shirt waist and long black moire petticoat. He threw things around and I struggled into my dress, and then had to start to meet them, half unbuttoned in the back.

If any place on earth I thought we would be free from unexpected visitors it is here, for no one uses this road except this sheep outfit. It was Mary and Patsy and their little girl [Patricia] and a Mr and Mrs Alex Laing and their little girl. Patsy had brought them all out in the auto and why we didn't hear it I don't understand. The men went down to the cabin to talk business and the two ladies came in the wagon while the children played outside. It is almost impossible to keep a sheep wagon cleared up. There is so little extra space. But as they had both been in sheep wagons before (Mrs Laing said she spent a whole summer in one), I didn't mind as much as I might.

I gave them sweet chocolates and opened a bottle of olives and some ginger snaps. They stayed two hours. They were real pleasant but toward the end I began to wish they would get a move on.

The men were interested in that sheriff business that took Alec to town. It seems one of the herders had a fight with the herder of another outfit. The other herder said he was on his land and took up his gun and shot a sheep. The herders in this outfit are at a disadvantage as they are all Basques and don't speak English. So the others take advantage of them and get the best grass for their flocks. It has happened several times and Alec wanted to make an example of this man to stop it.

He went to see the herder's employer. Also his own lawyer before he saw the sheriff. They are going to fix it up some way so as to stop this constant taking advantage of these foreign herders. Unless stopped now it will assume big proportions and they won't be able to get men to be herders.

You asked if I noticed any difference in my breathing on account of the altitude. No I don't notice any difference at all and that very sleepy feeling is leaving me now.

While I remember it, I haven't a copy of Kipling's Captains Courageous so don't change that one that was sent me.

I must tell you now about the sheep as I haven't said a word about them and they are a very important element in our lives.

The first evening I got here I saw my first herd of sheep. They were directly across from here on the side of a hill shaped like this. [Edith is referring to a missing sketch.] They looked just like a lot of white ants on an ant hill.

There are nine camps in this outfit, with three herders and horses and dogs in each. Each camp has about three thousand sheep to look after. At this time of the year when the lambs come, the big herd is called "the drop band." Each day when lambs are born, the ewes and lambs stay together and the rest of the band moves on. They have to have extra men to watch these little bunches to find a sheltered place for them at night and see the coyotes don't get the lambs. When the lambs are fairly good size they join several of these small bunches. Sometimes they start a drop band from two camps and join them when they get small enough for one man, with horse and dog, to handle. In the day time all the sheep are moved so as to have good feed and near water. At night flags are put out around the bunches as their fluttering scares coyotes. At night also they put lanterns to show where the different bunches are to aid a man called a "nightshooter". There is one in each camp and his duty is to go at sunset, and all night long, walk with a lantern around the different bunches, and fire a gun at certain intervals. He sleeps all day.

Most of the outfit are ewes. In fact twenty-nine thousand ewes and one thousand rams. Just now the rams are all in one bunch. They used to have forty thousand sheep but sold ten thousand last fall as the outlook for winter feed was so bad. This spring looks very good. The water was getting low but it rained and snowed last night so the springs have filled up. It was hard on the lambs that were born in the night though. They do the best they can for them though, get them in sheltered places, but a sheep doesn't seem to have any sense in trying to keep a lamb warm herself. A certain breed of sheep have to be watched very closely as the ewe will walk away and leave her lambs to starve unless looked after.

The men have long poles with curved iron pieces on them so they can catch a sheep by the foot to bring her back to feed her lamb. These are called, shepherd's crooks. When a man is on horse-back with one of those things, they look like pictures of Knights in a tournament with long lances.

The lambing season is most over now. They have at present about ten thousand lambs and they are getting ready for the shearing season. Each one of these herds has to be brought to the ranch. They have to time it so one herd comes in as another goes out. They have engaged twenty shearers, who arrive at the ranch May 20th.

They have a gasoline engine at the shearing pens and a man is hired each year to come from Chicago to run it. Alec & Patsy have all they can do to see to other things at that time. The shearers are paid nine cents a sheep and one Australian, Alec said, last year averaged two hundred and fifty sheep a day so you can reckon what his pay would be. These shearers travel together and start shearing in February in California and work east getting here the 20 of May and then go up from here to Montana.

Now, another big item of the business is that every man in the outfit is fed. Herders get from forty-five dollars a month up, and their food. All the shearers are fed too. In lambing time there are over fifty men to be provided with three meals a day. The rest of the year about thirty. That in itself is no small item. Alec does that. Every order goes through his hands and is signed by him before the goods can be purchased. Most of the buying he does himself, the herders suggesting what they want.

It's no joke to keep nine camps supplied with food and
drinking water in barrels. They have very good things to eat too,
most anything they want.

There will be forty to feed at the ranch for a month.
They are going to take the cook from here and give him two
assistants. Four dollars a day is what the head cook at shearing
time gets.

Where there are several herds within several miles of
each other, they have a central camp at this lambing time and
a cook. That's what we are here at Dry Creek. I guess there are
about five cooks now working.

This one is a character. I talk to him by the hour. He is
about forty-five I guess, maybe older, and has quite an Irish
brogue. I know now how to order my breakfast in the proper
way. This is what I have. "Two in the water easy, with a strip on
the side", or "Two on four", or "Bacon in the country". The first is
"two soft boiled eggs with a piece of bacon." The second, "two
dropped eggs on four small pieces of toast, each with a piece
of bacon on the top." Third and last. Some slices of bacon put
in the spider and when nearly done drop the eggs on top of
them and fry all together. That is fine because the bacon is all
through the eggs. They have "Ham in the country" too.

Well we have a stove in our wagon and plenty of fruit and
canned things but this cook is so obliging he lets me come and
have a meal anytime I want. I don't like to eat when the men
are there. They are a pretty dirty looking set, although they
have nice faces.

He makes nice hot biscuits and macaroni and cheese
with tomato in it. Gives them all kinds of pie, doughnuts,
and pudding, cake, coffee, tea, and chocolate, good canned
vegetables, lamb with potatoes, bread pudding. Really
everything very nice.

Well this cook is a character. He wears an old undershirt
which once might have been red, but is now pale pink. Over
this are black suspenders, one end in the back fastened with
a nail. Old pair of trousers covered with a white apron. The two
top buttons of his shirt are old, on purpose I think, to disclose

a large tattoo mark on his male chest. It is one of the most elaborate designs in tattoo (and probably the most painful), called "The Rock of Ages." There are similar designs on each arm. He was a sailor first, then fought under General Lawton down in Mexico in '85-6. He has been all over the world. To England, Ireland, & Wales, to Sweden, Antwerp and all the seaports of France and Spain, Bermuda and most of the coast towns on the Atlantic and Pacific, Honolulu, China and Japan. I spoke of what a poor sailor I was. He said, "O you'd soon get over it." I said, "Well I went from Boston to Naples once and didn't get over it." "Boston!" says he, "Were you ever there. That's my home town. I was born in Boston."

Now what do you think of that!!! He was born in East Boston and went from there to sea when he was a young man. He's been wishing ever since, he could bake me a pot of real Boston baked beans. He hasn't been back there for nearly twenty years.

Now I guess I've told you most everything I know myself. Alec says he thinks we have to go to town tomorrow. Powder is giving out for the nightshooters and also water is low in this camp and one other.

I tell you what. I think this is a pretty big business for two young men to handle. I guess it's lucky for them their father was in the business once and they call on him for all sorts of advice. And when the blizzards came winter before last, he took the first train from Ogden and came himself and worked as hard as they did. He certainly is a pretty fine father to them. Alec seems to think he's the finest father that ever lived. But I know another who was just as fine. Must stop now and go for a horseback ride as Alec has just appeared with both horses.

Affec
Edith

Buffalo's Post Office c. 1905-1910: Edith's lifeline to all that was familiar
and a receptive audience for tales of her adventures.
Credit: Johnson County Library.

CHAPTER 6

BACK IN BUFFALO

MAY 19 TO MAY 21, 1911

ALEC SATISFIED WITH HIS WIFE
DEALING WITH RELIGIOUS DIFFERENCES

The Occidental Hotel
Buffalo, Wyoming
May 19, 1911

Dear Mother Holden,

I want to tell you that I am satisfied with Edith beyond all expectations. She is one girl who hasn't a single fault that I can see. I wouldn't want her any different.

Edith will stay in town for a few days at least. We have no cook at Dry Creek now and I have to be away from camp so much, and she can hardly go with me on account of rain and long journeys, so we thought that she had better stop at the hotel until I get located again. We start shearing tomorrow.[44] Edith may come down to the shearing plant to stop when we get underway. Edith reads most of your letters to me. I'm awfully glad that you are so cheerful. It makes it so much easier for Edith to know that you can be so cheerful in her absence. It is fine that you have so many clubs and societies in which you are actively interested.

In closing I will repeat that I am perfectly satisfied with my wife.

Affec.
Alex

———

Sunday afternoon
May 21, 1911

Dear Mother.

Well, here I am sitting on a balcony which is just down the corridor from my room. It is a lovely place to sit. Two stories up and shaded by trees, while the creek goes rushing by underneath. Clear Creek. It is rightly named, for you can see every stone at the bottom. Not like those rivers we saw in Europe that came from melting snow. On second thought they came from glaciers, didn't they and that accounted for their grey, muddy look.

It is a wonderful day. Quite cool, but clear out and the mountains stand out wonderfully distinct. There is one place looks just like the Jungfrau, only a little different shape

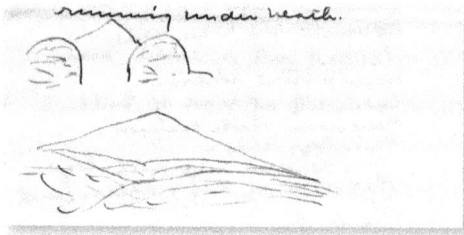

That is the shape of the Jungfrau; this is the shape of the one I'm looking at. The scratching part is meant to represent the dark green foothills, in the foreground, which makes the white snow stand out so much more. It certainly is beautiful. I can see it from my back window, but not from this window. The trees hide it.

All the trees there are around this section are concentrated in the town. Mostly along the main street and the creek. They are cottonwood trees and have become a mass of fresh green since I arrived here.

Well, I went to the moving picture show last night, as I said, and found Miss Hartman and Mr June there, and they called over to have me sit with them, and I had a real jolly time.[45] The pictures were very good. They are a long series of films acting out regular plays.

This morning I slept so late I almost missed my breakfast. Then I wrote a letter to Belle Bartlett thanking her for those runners and I washed out my crepe waist, the one that Miss Curtis made the things for. Those two waists have been invaluable to me.

At twenty minutes past 10, I started for the Episcopal Church. When I arrived, I found Sunday school in progress. I took a back seat and stayed. When they were having the lessons, the lady who is superintendent came and spoke to me, also another lady who is a teacher. I found out that since their rector died a year ago, they haven't had any, but hold service every other Tuesday evening when the rector from Sheridan comes over.

They are working for a fund to build a rectory, so they can call a man. They have two women's societies, the Auxiliary, which raises money to support the Sunday school, and the Guild, which supports the church. Then the two work together for the rectory fund. They were very pleasant ladies, about seven of them. She insisted I should stay after the Sunday school and meet all seven. Mrs B. S. Langworthy was one, sister-in-law to the other Mrs Langworthy, who is away just now. This Mrs Colgate, who spoke to me first, said she was coming to call on me for she thought we would have more than church matters of mutual interest, as she came from New York City. She was very pleasant. About 45, I should think. They had a little discussion as to when and how and who would see to cleaning and putting the church in order for the summer, which sounded just like the Alliance.

I didn't sail under any false colors. I said right out, when they asked me to take a class in the Sunday school (no, I guess they didn't ask that, but I thought they sounded as if they might) that as there wasn't a church of my denomination in town, I had decided I would like to come there to church and help in any way I could. I said I couldn't teach in the Sunday school because, of course, I couldn't teach anybody what I didn't quite believe myself.

I told them right out I was a Unitarian, but it didn't seem to bother them much, and I can plainly see I shall be playing in the Sunday school before I know what I am doing.[46]

They were very cordial. Counting teachers and scholars, there were 41 present. Doing pretty well, I thought, for a little church without a minister. I got home about 12, and got out my fiddle, and practiced awhile, then went down to dinner. Very good dinner, this noon, with chicken pie, and vanilla ice cream with fresh strawberries around it.

Jack Rice, that fellow Marion Cushing knows, came over and ate dinner with me, as he was all alone too. He is going out to the mountains for a six week surveying trip. Starts this afternoon. He said two men registered last night from Shelburne Falls, and he went up and spoke to them. They knew his uncle and a lot of other people he did. Where on earth is Shelburne Falls? Is it near North Adams?

After dinner, I read the whole of Molly Make-Believe.[47] You want to read it. It's an awfully cute story. Then I took a nap, and here I am. This balcony overlooks the street, too, and I am constantly looking at the people and teams that go by. The Clearmont Stage has just gone, along with its four horses, and its white canvas cover. That means they must get mail on Sunday. I guess I'll go to the post office later.

Now, about the momentous question about a house for us. We will try and find a furnished one for the winter, and then build next spring.

The other day, Mrs Mather said she wished we could have the lot next but one to her. I wish we could because it seems to me that's the desirable end of town, all new houses, but I guess that lot would be pretty expensive. Luckily it is owned by a man who is in the sheep business, and who Alec does business with, for they hired some of his range this spring.

I am anxious to talk it over with Alec and see what he thinks. Then too, it would put me in the opposite end of the town from Mary, which would be a good thing, I guess. Their lots are in the old part of the town, and I think they intend building soon. So much for that. Now what kind of a house.

Edith and Alec participated in St. Luke's Episcopal Church, as their faith—
Unitarian—had no church in Buffalo. St. Luke's, whose cornerstone was laid
in 1889, remains an active parish. Credit: Johnson County Library.

When you go to Portland, I want you to go out and see Ethelyn's house again and look at it from a critical standpoint and see what you think of one like it for us. I suppose it would be easy enough to get the plans.

It seems to me it is the prettiest bungalow I've ever seen. Of course there are some things I couldn't get out here. Fancy windows, etc. The only drawback I can see, is where the bathroom is. In case of a party, you have to go through the bathroom into her bedroom, and in case someone stayed in the bathroom sometime, you couldn't get out until they did. However, you don't have a party every day, so perhaps it would be well to build for every day. Then she has three rooms with closets upstairs and space for a bathroom. In the winter, if that wasn't needed, it could shut right off. I think I should like the living room just a grain broader. I don't think the den necessary. You see if you think the den could be part of the living room.

Another advantage in Ethelyn's house for me would be that I know exactly what it's like when it's done, and with these plans on paper, you don't. Now this bungalow here. Two square rooms opening out of each other. I didn't like it at all. I had rather have Ethelyn's house than that one we saw in Watertown any day in the week. You see what you think.

I'm going to get your letters and see if there's anything to answer. A nice long letter from Bertha Smith. Wasn't she nice to write. Also Mrs Piper.

Won't you have Nellie and Florence King, 103 Elm Hill Avenue, Roxbury, and May Young, Fuller Street, Brookline, and Lillian Raymond, Roseland Street, Cambridge, and Florence Collins, 33 Cypress Place, Brookline, over some afternoon. (I haven't written to one of them.) And tell them to bring their sewing and you'll read some letters about the sheep wagon to them. Tell them just what time the reading is to begin, so you won't have such a broken up party as you did with the others.

Ans. I. The sheep and cattle drink the water on the range. They don't mind it, and it doesn't hurt them.

Ans. II. The cook made bread, and I seldom eat it anyway, and I had all sorts of crackers—Uneedas, graham, oatmeal biscuit, ginger snaps, etc. If we got any meals in our wagon, Alec did the cooking. He insisted, and far be it from me to stop him. We bought a little alcohol stove. It will heat a quart of water in nine minutes.[48] Fine for a hot water bag, or for making a cup of coffee or chocolate, or heating soup.

My gracious, a boy has been fishing in this creek just opposite me, and has just landed a big trout. I suppose I ought to tell him to stop jumping around and throw the trout back in the stream for it's a Sabbath day, but I guess I won't.

Those pictures Alec sent me do not give you any idea of the country. They make it look flat and uninteresting, whereas it is cut into all sorts of hills, and with its vivid coloring, is extremely unusual and striking. The drive to Crazy Woman from Dry Creek is wonderful!

The temperature here fluctuates about as in Boston. Day before yesterday, I thought we would have a snow storm, and just now, several girls have gone along street in white muslin dresses. One day it was quite warm while I was out on the range, and the sheep looked so funny. One sheep, of course, in a certain position, cast a shadow. Another saw it, and put his head in that shadow, then another came and put his head in that one's shadow, and there was a whole long line of them, all in the blazing sun, when just below, was a gulch where one side was all shady. If that row of sheep didn't look silly! Foolish.

I am glad for Mrs Wiggin that she has rented her house to such good tenants. Always glad to hear about Marion.

Isn't that Michael McDonough the limit! Think of the time you gave him to get that road done. Yes, I should think it would be hard for the Millers.

I just saw the clerk of the hotel come along the street (in his shirt sleeves) with his arms full of mail, so I went and got my hat and jacket, and went to the post office. Got a letter from you, and the card case from Miss Vinton. I will write her tomorrow. Wasn't it nice it came just now, when I haven't any, and need one so much.

Too bad Aunt Lucy feels so horrid. Excuse me from a honeymoon on the briny deep. What a horrid time Mary

Wetherbee must have had.

Just saw two dandy looking white serge suits go by.

When I was at the post office, I met Mrs Van Houten, who asked me if I was to be in town now for a few days. She said she wanted to come and see me.

What a surprise to have Sarah Studley really say she was coming to visit you.[49] I guess you would like to see her, you haven't for so long.

I can't imagine Maud Benedict marching.[50] I'll see you doing it next. Nice of Gladys Olmstead to call. No, I don't see how she can sing in tune if she's deaf. Makes it quite convenient for you to have the Huguleys go to B.B. so often.

It is now supper time and I shall eat mine, and then I think I'll take some books I borrowed up to Mary's. It's nice having a place I can run into every time I feel like it. I suppose her husband is down to the ranch now all the time.

It has been a wonderful day, and now the mountains are turning dark purple. Good night for the present.

Affec.
Edith

Haying on the Healy Ranch, about eight miles east of Buffalo
on Clear Creek. Credit: Johnson County Library.

CHAPTER 7

NEIGHBORLY VISITS

The Occidental Hotel
Buffalo, Wyoming
June 19, 1911

Dear Mother.

Well, we've had a fine day. We started about 10 o'clock
for the Simmons Ranch, which is the one beyond the Healy
Ranch. We would get there about noon, and Alec said of course,
Mrs Simmons would expect us to stay to dinner, but I don't
like to drop in on people unexpectedly on a hot Monday, just
at dinnertime, even if it is the custom of the country. So I got
some fruit, cherries and oranges, and some Uneeda biscuits, and
graham crackers, and sweet chocolate. Stopped at Mrs Van's and
put some milk out of the ice chest into our thermos bottles.

It was just 12:30 when we arrived there, and a Mrs Oliver,
who is keeping the ranch this summer, when she saw us turn
in the gate, ran out in her sun bonnet, and said, "How do you
do, Mr Healy. Put your horses right in the corral, and Mrs Healy,
let me help you out. Come right back, Mr Healy, because I'm
just about to put dinner on the table." How's that for ranch
hospitality. I learned later they hardly ever sit down to a meal
that one or more don't drop in, mostly strangers too. Mrs
Simmons said that winter before last, when the weather was so
bad, she and Mr Shad always had about six extra to every meal.
She always set the table for eight. Just think, and they would be

insulted if anyone tried to pay for it. You see it is on the direct road between Clearmont and Buffalo.

We ate the cherries on the way out there, and drank the milk at about 4 in the afternoon, and it was still cold.

Mr and Mrs Simmons have filed on a homestead that adjoins their ranch, and the rule is you have to live on it six months a year for five years. So they have a log cabin on it, and live there in the summer, at least eat and sleep there. The rest of the time they spend in their own house. They got this Mrs Oliver to run things during the summer. This is the last of the five years, so next February that extra land will be theirs.

Alec went out there to get a mare and colt he wanted to bring to town. He took along my saddle horse too, to see how she went. Tied her side of the span. After dinner, he and Mr Simmons went to round up some horses and get the mare and just as they were turned back, Alec took a picture of them. A lot of them belong to Healy Bros. Hope it's good. Also took a picture of the procession with me in the buggy, three horses in front and mare and colt being led behind.

When we got to our ranch they were getting in the alfalfa and used such a fine new apparatus I wanted a picture of it, so he tied the mare with colt to the gate and we drove in, and I hope those pictures turn out well. I took three. When we were coming back, I said, "There go your mare and colt!" And sure enough, two little specks in the distance were racing back as fast as they could go.

Alec jumped out of the buggy and onto my saddle horse, and went after them. He never caught up to them until he got way back to Simmons! The mare had broken the rope of the halter. I guess I had to wait an hour for him to get back, so it made us very late getting back to town. He said that little horse of mine was a dandy.

We had a fine time last night at Mrs L's. Didn't get home until after 12. Had orange sherbet with whipped cream on top and angel cake. People stay so late at parties because there is no last car or train to catch.

We called on Mr and Mrs Stein the evening before. It's going to be awkward liking them both so much. I like Mrs Bert best, and Alec likes Mrs Stein best. Didn't get the mail yesterday, as it was Sunday, and today we were too late, so haven't heard from you for so long.

Must stop now, as I am sleepy.

Affec.
E.S.H.

Even in 1911, shearers at some ranches, like the Healys,' used electric clippers operated from a gasoline engine. Bellies are shaved first, with the struggling sheep quieted by being tucked into the shearer's arms and legs. Fleeces are bundled inside

out with the clean wool on the outside. These sheep are a desert breed descended from the Spanish Merino, known for their fine, long-strands of wool. Credit: Johnson County Library. Unidentified ranch, unknown date.

Edith's snapshots of seemingly fat, fluffy sheep waiting to be shorn, contrast (below) to the gangly looking, shaved sheep waiting to be herded up to mountain pastures for fattening up.

Patricia Healy, 6, cuddles a black lamb for Edith's camera. Below, fleeces crammed into large bags are hauled to the railroad for shipping to the Eastern woolen mills. Credit: Johnson County Library.

Abundant rainbow trout made fishing for dinner a
quick and relaxing task for Alec and Edith at the end of the day.

CHAPTER 8

BILLY'S FLAT

JUNE 25 TO 30, 1911

LIFE IN A SHEEP CAMP

Although much of the grazing in the Big Horns in 1911 was on public range, not long after their arrival in Johnson County in 1892, Healy & Patterson purchased the high meadow in the Big Horns known as Billy's Flat for their summer headquarters. The name came from the original homesteader, a fastidious person known as Uncle Billy. As Dan told it, "The story goes that he wanted to kill himself so he put a wash tub on the floor of the sheep wagon and cut his throat in such a way that he would bleed into the wash tub and not mess up the wagon."

From Billy's Flat the Healy Brothers could oversee their herds, totaling about 45,000 sheep in 1911. To care for that many animals, the sheep were grazed in bands, each with a herder. According to Dan, 45,000 sheep need 100,000 to 150,000 acres, depending on whether it is a good grass year or bad, and if they're at a low elevation or a combination of high and low elevations.[51]

Billy's Flat Sheep Camp
About June 25, 1911

Dear Mother.
    We have just arrived here. It is noon and we started from Buffalo yesterday morning at 8:30 in the morning. We expected to make the trip in one day, but there have been two heavy storms this last week, and when we got quite a distance out,

we discovered two bridges washed away. We forded the stream in one place, but when we came to the second, Alec was afraid to try it, for the wagon was so heavily loaded he was afraid it might break the springs, the banks were so steep. So we turned in Joe Todd's ranch and inquired if the road that led through his ranch would take us in the right direction.

He came back to the wagon with Alec and insisted we come in for dinner. Said they were just sitting down to the table. So in we went. He is a well educated man about 35. They sent us a wedding present, you remember. His wife used to live on the ranch, but they have four children and so they moved into town so the children could go to school. Mrs Todd called on me a few days before. She reminds me of Philip Nichol's wife. Joe Todd has 2,000 acres, most of it under cultivation. A sister of the woman who was on the Healy Ranch was on this one, and we had a real good dinner. Bacon, stewed tomatoes, potatoes, onions, and lemon pie. Then we started on.

The worst hill road in the state of Wyoming comes six miles beyond Todd's Ranch. It is called Crazy Woman Hill.[52] Everyone has told me how awful that hill was ever since I said I was going to the mountain. Mary said she preferred to walk up. That's the way the road goes. [Edith is referring to missing sketch.] Well we had about a thousand pounds weight in that wagon, counting us. So Alec said he'd like to get on his saddle horse, hitch a rope to the wagon, and around the saddle horn, and help pull, if I'd drive. So that's the way we went up.

It took us two hours to climb that hill, and just as we got to the top, a thunder storm struck us, but we had gotten over the bad part. Really, I never saw such a road. Full of rocks. Great big ones. Ledges that you had to drive over. Had to constantly put the brake on and stop to give the horses a rest. You weren't afraid of going over the edge. All you were scared of was that the wagon couldn't stand the strain. We passed two freight teams on the side of the road minus wheels. It would be impossible for an auto to go up. We met a man just coming down who told us to use his sheep wagon for the night, a Mr Stapler whom Alec knows.

It was raining hard and blowing, so we said we would,

CRAZY WOMAN CANYON

Edith wrote: "The worst hill road in the state of Wyoming...is called Crazy Woman Hill. Mary said she preferred to walk up." Top: Entrance to Crazy Woman, 2012. Left: By the 1930s, the narrow curved road was smoothed, but tight limestone overhangs still remained spectacular, as they are today. Credit: Johnson County Library.

although Alec said we could go to the first ranger's cabin, which was only two miles away. My hunting suit had a chance to prove it was waterproof. Before we got to Stapler's sheep wagon, it stopped raining, and the sun came out, so we went on. We also met that Mr Cook on horseback going to town and he told us we were welcome to his sheep wagon. They are apt to be pretty dirty places, so I didn't want to go in them unless I had to.

Well, by 6 o'clock there was still two hours and a half to go, and the horses were so tired we had to stop. We stayed near the Road Ranch, which used to be like an inn, but when the new liquor law was passed prohibiting a saloon except in an incorporated town, this was abandoned.

It was a wonderful night, and Alec had his bed that he uses on the range, so we spread it just beside the fence, so the cattle and horses wouldn't step on us. We had hot coffee and milk in the thermos.

———

Sunday, June 26, 1911
Altitude 8,000 feet. Feel fine! Mt. Washington, 6,000 feet.[53]

Dear Mother.
    A freighter started unexpectedly for town yesterday, and I just had time to address an envelope and put my unfinished letter in it. Another freighter has just stopped at the cabin, and while he and Alec are talking, I'm going to drop you a line although I may have to stop at any moment.

We are both feeling well. One of the men has our sheep wagon and we had to stay here last night. We put our bed on a spring couch out in a little tent, which was just big enough to hold it. Last night there were about 10 men, herders, camp movers, and freighters here. And they were all in the cabin playing cards, smoking, and playing the phonograph. These stories of the lonely herder's life and going crazy without someone to speak to aren't so in this outfit anyway.

By the way, will you tell Mrs Furber[54] that we used her leather case with thermos bottle, etc. and there isn't any inside stopper to the thermos bottle. We put in an ordinary cork, and

Friday night when we camped out at the Road Ranch, we made coffee enough for both bottles, so we wouldn't have to build a fire in the morning, and the coffee in hers was stone cold and in the other one was so hot, you had to put your handkerchief so you could hold it without burning your hands, which proves that there ought to be a certain kind of an inner stopper. Would you ask her to see if she can get one and send it out because we have only those two and I thought two enough.

Love,
E.S.H.

––––

June 26, 1911

Dear Mother.

I'm sitting in the buggy waiting for Alec to come back. He is surveying a section of land. It is a great thing for him to be able to do his own work as a civil engineer. His training as a mining engineer may not sound as though it would be much good to a person raising sheep, but often times it is a great help, like at the present time. Most ignorant people have a wholesome respect for knowledge, and just the sight of a survey's outfit makes a great impression.

Alec filed on a piece of land and there is a man who has a ranch on the other side of the mountain who is on it with sheep, who says it is his. After surveying it and being sure about it, Alec will send a notice to him to get off, or he will start suit. It seems to me people spend most of the time in this business defending their land rights.

I am writing this not knowing when it can get mailed. I'm going to always try to keep a letter on hand in case we meet a trader or someone going to town.

Let's see, where did I get to the other day. Oh yes, we spent the night in the loveliest field just carpeted with flowers. There are clumps of lavender, larkspur just thick everywhere, and lots of yellow daisies and small white flowers. When I got up in the morning, I never saw anything so pretty as that field was.

It took us about two hours and a half to Billy's Flat, which is sort of a headquarters camp. When we got there, we couldn't find our sheep wagon and learned one of the herders had taken it, and moved it three miles away. Well, Alec didn't have any other wagon to give him, and his bunch of sheep wasn't very near any other, so we stayed that night at Billy's Flat and until the next afternoon. Meanwhile, Alec moved that man's bunch of sheep near another one, so he could be with another herder, and sent someone to move the wagon near where he thought we'd better build our cabin.

That afternoon when we got to the wagon, we immediately got on our horses and looked around for sites for a cabin, as he had told two herders to come the next morning and help him locate good timber and cut it.

Right here let me tell you I'm in love with my horse. He is just so gentle and his gait is fine, although I can't ride yet long at a time. At least go fast for long at a time. The first three times I rode him, Alec had him by a long rope because he wanted to be sure a girl's skirts flopping against him didn't scare him. Apparently it didn't bother him a bit.

Out here in this Western country, when you are not using a horse, you turn him loose to graze. The only fault this horse had is he was hard to catch. Alec worked almost three-quarters of an hour before he could get him, and when we were at Billy's Flat, he had to run him into a corral in order to get him.

Well, the other day we rode down near the river, and Alec was fishing, and he thought the horses were going a little far down the bank and told me to go head them off. I went, and much to my surprise and amusement, when I got around in front of them to turn them back, my horse began walking towards me. I walked up to him and when we got close to each other, he stopped, and I put my hand on the bridle, and he didn't move. The joke of it was, I didn't want to catch him either. Alec was so amused. After awhile I heard them go off again, and this time when I walked up to him, he stood still and began to raise his front leg to shake hands with me, a trick someone had taught him. Alec doesn't waste any more time trying to catch him. When he's wanted, I just walk right up to him.

We have four horses with us all the time. Two for the buggy and these two saddle horses. Whenever we go anywhere, we tie a saddle horse on each side. Lots of times while we are driving along, Alec will see a bunch of sheep quite a distance off on a hillside, and want to speak to the herder. He just jumps off onto his saddle horse and gallops up to the herd, and I sit in the buggy. Soon I shall be able to go too, but just now we bring my horse along so it will have the exercise.

At night we put a big horse bell, like a "cow bell" on the most popular horse, and in the morning you can tell what direction to go for them because up here in these mountains, there's a lot of timber. Fine, tall pines.

We'll go back to that afternoon. We had a fine ride, just going where we pleased, crossing and recrossing a small stream and up the side of a hill covered with underbrush. Finally we came to several ledges of rock, so we got off our horses and led them. Alec is very careful and watches me all the time so I am not a bit afraid. He found a splendid place for our cabin in Grizzly Gulch, near a spring, and also a good place for a hammock, and also near one of the finest trout streams in this state. It (the stream) is about as near as Mrs Huguley's house is from ours; in fact you can jump down there in about two minutes. The cabin site is at the head of the gulch and you get the view down the whole length. I'm going to try for it with my camera.

They have to haul logs about a mile, though, because there isn't big enough timber right now. Those two herders are so interested in building this cabin. Alec wants to give back this sheep wagon to the herder. That's why he's in such a hurry to get this cabin built. There is a cabin they own over near where I'm sitting now, that is never used, so they are over here, tearing out all the planed planks so we can have them for a floor and help out the roof. They have the logs all cut and will haul them tomorrow. One of the freighters is to bring up our cow and calf. They ought to get here tomorrow.

That night, after getting our cabin located, when we came in, Alec said, "Would you like some fish for supper?" It was then quarter of 6, and I said, "Yes, but I was hungry, and I'd like my supper by 7 o'clock, and if he started then to catch them, it might take forever to catch them." He said yes it might, but he was going to try it. In 20 minutes, he had caught three beauties (trout) and at 7, we were sitting down eating them. Dipped in flour with a little salt and fried in butter with a little lemon juice squeezed on. I never tasted anything so delicious.

Last night after supper, we went down, and he fished until he caught four (one was so big, he broke his rod getting him landed) and we had those for breakfast. We aren't going to eat them but once a day because we are afraid we will get tired of them.

Yesterday noon we had to ask those two herders to dinner as they were working so near. I peeled and sliced a whole big spider[55] full of potatoes and sliced an onion up with them. It took forever to fry them there were so many. I fried a lot of bacon first, and then used that fat for them. Meanwhile, Alec made two pans of baking powder biscuits, and those three things with tea were all they got. As there was plenty of everything, they seemed satisfied, but it was a nice, indigestible meal for us, although we didn't feel any bad effects.

We warmed up some of the biscuits in the oven at night and had them for dessert with honey. They were good too. Twice we have had broiled lamb chops, but that was at Billy's Flat. We haven't any meat with us.

Today for our lunch, we brought three boiled eggs apiece, graham crackers, Uneedas and peanut butter, and dates, hot coffee in a thermos bottle. And cold tea with slices of lemon in the other bottle is waiting until Alec gets back. Mrs Furber's case is a great thing. We took out the sandwich box and put the two thermos bottles in it. We haven't any bread to make sandwiches, so we don't need the box so much. That case is great because it keeps the bottles from rolling around the wagon and getting broken. I like my whip too, tell Holden.

This wagon isn't much on looks, but it certainly is very comfortable and strong. It would hard to be to live in this country on these roads. Half the time, Alec doesn't keep to the road, but just makes a beeline for where he wants to go, and we ride over sagebrush and anything that happens to be in the way. It often seems to me it is easier going than the regular road where the rain has washed so many gullies.

I don't notice the altitude at all, and just think we are 8,000 feet above the level of the sea.

I am in love with those riding boots you sent. At first they were so stiff they hurt me at the heel, but now they are broken in. I like to wear them all the time, the way Alec does his. In walking through the grass you don't have to look out for thistles and cactus. I don't know what I should have done without those chamois riding gloves Aunt Georgia gave me. I have worn those constantly since I have been out on the range with Alec. Even in driving you need gloves because the dust is so alkaline it dries your hands, and these are so large they don't make your hands feel hot. And of course in horseback riding, they are indispensable.

I have my crash[56] riding skirt with me, not the other, and I wear that and the boots in driving, so in case I want to get on my horse I can. I have them on now. My little black hat with the feather smashes so easily and shows the dust. I didn't bring it out here, it was so in the way at the Dry Creek camp. I wear one of Alec's Stetson soft felt hats that all the men wear out here. It stays on very well. Alec prefers a Panama in the summertime. I tell him he doesn't look like wild and woolly Western at all, but he says I look enough like it to make up for him, so I am providing "local color" for the landscape.

They are coming now, so I must stop.

Affec.
E.S.H.
P.S. Yesterday on the way out to Billy's Flat we met a buck herd of a thousand head. Of course, I didn't have my camera. They are the first bucks I ever saw. Most all had long curved ram's horns. I heard a noise like the report of a gun, and said to Alec, someone must be shooting around here, and he laughed and pointed. I looked and saw two rams fighting. They would back off several yards apart and run for each other, heads down, and when they came together, it sounded like the report of a rifle.

FROM CAMPING TO A CABIN

Top: The newlyweds spend the night in a field of wildflowers.
Above: A herder helps Edith move from the sheepwagon to the new cabin.

They sometimes kill each other that way, and I should think they would.

Affec.
E.S.H.

———

June 30, 1911
Sheep Wagon

Dear Mother.

A freighter is going down tomorrow, so I want to write a word to you, so we can take it over to Billy's Flat after supper and give it to him.

I was over there all day yesterday, for two bands of sheep got mixed and Alec had to be over there to help sort them out. They have big corrals right side of the cabin at Billy's Flat, where they do this. The sheep are all put in the corrals, and then are run down a shoot toward a gate. Alec stood at the gate and swung it back and forth, fixing it each time, so the sheep of one brand would all be in the same corral. There were some over 5,000 sheep to be separated this way, so we were most all day.

While there, the freighters came from town and brought me four letters from you, and some pictures I had had developed. I'm so pleased to send you such good ones. I'm going to send the films along too, as I don't want them, and perhaps there might be some you'd like to have printed sometime and send someone.

Now, I'll answer some of your numerous questions.

We have some of the finest cold water to drink that comes from a spring just below us. Comes right out of a rock.

There are no rattlesnakes on the mountain, and I haven't seen an ordinary snake. I wear my high boots all the time, the way Alec does, so I have no fear in walking through the tall grass.

The horses are turned loose all the time when not in harness. The most popular one has a bell on its neck, and they all stay together.

Yesterday we did not take the saddle horses with us when we went to Billy's Flat, and at night when we were nearing home, I grabbed Alec by the arm, and said, look, and there, standing in the middle of the road, grazing in the direction that we would come, were those two. When they caught sight of us, they galloped toward us, and seemed to be saying, "Well, we thought you'd never come home. Why did you stay so long."

When Alec got the harnesses off of the team, the four of them ran down together to the creek and we didn't see them again until this morning.

That freighter didn't bring our cow and calf and Alec was furious with him. I guess he thought it was too much work. He's getting pretty independent, according to all accounts. Alec told him in a very quiet, firm voice that he could rest his horses a day, and start the next day for the ranch, and could come back with that cow and calf, or not at all. He's apparently as meek as Moses today, and is getting ready to start for town tomorrow morning. When we get them, we will tether the calf by a long rope, and the cow will graze around everywhere, but she will always come back to the calf. There is wonderful grass up here this year. Alec says he knows how to milk.

He has gone now over to where they are hauling logs for our cabin. He came back for his surveying instrument so as to get the house level. That instrument cost $325 as it is an especially fine one used by mining experts.[57]

We are getting along famously with regard to food. One of the herders killed a deer the other day, and we had as fine a steak last night for supper as I ever ate. We broiled it on the grating out of the middle of the oven of the stove, and had Lyonnaise potatoes to eat with it, and cocoa. Candy for dessert. The grocer sent me a lot of candy as a present when Alec paid his bill. Also gave him a box of fine cigars to bring up here.

(I happened to offer some of our venison to a man who was here yesterday, and I almost got our herder into trouble, for the law is on deer, and you mustn't shoot them until Sept. Nobody told me to keep still, so it was a narrow escape.[58])

For breakfast, we have every morning, shredded wheat,

bacon, boiled eggs, and coffee. Alec insisted on trying to make some bread the other day. The biscuits were fine, but the loaf wasn't good. I'm going to try it next time, and see if I can't do better. That's the way we do things, and the competition is fun. We had for lunch this noon, some Campbell's oxtail soup with Uneedas and hot tea with lemon in it, and a cornstarch pudding with a caramel sauce. We both made the pudding, and I made the sauce. Tomorrow for dessert we are going to have some jelly and I'm going to melt some marshmallows for sauce as we haven't any cream.

We have plenty of potatoes and onions and turnips. The two latter, the freighter brought yesterday, as we left word with the market at Buffalo that every time the freighter was in town to send us up some fresh vegetables. They are two days on the way, so they must be fresh when they start or they are no good.

You spoke about living at the hotel next winter. It costs us $5 a day there, anyway. I can generally get enough to eat breakfast and supper, but dinner is often impossible. The meats I stopped eating. They were always tough and unappetizing. Generally I could eat the soup and some dessert, often it was only pie, and often custard pie was the only kind I could eat, as the pastry was so indigestible. I could stand the table for awhile, but month after month, it would be hard.

There is a house about five doors from the house we have taken for next winter where they give meals. Most of the young men and several of the school teachers eat there, and Bob Alling says it is better than the hotel, so if we got tired of doing our own cooking, we could get our one hearty meal there at noon. There is nothing to my mind so unhomelike as a hotel bedroom. I told you they are only prepared to accommodate men for overnight. Hardly anyone stays over a week. The rooms are neat and clean and comfortable, but it is impossible to make one look homelike or cozy. There aren't any connecting rooms, and most of them are quite small. The one I had the longest was the best room for size and pleasant view in the house, but it was right over the kitchen, and just before a meal, the smell of cooking was almost unbearable, and sometimes the room was thick with stream from frying. I put up with it for the sake of the view and closet, but when the warm weather came, and Alec came home from being on the range, he stayed there about 15 minutes, and then went downstairs to try and change it.

We got a small, cool room with no closet, as the latter are in only a few rooms, and the proprietor let me keep the closet in the other room. But sometimes that other room was occupied, and then it was embarrassing to be wanting things in there all the time.

I was interrupted later by Alec coming in to say he had found by using his surveying instrument the site we had picked out for our cabin was impractical. The ground sloped too much, although it didn't seem so to the eye. However, he had found another spot near there, and wanted me to get my raincoat and hat and come right along as the men were waiting to get to work. It was raining, but he seemed so earnest about it, I grabbed my things and went. The place was all right, and I stayed the rest of the afternoon watching them. Martin was there working like a beaver. (He's the man who didn't bring the cow.) When night came, Alec had relented and told him he needn't go today, but could rest over another day before he went. So that is why I didn't finish this letter last night.

I never saw such a popular piece of work as building that cabin is. Two of the men have been cutting and hauling logs, then yesterday, Martin joined them of his own free will, then along came another herder – Antoine Silva (his wife was the one who called on me) and asked if they needed any help. Alec said he didn't think so, at which he got off his horse and stood around and watched for a few moments, and then he couldn't stand it any longer, but grabbed a hammer and began to pound harder than anyone else. Counting Alec, it made five men at work. None of them seemed to know much about it, and each has a different opinion and goes to work in his own sweet way.

I'm wondering what it's going to look like when it's done. I see where the sheep will eat poison weed and wander all over the country until this cabin is done.

It is just below here, so the men come and go to their

meals by this wagon. Then too, Alec being in charge of the outfit, men are constantly coming over here after him. So instead of feeling like I'm alone in the wilderness, it seems as though this were a howling metropolis. Such wonderful bracing cool air. It's great this morning.

Yesterday we had a call from a man they call Red. I don't know what the rest of his name is. He has red hair, and that is the man Alec said Lucille could have. He certainly is a character. He is in charge of Joe Todd's sheep. Has been here 22 years, and was here at the time of the Cattle War. He was an entertaining talker, and he stayed about an hour and a half. He was on his way to fish in our creek, which by the way, is the north fork of the Powder River. Powder River, which flows into another river, which flows into the Missouri, which goes into the Mississippi, and so to the Gulf. Think of it.

Alec is gone to find the forest ranger. Something about a water right for the sheep on the other side of the mountain.

I think those wallpapers are lovely. I'm crazy to see them on the walls. It was nice you had such a good time at the Phelps. Miss Simmons showed me that hat. I think it's a beauty. I don't understand why M. Treadwell gets so many telegrams. Is he too lazy to write? More money than brains, I guess.

Had a postal from Mary. Bert had a relapse. Just think what that poor girl has to go through. I suppose when he isn't working, the income stops too, and that must add to the trouble.

That is a lovely postal of Miss Walker's. They have frames for postal cards. I wish you could send me one. I'd like to frame this one for next winter. Had a long letter from Ethelyn.

We start day after tomorrow for the Webb's ranch, and the Fourth of July celebration.

I sent two letters to you. By a herder who was going to walk to town. He had been discharged so I don't know as you will ever get the letters.

Your last one with the wallpaper had two cents due on it. I'm glad they didn't hold it in the post office, but let the man bring it up.

With love from E.S.H.

Ranchers and townsfolk traveled for miles for festivities such as
Jannette and Lew Webb's all-night 4th of July party, using vehicles such as this
buggy in the Hole-in-the-Wall country. Credit: Johnson County Library.

CHAPTER 9

FOURTH OF JULY

By horseback, buggy, and wagon, everyone converged at Lew and Jannette Webb's ranch for their all night Fourth of July picnics. This was a big, annual event that took the Webbs all week to prepare.

The Webb's spread lay about thirty miles south of Buffalo as the crow flies and about twenty-five miles north of the famous hideout for Butch Cassidy and the Sundance Kid into a protected valley through the "hole in the [canyon] wall." The ranch was nestled in an area called "The Horn" by locals, at the southern end of the Big Horns on the North Fork of the Powder River. To this day locals call the wide-open, welcoming entrance to the canyon Dance Hall Flats, according to Jerry Sanders, author and photographer of *Bighorn Country, An Introductory Guide (in Wyoming)*.

Descending from Healy Brothers' mountain pastures, Edith and Alec had to take the long way around because they couldn't just drive down the canyon of the North Fork like other canyons Edith described, such as Crazy Woman. That's because although the summit of the North Fork is open grasslands, the canyon remains impassable. "Let me tell you about it," said Jerry. "Slabs of limestone peeled from canyon walls litter the bottom, leaving a hiker the choice of crawling under the slabs in the water or skirting the mess by inching across the top of the scree slope and kissing the sheer face." Jerry crawled the one time he trekked down the canyon.

The barn for dancing that Edith described has long since disappeared. So has Edith's letter about her first Fourth of July at the Webb Ranch. As it turns out, however, we do have her notes. Interestingly, she did not spontaneously scrawl the 2,500-word letters she mailed home; instead, like a reporter,; she noted questions and responses and the details she observed on the same thin sheets of 6″ x 11½″ paper that she used for her stationery. These are the notes Edith made on the July 3-4, 1911, trip coming out of the mountains.

> Barbeque. Gloucester,[59] hammock between two pines. Moonlight.
>
> Packed up things in buggy, suitcase, a pailfull of eatables, camp bed, violin. Got started at 1:30.
>
> Alec lighted a cigar and said he felt as though we were going on a vacation.
>
> Billy's Flat, headquarters camp, one hour ride. Get a teepee there.
>
> Basque herder rides hard and says he saw another herder's sheep in gulch.
>
> Arrived at cabin. Bill rode in calmly, puffing a pipe, and said he hadn't any more sheep than a rabbit. Said he hadn't seen them since he went in to supper. They went in the timber and he couldn't find them. 2,500 sheep gone from 7 at night until 3 in the afternoon.
>
> A. caught a saddle horse and rode in opposite direction. Sent in herders in all directions. Sheep found. Go back to wagon for book to payoff herder. Eat beans, pickle, cocoa, and bread.
>
> All sheep come in. Count blacks, start out (man looks ugly when discharged).

Started at 7:30. No water because we were to cross and recross Bear Track Creek. Bright moonlight, cattle country. Expect to see creek but don't. Horses need water, and we need water for coffee. Black woods. Road turned and twisted every few years. A. had to get out and see which way it went. I didn't like it. Afraid of bears.

Quarter of 11 we camped. Flashes of light may be a day late and fireworks. In sunbonnet. Bird lights on face in a.m.

Wrong road. Wondered if the road would land us too far away to drive to Webb's ranch in a day.

Came to edge of mountain. Wonderful view. Can see on clear day smoke of a train 125 miles away.

No trees except where they outline the creeks and ranch houses on the creek. Wonder if any were Webb's.

Descend the mountain on a road that kept disappearing. Ford creek at bottom and man fishing.

No I can't tell how many feet away the house is. All I can say is you're inside his fence now.

Road down mountain is cattle trail. Shortest route. Asked the man what day it was. He said "It's the Fourth of July." "Say, where did you people come from?" He gave us four fish for breakfast. Drove up to house at 8:30. First arrivals.

Set our tent up in front yard. Two tents already there.

Helped pack biscuits, etc. to carry two miles to campgrounds. Kept hearing hooves, and look out to see groups of people on horseback cantering by, waving their hands. Changed dress to white one and pink sun bonnet. Ford creek with steep banks on both sides. All the cars got stuck. Had to have four horse teams pull each up bank. Friends at grounds. Barbeque yearling steer on wheel over fire. Basted it with liquid made of vinegar, mustard, salt, pepper, and sugar. Did look good, and I didn't think I wanted any. Had a hunk and it was great! Tender, juicy, and wonderful flavor.

Fried 500 trout. Fresh bread, biscuit, ranch butter, potato salad, fresh strawberry pie and ice cream, and four or five different kinds of cake.

200 there. Fried more fish and plenty of everything for supper. After dinner everyone rested. Took naps.

Square building with little platform only used July 4. Organ. Asked me to arrange program. Star Spangled Banner. Two judges from Sheridan speak. Dec. Ind. read, ended with America. I played with the songs. Watched fancy riding by cowboys. Foreman's girl was watching, so he did extra fine stunts. Then the dancing began. Organ and fiddle for music. Four different ones changed off. Lucky, two were awful.

Supper at 7. Then the dancing continued until 7 the next morning. At 10:30 we had enough and started for our tent in Webb's front yard. At 4:30, we heard honk honk, and there were some of our friends, just starting home.

Breakfast at ranch house, burnt cream of tartar biscuits, fried ham, strong coffee, strawberry preserve, canned peaches, and applesauce. 8 o'clock, last people passed. 25 miles to ride to ranch after dancing all night. Babies and children rolled up and under seats, sound asleep with all that din. Coming through the Rye. Take blanket and roll up in it, sleep an hour or two and go to dancing again. Western men hop more and tire you.

Go back same way. Not so bad going up. Made fire and heated some Campbell's vegetable soup. Had olives and Uneedas, sweet chocolate, and dates. A. smoked a cigar and went on in one and a half hours. Landed home at sheep wagon at 7 o'clock. Two saddle horses on the road watching for us.

When freighter arrived, he was driving eight horses with a saddle horse on his side. Two freight wagons hitched together,

and a cow and calf tied behind. A. builds corral for cow while
I sit under tree handing out advice, which he laughs at and
ignores. The cow goes out to graze in daytime and calf stays in
pen. At night, the calf goes out.

————

While Edith's letter about the Fourth of July celebration at the Webb
Ranch is not in the family collection, we do have details from Jannette
herself, who mentions Edith playing the violin "wonderfully." Mrs.
Webb described the all day, all night event in an oral history she gave in
1954 to the Johnson County Library in Buffalo.[60]

Mrs. Webb's Oral History
The picnics we had at the ranch![61] The men would try to
finish with their first cutting of hay by the Fourth of July, and
then they would go for a week's fishing trip up the canyons
beyond our ranch. The gatherings grew bigger and bigger until
they became real celebrations.

We had two large celebrations, and then Mr. Webb put up
a big dance hall. It was 60 by 80 feet with a big door in each
end of the hall.

It took two men, beginning at midnight of the 3rd to
barbecue that beef. We had a great big pit with a bed of
coals in it, and iron wheels on top. They would split the beef,
a yearling, down the spine and lay it on the wheels. I fixed the
"dope" to baste it with—vinegar, brown sugar, salt, nutmeg and
mustard were in it. And then I would take a clean tea towel and
I would roll it around a stick and tie it on. They would have two
of those in the bucket and baste the meat with that. You'd take
a bite out of that meat and if you were standing up, the juice
would fall in the sand.

Fred Pettit would come a couple of days early and catch
all the trout for the bunch and pack it in ice.

I baked bread and made fresh butter. I had a great big

butter dish, granite, white and gold, and I would put that in
the river and the water would run through the butter.
It was wonderful.

I always made 20 gallons of tutti-frutti ice cream—fresh
strawberries, raspberries, lemons, oranges and bananas.

We'd have dinner at 1:00, supper, and then breakfast at
6:00 in the morning. Dance all night. If they would get tired,
they'd go out to the tent and rest awhile and then come back
and dance some more. Edger Simmons played for the dancing.

I got an organ on purpose for those picnics, and we would
play and sing. Mrs. Alec Healy played the violin. She was a
wonderful violinist—had played in the Boston Symphony.[62]
We would play Il Trovatore, popular songs, and other things.

———

Monday July 10, '11
Sheep Wagon
Big Horn Mt.

Dear Mother –

Since finishing your letter Martin has arrived bringing six
nice letters from you. Isn't that just great about Mary. I'm so
glad it is a girl. Had a letter from Stella Davis. She is in Chicago
visiting her Aunt.

Also Kate Hay's invitation, a note and some music from
Miss Hartman who is in Boone, Iowa. I guess there is no doubt
but what she is going to be married and come back here in
September. I'm so pleased.

What a fine letter that was of Miss Walker's. The last
letter of yours was written from Aunt Georgie's.

I'm so glad you heard from me before you got away from
876. Mail is so uncertain here. Martin was seven days making
the round trip this time. I wish I could have had a picture of him
as he pulled into Billy's Flat. We drove over in the early part of
the afternoon. It had turned suddenly cold and I put on all my
thick underclothes, my fur coat, my woolen hood and mittens,
and woolen scarf and I was nearly frozen by the time I got home.

Just before Martin got in, there was a snow storm! It began with hail and ended by snowing and blowing like in January.

Fortunately we were in the cabin all the time with a nice fire in the stove. We looked out the window at the storm and saw a man riding like everything. Alec ran to the door and helped him in. He was a horse trader and he said the snow was coming so thick he couldn't see the cabin. He was quite an entertaining talker and as we were nice and warm and I had a cat and four kittens to play with I didn't mind the storm a bit.

How that cat keeps those four kittens from being chewed up by the dogs is more than I know. I have seen ten dogs there at a time. They are every one scared to death of her.

When Martin came he was driving eight horses, four pairs with a saddle horse on the side, the lead two freight wagons, hitched together, full of things and a cow and calf tied on behind. He had another man to help him. He brought several Transcripts, two Registers, a little box with some awfully pretty cuff buttons from Aunt Georgie, a postal from Marion en route to East Sullivan for the summer, and a Ladies Home Journal. So you see we have quite a lot of reading now.

He also brought two bunches of asparagus pretty wilted but it has revived in water and we are to have it for lunch. Four cauliflowers, two of which are steaming in the fireless cooker for supper, three nice long cucumbers—(we have a bottle of Durkee's salad dressing) and two cantaloupes. We had one this morning and it was simply great. Also two dozen oranges and a dozen lemons. The melons cucumbers and lemons spend their time in an ice cold spring. The other (water) melon, I spoke of eating in that other letter, we brought from Webb's along with a dozen peaches. So you see for a few days after Martin returns we live on fresh vegetables. I was so afraid that cow and calf being brought from the hot weather down on the Flats would freeze to death in that snowstorm and that cold night but they are very much alive. It is a Durham cow which is supposed to give rich milk. It arrived over here at the sheep wagon last night.

Alec is at present building a pen for it and I am sitting in a camp chair under a nice shady tree watching him and handing out advice which he laughs at and completely ignores.[63] It is over near our new cabin. We are going to put the calf in it day time, and turn the cow loose to graze. At night the cow goes in the pen and the calf goes out to graze. It's quite a large sized calf so it eats grass at a great rate. Alec milked this morning, and we had about two quarts. By night there ought to be cream on it. He is going to get two quarts night and morning and let the calf have the rest.

He has selected a nice little grove of pine trees that is round. He is cutting out the center ones and nailing trees all around the outside, so the calf can have nice shade at any time of day. Great scheme.

Before I forget it I want to say snow storms in July are not common up here. Martin has been working on this mountain every summer for eight years and he never saw a snow storm until late Fall. Tradition says there once was one in August but not lately.[64]

This letter from Edith written to her father's cousin-in-law, Aunt Georgie Sampson, is missing pages.

. . . that flows right out from the side of the hill in the sage brush. The spring is fenced in to keep the cattle from the place it comes out. The horses were unharnessed and the only shady place was under the buggy, so I crawled under there with a robe two sofa cushions and a rain coat to cover me.

We ate our lunch under there too and I have just discovered I must have taken my nap in some soup that was spilled on the ground. I have scrubbed the spots with water and the sun is fast drying them out.

I can see Alec and Mr. Schoonover returning. They look like little black flies in the distance so I must begin to pick up things so we can start for home.

I don't care to travel these roads after dark and we are quite a long way from home which is our sheep wagon at present.

Our cabin in Grizzly Gulch is progressing slowly. Two herders are working on the fire place today but as neither ever built one before I have my doubts about results but they don't seem to have any.

Thank you again for the lovely cuff buttons. Give my best love to Aunt Celia and of course to Edna & Leslie, Eliz and Grace. I hope I can have time to drop them a line someday soon.

Affectionately,
Edith

Artist Helen Healy Lynch, Alec's older sister, initialed and decorated
Bavarian china with gold as her wedding present for Edith and Alec.

CHAPTER 10

TEA PARTY

Up in Mountains.
August 1 (I think)

Dear Mother.

Martin will be going to town tomorrow or the day after, and I must have some letters written to go down with him.

I'll begin way back from where I last wrote from town.

The last afternoon I was there, Mrs Bert had Mary and a Mrs Mather and me in to spend the afternoon with our sewing. Mrs Mather is the one I told you about who is much younger than I, and has three children. With Mary's two, Mrs Bert's two, and these three, they made quite a children's party. Thank goodness they have a tent on the lawn to which they were dispatched without ceremony, as the confusion in that little house was deafening.

We had a real good time. Had tea and lettuce sandwiches, then lemon sherbet and angel cake.

They always to seem to have two courses at these little informal parties. I think it is unnecessary. I shan't do it. What I used to have when the girls came to play bridge was plenty enough for anybody. That party I told you about of Mary's where she had the dining room table set and all those elaborate things to eat was only the same kind of a party. Just Mrs Bert, Mrs Mather and our sewing. It seems absurd to me. You ask if it were a luncheon, and I don't wonder.

Well, the next morning we started at 9. Somehow it seems as though we never can get an awfully early start. We had to go to different stores to put up things.

However, we got to the top of Crazy Woman Hill at 1:30. I drove up again. Alec got out to lighten the load.

It is nothing to drive up, side of what it is to drive down. That is perfectly awful!!! Next time I'm going to be blindfolded and let Alec drive me down.

We met Pete and Jack Balden on the way up with a sheep wagon and a supply wagon. The two wives were on ahead, on horseback. We stopped and talked with them, and I was fascinated listening to the English accent of Jack Balden's bride from Liverpool. Pete hasn't been married but four years, so both the girls are young. They are to camp up here for the month of August, and said they would come over and see me. If things seem strange to me, what must they to that English girl, and I don't believe she is more than 24. I'd like to know her better. Well, we arrived at our sheep wagon at 7 that night. I was pretty tired, for there are so many rocks in the road, you bump so. The next morning at 10, the camp mover came for our wagon, which meant we had to move into our cabin at once. They hitched a team of horses on the wagon, and drove it down beside the cabin door, so moving was an easy matter. But such a looking place. It would make your hair stand on end. Everything dumped all over the floor. Alec proceeded to put up the new stove outside, and put a roof over it. Then he made a table and covered it with oil cloth, and nailed up a box to keep salt, pepper, etc. in. We eat outside, except when it rains or is too cold. We shall only get this part of the house done this summer. The kitchen and bedrooms will have to wait. It took them so much longer to put this up than we thought, but it certainly is mighty well built and substantial.

It is 20 by 16 feet. The door is at one end of the long side. The fireplace in the middle of the other long side. Long big windows in the center of the shorter sides. They are called "lazy windows" in this country because they are laying down, I guess.

[SKETCH MISSING]

That is the shape of an ordinary window. Well, they take two like that and it makes this kind of a window. Fine and big. To open, one frame slides by the other.

We have a fine big couch with spring and mattress that Alec had at the ranch. That is in one corner now covered with a dark green couch cover which has a pretty oriental stripe around it. It is made of a pair of heavy window curtains sewed together. I like these curtains so much better than any couch cover they showed me, and conceived this plan. It makes a very wide cover, so we can have the couch open to its full width. We have a nice big table one of the herders made, and I have that covered with garnet burlap. Two pieces sewed together and raveled out four inches for fringe.

In one corner Alec put up a willow rod and I made long dark green denim curtains for that. We hang clothes behind that. So you see, I have been busy too. Alec made two shelves for dishes, and under a seat in a corner, we put all our canned goods. Soups, beans, corn, and tomatoes. Then he nailed up two boxes with shelves in them for our toilet articles. The steamer trunk is covered with my green steamer rug. He has also put ropes from two big logs in the ceiling and we hang the hammock in here. It looks awfully cozy with the three sofa cushions I have. You don't know how attractive and pretty the room looks.

The fireplace is a huge success. When they first finished it, it smoked and they decided the opening was too big, so they took an iron tire off an old wheel and bent it (horseshoe shaped). They got the prettiest curve and only had an ax to pound it with. They sat that in, and got small stones, and built in all around the outside edge, so that is the shape of the fireplace now, instead of being square. It is so pretty. They got one big block for the top, which makes a mantelpiece. It is a little over six feet long and a foot deep. It took four men to get it in place, so you can imagine the size of the fireplace. We have a fine big log in there now, and that will last two or three evenings. On our table, we have a lamp, books, magazines, and two cameras. My violin and Alec's rifle are also in evidence.

We have two camp chairs with backs to them, and I forgot to mention I cut out the cover of The Delineator for July and have it pinned over the fireplace. It is a lovely picture and if it doesn't get ruined, I'm going to get it framed.

We had quite a little excitement last night. The cow and calf got loose. That scheme didn't work, having the cow loose all day and the calf in a pen, and vice versa at night. The calf didn't get enough to eat and wouldn't go get a drink in the dark alone. So we have to keep one tied up all the time. Somehow the calf got its rope loose, and they were both gone. It looked absolutely hopeless to think of finding them, for they could keep on the banks of this stream for days under these thick willows, and you couldn't see them. Besides, they belong to brother-in-law and are kept at the ranch, so we didn't want to lose them. Well, I knew they hadn't been gone long, as I saw them about 4 o'clock, so we started, one on each side of the river. Finally, Alec found them way down the gulch on the other side of the stream. Perhaps we weren't glad. Alec said she would finally show up at the ranch when cold weather came, so she wasn't lost for good.

Anyhow, it makes us appreciate the milk even more. We get about four quarts a day. That is all we can dispose of. Such whipped cream for coffee and shredded wheat. Alec does the milking.

He is away today. Has gone over to Bader Gulch to have a look at four herds. Most of the herders are Portuguese, French and Spanish Basques, and about four Americans.

Most of the foreigners are earning their money to go back to their country and buy farms, etc. so they don't want their money except once or twice a year, and then they send it over there. The Outfit keeps their money for them and pays them interest on it. All this entails a special set of bookkeeping for Alec. Whenever they go to town, they go to a store and get what they want in clothes or anything, and charge it to the Outfit. They bring back a slip and Alec puts it down to their account. All different kinds of tobacco are bought in town and brought up, and the men buy them from the Outfit. We have most of it here, and when they want any, they come and take it and it is charged up to them.

Now today a man came with an order from two herders to pay him $5 dollars for one and $8 for the other. So Alec had to make out a check for $13 and charge it up to these men's accounts.

The stores in town keep their slips, so he has to go over his accounts every now and then and compare. He has just had a lot of slips printed with a formula on top, signed Healy Bros. and all the stores have orders not to deliver any goods to a man unless he writes out one of these slips. Unless you have something like this, the Outfit would be imposed upon. Several times after a man has left, a bill comes in from the store for things he has bought. So as now, the stores are obligated to send Alec the slips at once, that won't occur so much.

I have tried to just wear my full green bloomers I have in camp, for they are so comfortable, but I've given it up. It seems to be a signal for someone to appear and I have to dash behind the door and put on a skirt. You never can tell when someone will walk in, ride in I mean. The other day we had four visitors all at different times.

It rained pouring day before yesterday in the afternoon, and Antoine Paradie, a Portuguese, came. His sheep were right here in this gulch, and of course I couldn't drive him out in the pouring rain, so he stayed two hours. Alec was over at Billy's Flat, so I conversed two whole hours with a man who can hardly say a whole sentence of English. Poor fellow, he seemed so delighted to have a senora to talk to. He is about 40, and has a wife and seven boys in the old country. He stayed here five years, then went back to Portugal for one, then came back and will stay five years longer.

These foreigners have such gentle, pretty manners. They see a woman so seldom, they would all do anything for me.

You asked me if all the horses are shod. Those the men use, like herders' horses, camp movers', and freighters', are shod. Those used at the ranch are not, the ground is so soft. Those not working that are running wild on the range are not. They have a horseshoers' outfit at Billy's Flat and can shoe their own horses if they can't get to town. I don't think you asked any more questions.

We had six trout fried in butter with cucumber and French dressing again last night. My but they were good. Cornstarch pudding, caramel.

Affec.
E.S.H.

———

August 24, 1911
10 days alone on the mountain from 5 o'clock to 6 or 7, working sheep

Dear Mother.

We are going down from the mountain for good, so I shall mail this letter myself from Buffalo.

There are two reasons why we go before September 1. The first and principal [sic] one is that it is getting so cold up here. The last few days I have had to stay in the house all the time, and we have taken the hammock in the house for good. I simply froze outside. In the morning, there was a thick cake of ice on the water bucket and slush in the tea kettle. We had to keep a fire burning in the fireplace all day. My but it was pretty. We found lots of big stumps to burn and we baked potatoes in the ashes.

The other reason is that Alec thinks his father and mother may be in Buffalo, and he wants to see his father about some business matter.

Another reason is, we want a few days at the hotel for a breathing space from getting our own meals before we tackle the little house. Our menus up here have been pretty limited.

Also, there is no absolute need that Alec be up here.[65]

. . .

Now that we are going, they are sending a herd of sheep down this gulch. Last night they arrived, along with a sheep wagon brought by a camp mover. Later the herder arrived. He is a Portuguese and can't speak any English. As he came along, I saw he had his coat over one shoulder and was carrying something in his hand. He came up to the cabin door, and said what I suppose was meant to be good evening. And then he proudly displayed what he had. I jumped inside the cabin! What do you suppose he had by the neck stroking it and patting its head, but a skunk!!!!

He had been carrying it by the neck as you would a kitten, and why it hadn't covered him with scent was a mystery. Alec told him to go away with it, and he smiled sweetly and went on patting it, showing he didn't understand and thought Alec was praising it. Well, it was the handsomest little animal I ever saw (out of the window). Black long hair like a lynx with a broad white stripe right down its back from the tip of its nose to the end of its tail. There must have been something the matter with it, for it didn't know its scent at all (it smelled strong near, too) but Alec was afraid it would cover the poor unsuspecting Joe sometime, who was tickled to death with his new pet.

So he set out to find the camp mover who was a Portuguese too, and who could explain to him in his own language. When he was found, he grew as excited as people of that race generally do, and with much waving of hands, and pinching of the nose, he made him understand, and they killed it. What do you suppose. He found it in his bed and had been carrying it around a long time. I'm glad I'm going home. I'm not crazy about finding a skunk in my bed.

Must stop now and pack. Haven't had any mail for ages. The last letter was where you had just been with Aunt Emma Williams.

Affec.
E.S.H.

Alec pauses by the front gate of the Healys' new home.
Sheepmen from Utah were known throughout Wyoming for dressing well.

CHAPTER 11

NEW HOME

AUGUST 29 TO OCTOBER 1

BACK IN BUFFALO – MEETING THE SENIOR HEALYS
DECORATING – FAST PACE IN BUFFALO

By the time Edith wrote these letters, she was pregnant with her first child, Alec, Jr., who joined the family in Boston on April 5, 1912. In these letters, people in Buffalo seem to use the phones often. Alec even called Edith long distance from Omaha. Fortunately for this book, the farthest long distance call possible with 1911 technology was between New York and Denver. Boston was still too far from Buffalo for a telephone call.

> Occidental Hotel
> Warren & Co. Props.
> Buffalo, Wyoming
> August 29, 1911
>
> Dear Mother,
> Well, Alec has gone, and I have just finished doing up soiled clothes to be washed and am sitting by my window in a rocking chair.
> Well, I had put the stamp on your letter Sunday afternoon, and Alec was reading out loud to me out on the balcony overlooking the street when all of a sudden he jumped up and said, "There's my mother," and dashed downstairs. Sure enough there they were, and we were all so glad to see each other. We had a chat in the office, then she called up Mary, but we couldn't get her. After that, we went in to supper. Before we had finished supper, Mr and Mrs Hill had come down to see them. John Hill had seen them getting out of the auto and went home and told his mother, so they came right down. Mr and Mrs Steve Langworthy happened to look in the hotel as they went by, and came in, so we all had a jolly chat. A little after 8, Mrs Healy got

Mary on the phone, but as the children were in bed, and they were tired, said she would be up the first thing in the morning.

The next day she wanted me to go along with her to Mary's, and then go on to Mrs Hill's, who had asked us both to come up. So I went. However, I thought after we had been there a little over an hour that I had better come back to the hotel, as I had some things to do. Patricia wanted to walk back to the hotel with me, so she came along, and when we got to Adams & Young's grocery store, we looked in and saw her grandfather, so went in. He asked her if she'd like some candy, and she said yes, and proceeded to pick out all kinds of fearfully cheap stuff that I knew would make Mary's hair stand on end. I ventured to remark she'd better take a better kind, but she wanted those, and Grandpa said she could have what she wanted.

So she came along with me with a huge paper bag full of the most awful looking chocolate colored animals, which she proceeded to put out on my bed in rows. She cut out paper dolls out of my Ladies Home Journal, and before we knew it, it was lunchtime, and Mrs Healy was back home. She didn't go Mrs Hill's after all, and said Patricia could stay to lunch with us.

I had just come up to have a nap when Mrs H. came and said Mr Oliver had just invited us three, Mr and Mrs and me, to go out to the ranch in his auto and she wanted me to go. So I turned my hat backside so it shaded my eyes and went.

Alec had had to go out there that morning, and we passed him on the road as he was coming in. He was so surprised to see us. The ranch looks fine. They have had a good crop and just finished getting it in. 885 bushels of wheat and over 7,000 bushels of oats. About 8,000 bushels of grain in all they will have. The ranch is being run on shares this year, so all that isn't Healy Bros., a certain percent goes to the farmers who have done the work, but they consider it a very good crop.

When we got back, Mrs H wanted me to go up to Mrs Hill's with her, but I thought as long as Alec was going away for three days, I'd stay with him, and then he disappeared. It seems he took his father in his buggy out to see the buck herd that was on its way down from the mountain and only two miles outside of town.

I took a little nap then, had a bath, and put on my white (Filene[66]) lingerie dress and white shoes and stockings for supper, as it had grown hot and it was about the only clean thing I had. It really looks very well. I wear that deep pink chiffon scarf with it.

When I wasn't quite dressed, the bell rang in my room, which means I'm wanted downstairs. I slipped on my long white coat, so it wouldn't show that I hadn't buttoned my dress, and ran down to find Mrs Healy and a Mrs Redmond whom she wanted me to meet. We had a pleasant chat. Mrs R has the ranch next to "ours" on the way in to town. The Healys invited Mr and Mrs R to stay here to dinner, so we six had a very jolly time.

After dinner Mrs Hill arrived, and we four ladies went to the picture show. They had some extra music; three Italians who really played exceedingly well, so the show lasted longer than usual. It was nearly 10 when we came back to the hotel, so now you see why I didn't get a chance to write you.

Mrs Healy brought her trunk tray full of cantaloupes and peaches for Mary and me. A dozen cantaloupes and about six dozen peaches. She brought the baby [Patrick III] a dear little gold ring with a tiny diamond in it and a silver bib chain. She brought Patricia a lovely silver button hook, of a pattern that she's giving her [as] a set of bureau things. She brought each Mary and me a lovely drawn work center piece, and Helen sent me (Mary wasn't to know) a wooden box of jellies, preserves, and pickles, they two put up, and John the baby sent me a dandy box of candy.[67] Now aren't they kind. I am especially pleased at that box. It was awfully good of them to give me things like that that they had slaved to make.

Well, this is what I've been doing up to date.

I think that's a joke about Aunt Lucy. She'll have all of Europe she wants this trip. "They do things so well in Europe." Especially strikes.

Must stop now and hem some napkins. Some of those that came from here for a wedding present.

E.S.H.
Hope you'll rest now.

Patrick Sr. and Mary Ann Healy, visited Buffalo fairly often.
He was about 64, she about 55 in these studio portraits taken in Ogden.

Birdie Childs Williams and Mollie Miller Ellis not only knew everyone's phone number but kept tabs who was where, so anyone could call the women and locate someone. Below: Often the men were at Adams & Young grocery store, c. 1908–1920. Credit: Johnson County Library

The Occidental Hotel
Buffalo, Wyoming
August 30, 1911

Dear Mother,

I had the nicest time yesterday. Mr and Mrs Healy came down to dinner here at noon, and then Mrs came upstairs with me and spent the afternoon. We had a fine time talking over the wedding, my first opportunity, because I don't count Alec. All he seems to remember about it is that it was legal.

Her friend Mrs Hill had telephoned in the morning and asked me to come with them up to tea at 5:30. She said it was just informal, and she couldn't promise much to eat, but she'd love to have me come. So about 5 we went up. She had invited Mary too. She has a husband and two sons, college boys, and we did have such a jolly supper. One thing we had I never tasted before was boiled rice with melted cheese on top. It was delicious. Done in a baking dish. Two ladies, Mrs Young and Mrs Lang, both about my age (each have two children), came in for a few minutes. They live next door, and they had been out making calls, and had called on me at the hotel. Well, we persuaded them to come back and go to the picture show with us, so at 7:30 we went.

Mrs Bert Langworthy's sister, Miss Norval, had asked me to come up there in the evening, but Mr and Mrs Bert got home at 5 from Denver in their car, and as I wanted to stay with this crowd, I telephoned up and said they must be tired, and wouldn't they rather I would come the next afternoon, and they said to be frank, they would. So that fixed me all right. Mrs Bert said they brought home with them a friend and her husband from Denver to make a little visit, and this friend had brought the very best love of a young man in Denver to Edith Holden. Now the only man I know in Denver is Harold Bosworth, so it must be "Bosey." Isn't the world small.

The picture show was good, a change of pictures, and more very good music. All the pictures are approved by the national board of censorship and are fine. Interesting, funny, and pleasant. Afterward we all went up to the drug store and had some ice cream on Mrs Healy, and I got back to the hotel about 10:30.

I was so sleepy in the drug store they all made all manner of fun of me, saying the rapid pace of Buffalo was killing me. As for them, they had only just waked up.

Mr and Mrs Hill come from Kentucky and are just as jolly and pleasant.

One of the boys here spoke to Alec and me about getting up a bridge club for next winter. Just two tables. Mrs Steve Langworthy, Martha Post, the librarian I like so much, and I, are the only ladies who play bridge (Mrs Bert doesn't play cards) and five fellows, Steve, Alec, Bob Alling, John Hoffman (Princeton fellow who spoke to us about it) and Bob Kennedy. I think it would be lots of fun. Just meet when we felt like it and have a rarebit[68] for refreshments. I wish you would write out your receipt for rarebit for me. I've made it, but I can't remember the proportions.

Tonight there is to be a dance, and Alec on the mountain, but we are all going just the same. I have my white (Filene) skirt with the buttons down the front and G. Wilde's waist with blue collar and cuffs this morning. I wore the white lingerie dress yesterday with that Irish lace thing May Young gave me with the little rosebuds on it. It looked very pretty, and my pink chiffon scarf just matched it. Guess I'll wear my blue (Swiss) muslin tonight.

Mrs Healy certainly is a stunning looking woman and dresses beautifully. She had on a most embroidered white linen suit yesterday that she got in Florence. Just heavy chrysanthemums that went up each panel. Perfectly stunning. Well, I must stop and hem napkins.

Affec.
E.S.H.

Occidental Hotel
Sept. 5, 1911

Dear Mother.

Another day has passed, and I haven't written you the nice long letter I promised you. This morning after I got through doing my housework (ahem!) I thought I'd get my violin and do a little work, and when I finished that and was starting to write, Mrs Healy called me and wanted me to find Mr H. and bring him up to the house, as she wanted us all to go to Mary's boarding house with them for dinner. So I started right out, but found Pa Healy had gone to the ranch in someone's auto

This afternoon we spent calling on Mrs Hill, and then I had some errands, and an awful storm came and we just had time to get to the hotel when it came down in sheets. Had supper with Mr and Mrs H here.

Alec had to leave yesterday. They decided to ship some lambs. He has to separate them at the ranch, get them to Clearmont and load them and take them to Omaha. Patsy [Jr.] isn't back from Omaha yet.

He (A.) is taking 4,000 lambs. Fifteen cattle cars it takes, and they hire an engine. They (the cattle cars) are made with a platform in the middle, so there are two layers of lambs in each car. Keep this from Mrs B and Aunt Lucy or they will burst into tears, as usual, when animals are mentioned.

He will have two men to help him. They have to unload to feed and water them. He will be gone from ten days to two weeks.

Miss Post, the girl I like so much, stays with me nights, and I get my own breakfast, and have lunch and dinner with Mr and Mrs H who say they will stay until Alec gets back.

I am feeling all right

That Portuguese woman is making me a dozen glasses of the most elegant crab apple jelly.

Mrs Healy had a big basket of grapes and eating apples sent up to me yesterday. I am writing this in the hotel office, and there is so much confusion must stop.

Affec.
E.S.H.

Engine No. 301 pulls livestock cars with open-slated sides in January, 1945. One or the other of the Healy Brothers delivered their sheep to buyers in person. In September 1911, when it was his turn, Alec hired an engine and fifteen double-decked livestock cars to take lambs to the market in Omaha. Credit: Johnson County Library.

Alec bought an Excelsior auto-cycle in October 1911 to ride out
to the Healy Ranch rather than a horse to check the sheep.

Sept. 6, 1911

Dear Mother,

Well, at last I have settled down to write you a letter.

Mrs Healy has been perfectly fine about helping me get settled. We both got pretty tired, but everything is done now and it is such a relief. I kept one trunk, Alec's big one, and put everything I didn't need now into it. Fur coat, table linen, etc. That is in my room. All the other trunks are empty and are out in a shed in back.

The living room has a piano, a couch, tea table, stove, and four large comfortable rocking chairs.

The bedroom has bed, bureau, table, trunk, bookcase, closet, a good big one. Dining room has table, chairs, sideboard, and sewing machine. Spare bedroom, bed, dressing table, two chairs, commode, wardrobe, and closet. There's a small cellar.

Things are pretty badly out of repair. The carpets are very much worn, but I'm thankful it is as good as it is, and I think we'll be very comfortable. The pictures are all hung. The Amalfi over the couch with Murillo's Madonna under it. Looks just great. The Venice one at the head of the couch with Duchess of Devonshire in gold frame that Lillian Raymond gave me under, and the two little ones of St. John in the fancy wood frame and that little girl that used to hang over my desk, one on either side. The Jungfrau between the front window and door, with small, fancy colored one under it. The sheep picture and several others I had before are in the dining room.

On the left side of the bureau is Holden, on the right, the picture Aunt Celia gave Alec that she thought looked like me, and under it, the six girls.

The two mirrors, one is in the living room beside the piano, the other in dining room. On one corner of piano (mahogany case) is the brass book rack with the best books in it. The other books are piled on the table in the bedroom.

Cut glass fruit dish is on the center of dining table. I found out who gave me that sideboard cover. It was Mrs Savage.

White net curtains with a border at all windows. I have

the plant Mary gave me in the brass jardiniere on a little stand in the window between the foot of the couch and the piano. It really looks awfully cozy and pleasant.

I put that pink velvet pincushion that Miss Lathrop gave me and the little pinbox, pink with the big bow on top, that Elizabeth Miller gave me last Christmas on the spare room dressing table, which is covered with white dotted muslin, and you don't know how pretty they look. Then I pinned the pretty postals Miss Walker sent you around and inside the mirror.

I can get that Portuguese woman to come and clean anytime I want her. Alec telephoned me this morning from the ranch. He can't get in, there is so much to do.

I'll send along the letter I wrote you Sunday, and didn't get a chance to mail. I used the electric stove this morning, and 15 minutes after I lighted it, the coffee was ready to drink. I want something hot with my breakfast now. I also made some fudge on it this morning. In fact, I haven't made a fire in the stove since Alec went, and I don't intend to, as I only get my breakfast here.

The Portuguese woman is to bring my kitty today.

Haven't had a letter for two days. I hope to get one today. Fair begins tomorrow.

Affec.
E.S.H.

———

Sept. 9, 1911

Dear Mother,

There was a cloudburst day before yesterday down near Clearmont and there are nine trains stalled there, so no mail went out or came in. We got a little of it in the shape of a big shower.

Well, yesterday noon, Mrs H. telephoned me and said we were invited to a 500 party[69] at Mrs Van Houten's that evening. I met Mrs H. and Mary at 4 o'clock to make calls on Mrs Young and Mrs Laing. They are sisters about 30, each with three children, and live side by side. We had a very pleasant time. Mrs Young has a lovely big house (too big, does her own work).

I wish you could see the set of china she has. A whole dinner set of white and gold like that Helen made me with a "Y" on each piece. Mrs Laing has a set too.

Mary has a girl now, so she invited me home to supper with them, and I went, for we were asked to get to Mrs Van's at 7:30. It was a neighborhood party gotten up on the spur of the moment that morning. The houses run this way, Mrs Van, Mrs Walters, Mrs Quick, Mrs Hill, Mrs Laing, Mrs Young. Mrs Laing had a headache when we were up there, so she didn't come. With the exception of the two (Y and L) I mentioned, the others are ladies about 50 and friends of Mrs Healy's.

We played 500. The idea was the four losers were to take the four winners to the picture show. Such fun as we had talking about it, for if you go this week, they have the extra music, and it's a quarter, while next week, it's the usual price, 15 cents. I had never played before, so they had great fun with me, for I had beginner's luck, and when we finished, was in the upper four. In fact, the Healy family are to be entertained with Mrs Young, for Mary, Mrs H., and I were all in the upper four.

For refreshments we had coffee, and jelly with sliced peaches in it, and whipped cream, and four kinds of cake. Mrs Van made the coffee, Mrs Hill the jelly, which she had meant to have for her own dessert that night, and Mrs Walters, Quick, and Young contributed half a cake they had each baked that morning.

It reminded me of the parties they used to get up at the lake at such short notice. Mr Van got his auto and took me home, for all that crowd live in the other end of town.

This is a lovely morning and some man has just telephoned and said he would call for me at 1 o'clock to go to the fair with Mr and Mrs Healy. It is 12 now, and I've got to get dressed and get some lunch, so must stop.

Affec.
Edith

Two nights up until 12. The pace of Buffalo is pretty fast.

———

Sept. 20, 1911

Dear Mother.

I didn't write you yesterday. Too many parties.

In the afternoon, quite an elaborate one for Mrs Healy given by Mrs Baker. I wore my green voile dress and Mrs Bert came for me in her auto, so I went and came in style. Mrs Healy has some beautiful clothes and looks stunning in them. She has the most beautiful embroidered white mull dress she had made in New York. She told me privately it cost $55. Well if she has the money and wants it, I don't know why she shouldn't have it.

There were 16 ladies there yesterday afternoon. We were asked to bring our sewing. I had plenty of napkins to hem, and by the way, Mrs H insists on taking home with her to hem, those two best tablecloths and half a dozen napkins that we got for a wedding present. She will send them back at Christmas when she sends our presents.

Well, yesterday at the party we had to eat: tomato jelly salad on lettuce with mayonnaise dressing and crackers, creamed chicken in ramekins with spiced pears and sandwiches and coffee, shredded pineapple mousse with cake.

A table for 10 was set in the dining room and one for six in the living room. This Mrs Baker is a young woman about 34 with two children and does her own work.

In the evening, we were paid back our picture show party and taken up to Gatchell's Drug Store for ice cream. There another party was organized. I don't know when I've laughed so. It was after Mr Healy had come in the drug store and said they couldn't go in the morning, not until the next day. So we are all to go up to Mrs Quick's to play 500 tonight. Each person is to contribute something toward refreshments. I am taking a pan of marshmallow fudge, Mary, a jar of spiced peaches her girl has just put up, Mrs H a big bottle of olives. (A crowd of nine children on horseback have galloped past most of them not older than Holden. They were on horses, not ponies. Sometimes two children on one horse.)

This afternoon, Mrs David Young entertained the Ladies
Aid of the Congregational Church at her house, and asked me
to come back to Mary's last night as their trunk was there, and
Patsy was going to drive them to Sheridan in his auto.[70] It takes
two days to get to Ogden from here. They have to go by way of
Butte and Billings.

We may get 14 quarts of milk for $1, but sweet potatoes
are 10 cents a pound. I ordered two pounds and just got six
medium-sized potatoes for 20 cents.

Mrs Hill sent me a glass of jelly. Mrs Steve L. brought
me two glasses, big ones. Mrs Van Houten promised me one
last night. Mrs Hill also whispered that she had a jar of pickled
peaches all ready to bring down.

Mr Mather stopped in with a big bunch of celery from
his garden yesterday and this morning before we were up, Mrs
Astell sent over a loaf of bread, hot out of the oven.

We certainly can live off of the neighbors. Aren't they kind.

That electric stove is fine. I made the fudge on it just now,
and it took about the same time as on a gas stove. We got
breakfast on it, coffee, boiled eggs, and toast, and warmed the
shredded wheat. Had a fine cantaloupe too, with enough cream
off yesterday's milk for the coffee and shredded wheat.

No, please don't send me that white felt hat. It isn't the
kind I want.

Have just come from Mrs Van Dyke's, a perfectly fine
dinner, well cooked and seasoned. Veal, browned potatoes,
tomato salad, corn jelly, gravy, and peach pie for dessert. 35
cents each meal. How's that. Ten counting us, people, all young.
Miss Post, Bob Alling, etc. Lots of fun. She lives right opposite
here. Must stop and go to the party.

E.S.H.

———

September 23, 1911

Dear Mother,
    I am enclosing some pictures of the Johnson County Fair.

I only had my little camera as I forgot to get some film for the big one, but I am so surprised and pleased to have these come out so well.

Bob A. didn't take any that day. He thought it too dark. I'm so glad I risked it.

I learned something last night that interested me. Talking about voting. Mrs Van Dyke said no one could be elected in this town without the women's vote. She said they (the women) didn't do much until it was necessary, but two different times when saloon keepers came up for office, the women got together, and defeated them so hard they never dared try again.

Next fall will be the presidential election, and I will have been a resident a year, so I can vote for him.

When I was talking to Mother Healy about how wonderful it seemed to me to be able to cook and serve a dinner for ten people, she said it didn't seem so to her, she'd done it so many times. She said, why we gave a breakfast for Margaret Armstrong in June, and Nellie [Helen's nickname] and I did all the work ourselves, and we had 20! The Japanese boy they have goes to school, so all he did was wash the dishes after he got home.

The breakfast was at 10 in the morning, and this is what they had. Cantaloupe, cream of wheat with cream, half a broiled chicken for each person, hot biscuits, creamed potato and peas out of the garden. And coffee, then waffles and syrup. Mrs H sat down to the table and Nellie and a friend of hers served the things. They have a round table that opens up and can seat 20 and she got a big tablecloth and napkins in Belfast. They had a huge basket of pink peonies on the center of the table, and Margaret's (the bride's) chair, they used a white enamel one, and fixed a wire arch over it, which they covered with sprays of white orange blossoms.

They said it looked lovely, and I don't doubt it. But think of the work, and all done by 10 in the morning.

Whew!

Yesterday morning, the telephone rang while we were eating breakfast (I won't say what time it was) and I jumped to answer it, as I expected Mrs Silva to call me up. My arm hit the handle of the coffee pot, and the entire contents went splashing across the floor, grounds, and everything. Alec swept up the grounds with a broom into the dust pan while I answered the call, and then I went at it. A large dark stain fully two feet long. The carpet is so old, it's almost in pieces, and I thought it would be the limit if we had to get a new one on account of the stain. I took a kettle of boiling water off the stove, and soaked and rubbed until I was weary. You can imagine how much water I put on when it didn't dry out until this morning. And not the sign of a stain. Isn't that luck.

I just happened to run across the receipted bill for those lambs took to Omaha. They netted Healy Bros. over $12,000 and they considered the market poor. Another load go October 5. I hope Patsy will go with those.

Alec came home yesterday and said Jim Gatchell asked him if he thought I could be persuaded to play in a small orchestra, first violin, Mrs Jeffers second, etc. I guess I'd like to. I'll wait until I hear more about it. I expect that girl any moment, Miss Bell, who is to try my accompaniments for next Friday night.

Alec has those pictures in his coat pocket and he is downtown, so I'll send them tomorrow.

It's a big joke and gone all over town, what I said to Alec a little while after we were here. He said he guessed he'd go down to Adams and Young's [grocery store] and I said, why, what do we need. I thought we got everything yesterday.

Now I understand the joke. This is just like the New England country grocery store. The village club. All the men congregate there and talk things over. In winter they have a stove and everyone sits around it on chairs or boxes and settle the affairs of the nation. If you want the man of your family, telephone Billy Adams or Dave Young, and if they aren't there, someone who is there knows where they went. Also Central[71] is most accommodating. She will locate any man in town for you. When she hears he's at the picture show, she telephones the hotel, and the clerk runs across the street and hauls him out.

We have a small barn that goes with this house, so Alec keeps his buggy and two of his horses there.

This morning we took a nice ride over to the fort.[72] When there was so much trouble with Indians around here, the fort was made. Now that the Indians are moved 20 miles above Sheridan, this is used for a soldiers' home and the soldiers are over near Sheridan.

Must stop now as I see the lady coming.

Affec.
E.S.H.

———

This is an undated fragment written from Edith and Alec's mountain cabin in early October 1911.

. . .The kitten is a dear, but not much use. She's too small. We got her to chase the chipmunks who bother us so. She does chase them, but she isn't quick enough to kill them, which I'm glad of.

I saw three big woodpeckers yesterday, and last night a hoot owl made night hideous. Yesterday, I also saw a bunny. Quite a big one. We have been living on prairie chickens lately.[73] My but they are good broiled. Alec also brought over some meat, and we have had plenty of lamb chops. We broil them on the grating that comes out of the center of the stove.

The other afternoon I was so surprised to see Bob Alling and another man and a girl riding up to our front door.

He was taking his vacation and camping with the McNeese's. They didn't know just where we were, and after riding about 30 miles, finally landed at Todd's cabin in Onion Gulch. They had dinner there, and Dudley, Todd's bronco buster, brought them over here. They stayed about an hour, but as they had a good 25 miles to ride back to their camp, they couldn't stay any longer. My what a ride. I'll bet that girl was dead the next day. She looked real cute, though, in a dark brown corduroy riding habit and a big straw hat tied down with a pale blue veil. I took a snapshot of them. I hope it turns out well.

There isn't much new to write about. Alec has to begin mouthing sheep the 15th and we are trying to figure out what's to become of me. Perhaps I shall have to go to town, but I don't want to. How would you like to look into the mouths of 40,000 animals. You see, when a sheep hasn't good teeth, it can't chew its food well, therefore it is apt to get thin and die during the winter from lack of strength. Those whose teeth are very bad have to be marked, and sorted out in the fall, and shipped to be sold as mutton. Those whose teeth are just beginning, have to be marked in another way, and put in a bunch by themselves. These are kept near the ranch all winter and fed easy things to chew.

Well they hope to do two herds a day at Billy's Flat. Day to these men begins at dawn, about 4:30.

Nothing would tempt me to stay here all night alone. So unless Alec can fix it so he doesn't have to begin so early, I shall go to town, and stay those ten days. However, he says he's sure he can fix it somehow, and I'm sure he can, for I'd rather be up here. I guess I'd better stop now and wash out one of my crepe waists.

Hope you are all right.

Affec.
E.S.H.

These pages were the last of Edith's honeymoon letters home. By the time she wrote them, she was three months pregnant and making plans with Alec to build their first home.

Edith doesn't mention her pregnancy or Mary's, her sister-in-law. She and her mother held Victorian–Edwardian sensibilities about proper subjects of conversation so it seems reasonable that either Edith just wouldn't talk about it or that her mother discarded letters that mentioned her pregnancy.

Given their experiences with childbirth and death, both women and their husbands were cautious. They wanted the added protection

ALEC, JR.

Edith in Boston with her newborn son, Spring 1912.

ALEC, JR.

Alec, Jr. probably in Boston for the birth of
his brother Dan, three years younger.

Alec, Jr. in Boston, in Buffalo, on the ranch, with his father, with his puppy, Rowdy, and with Edith's cousin, Lillian.

of more advanced medical facilities such as Boston and Los Angeles offered. The sisters-in-law naturally wanted their mothers with them for childbirth, and, of course, their husbands. Alec and Patsy spelled each other during the 1911–1912 winter so that first Patsy could join Mary on the West Coast and then Alec could be with Edith on the East Coast.

That winter was said to be one of the most severe in memory. The previous year's drought had continued, feed was scarce, winter arrived early, and the livestock suffered. On April 25, 1912, The Buffalo *Bulletin*[74] reported that carcasses lay scattered across the plains when spring finally arrived. The disastrous winter must not have started when Edith wrote from the mountain cabin, since she chats about woodpeckers, a hoot owl, and a big bunny, not a blizzard.

By the time Edith mailed her October letter to Boston, Mary—then seven months pregnant—had taken the train to Los Angeles with Patricia, Patrick, III, and probably Mrs. Sedwick, her mother. Mary had given birth to Patrick in Los Angeles two-and-a-half years earlier. While his family rode the rails West, Patsy, Jr., made an adventure out of the journey, racing his Willys-Overland[75] from Buffalo to Los Angeles with two other pals, each in his own car. Patsy, Jr., told the Buffalo *Bulletin* that the trio expected to make the trip in fifteen days; instead, it took them twenty-two.

Both families were blessed, and the mothers and babies thrived. Not only were the two Healy cousins, Stuart Sedwick and Alexander, Jr., to grow up to be great friends, but their sons, Stuart, Jr., and Tim, remarkably born only a few hours apart, also maintain a deep friendship.

Back in Los Angeles, Patsy, Jr., must have taken the train home because his son, Stuart, was born on December 26, 1911, and Patsy was back in Buffalo by January 3, 1912. Mary and the children didn't return until the end of March.

Edith didn't wait for her pregnancy to become as advanced. When she was five months pregnant, Miss Todd from Boston came to visit and on December 8, 1911, she accompanied Edith back to Beacon Street by train. Miss Todd was mentioned in the first line of Edith's first honeymoon letter. "Look what we just found at the office. That's from Miss Todd, isn't she the limit!" Most likely Miss Todd was a friend of Mrs. Holden's, since she wasn't an attendant in the wedding, nor one of the boarders in the Beacon Street house.

Since Edith and Alec thought the only time your name should appear in the newspaper was "when you were born, when you married, and when you died," the timing of their comings and goings during Edith's lying-in are uncertain. Presumably, Alec didn't leave for the East until his brother had returned from California, which meant that the honeymooners did not share their first Christmas together. They were together for their first anniversary, April 3, 1912. Their son, Alec, Jr., was born two days later on April 5.

The baby was healthy, Edith was healthy, and, like his brother, Alec probably made a quick return to Buffalo. Alec, Jr., told his son, Tim, that his father had been very anxious in Boston waiting for the baby's birth and worrying about the winter disaster on the range.

Edith's seventy-five-year-old mother likely accompanied her daughter and grandchild back to Buffalo. Like her sister-in-law, Mary, Edith probably waited to travel to Buffalo until her baby was at least three months old. If so, Edith, Alec, Jr., and Mrs. Holden probably arrived in Buffalo in late June or early July.[76] It may be that Edith would have made sure to return in time to celebrate the Fourth of July in Buffalo style—she always made much over Fourth of July gatherings. However, Alec may have telegraphed them to stay in Boston a little longer until Buffalo had cleaned up after a flash flood on Clear Creek destroyed part of the downtown area.

NEW HOME, NEW BABY

Top: Edith's shadow signals who is snapping the shot of her husband and sons:
Baby Dan and Alec, Jr. Above: A pair of 100-year-old pines dwarf the bungalow that
the Healys built on the corner of Lobban and Gatchell.

On August 22, 1912, the Buffalo *Bulletin* names Elizabeth Holden as joining in the two weeks of nonstop parties in honor of Alec's mother, Mrs. Patsy Healy, Sr., who was visiting from Ogden. Some of the parties, including a reception at Edith and Alec's on August 24, were also in Mrs. Holden's honor.

Elizabeth Holden returned to Boston on October 22, with snow capping the peaks and frost blanketing the grass every morning. By then, the Healy Brothers had loaded their sheep on seventeen double-decker railroad cars and shipped them to Omaha. Buffalo was settling in for the winter.

Edith's mother didn't create a journal book with postcards, so her reactions to the Wyoming countryside that Edith described in such poetic detail in her letters home are unknown. Elizabeth Holden must have loved the beauty of Buffalo and the Big Horns, with its tumbling creeks (even Clear Creek in town) and flowers bursting with color—pink hollyhocks, purple phlox, bleeding hearts, violets, snowball bushes, wild roses, shooting stars, Indian paintbrush, and blue lupine. Elizabeth Holden remained in Buffalo long enough to watch the procession of summer greens of grasses, sage, pines, aspen, cottonwoods, and the willows that turn crimson and gold in the fall.

As Elizabeth Holden read aloud her daughter's letters in afternoon gatherings at her home, perhaps the New England ladies shared the heady energy that Edith was experiencing as a pioneer helping to create a new world in a distant land, even as their forebears had upon arriving in America. Although Elizabeth must have endured moments of sadness that her daughter didn't live down the street, Elizabeth Holden was a practical Yankee. She probably influenced her Bostonian grandson, Holden Furber, who said on several occasions that he was "philosophical," about the separations that come with old age.

Edith and Alec filled their home with books, like the leather-bound
first editions from Edith's Grandfather Holden in the case behind, as well
as many colorful children's books for Alec, Jr. and Dan.

CHAPTER 12

CHRISTMAS WITH BABIES

DECEMBER 30, 1915

WORRIES ABOUT MOTHER – CHRISTMAS DETAILS ABOUT
BUFFALO'S NON-STOP CHRISTMAS WEEK

We assume that Edith continued writing frequently to her mother after her honeymoon letters ended in mid-October 1911, but only two letters to her mother survive: Christmas Week 1915 and October 8, 1916. The first letter describes Christmas and New Year's nonstop festivities in Buffalo (included in this chapter), and the latter details the annual state meeting of the Daughters of the American Revolution when a young Buffalo woman's design for the Wyoming state flag was selected (see Chapter 13).

While Edith's two letters from this period give a personal view of the Healy's lives, she doesn't touch on any of the life-changing forces set loose by World War I and, closer to home, the closing of the frontier.

Edith's relationship with her mother remained close. Mrs. Holden only made that one trip to Buffalo in 1912, but Edith must have spent considerable time in Boston, including attending the scientifically minded Boston Cooking School made famous by its publication, *The Fannie Farmer Cookbook*, which is still in print.

A year after Elizabeth's trip to Buffalo, Edith assisted Elizabeth— undoubtedly with Alec's help and advice—to negotiate the sale of her big, bay-windowed townhouse to the Second Unitarian Church in Boston. This was not Elizabeth's own church. Elizabeth probably belonged to the Second Church in the Brookline suburb near their Beacon Street home, a reasonable assumption given that the Rev. Arthur

W. Littlefield, the Brookline minister, married Edith and Alec. The Boston church also bought Elizabeth's two neighbors' homes, giving them large grounds that spread from mid-block to Audubon Circle, the diamond-shaped intersection of Beacon Street and Park Road.

By the time Second Church, Boston, opened its new red-brick, Georgian colonial style house of worship in 1914, Elizabeth Holden had moved to an apartment in Brookline at 86 Vernon Street about a mile and a half farther from downtown Boston, just off Beacon Street. The 1910 census shows 86 Vernon as having three apartments housing a couple, a family with four children, and a widow, 70, with her grown son, daughter, and a boarder.

Did Elizabeth Holden, 76, have an apartment of her own? Did she have live-in help, as she had for most of her life or did she become a boarder? Who moved out of 86 Vernon between 1910 and 1913? Did her neighbors include children or only adults? Was she on the ground floor to make walking easier as her legs began to swell with the onset of heart failure? Did her window look out at the towering trees in the triangular park across the way?

This visit must have been emotional for both women, knowing that their family home with so many happy and tragic memories would soon be leveled, yet the sale gave Elizabeth financial security. Given Edith's delight in telling her mother about arranging gracious homes (even a sheepwagon), it is clear that mother and daughter shared a joy in decorating. They must have decided, then decided again which pieces of furniture to move to Elizabeth's new apartment, to ship to Wyoming, to sell, or to give away.

Edith returned to Boston the following winter pregnant again. Alec, Jr., probably accompanied her, with Alec following later. On May 20, 1915, Daniel Sampson Healy was born. He may have been named Daniel after Alec's uncle, Daniel Healy.[77] Like Edith, the baby's middle name was Sampson after the Holdens' *Mayflower* ancestor, Henry Sampson.

Buffalo Wyoming
Dec. 30, 1915

Dear Mother -

Got your letter written from Waban[78] and was glad enough to know you were able to get out there, so now if you don't feel well you can be waited on and have good care. It troubled me to think you had to be up and about whether you wanted to or not because I know how hard it would be to get any extra attention at 86 Vernon Street. Also if everyone there had colds it would be just as well to get out of that atmosphere.

I hope you will stay until you get good and strong again.

Now I will go into a little detail about our Christmas.

We got our tree as we did last year, going out into the hills for it. This time to our Klondike ranch, which is so near the mountain we got the tree just outside the ranch fence.

We went on Monday – Tuesday evening was our dancing class. Wednesday evening Mrs Langworthy gave a dinner party – this was for Mary's mother, who has failed very much in the last year and who looks sick to me. She had Mary and mother and Patsy, Alec and I, and Mr West who is the new Episcopalian minister and his wife.

They are a very attractive young couple who have only been married a year. Her table was all pink with candy baskets and place cards to match – oyster cocktail first, then clear soup, then chicken in casserole, mashed potatoes, and cauliflower and cranberry sauce. Salad of head lettuce with tiny French onions. French dressing. Dessert of some kind of frozen custard with cake and coffee.

Being Christmas week we were all rather tired so we were glad to spend the rest of the evening drawn up around the open fire. Didn't do anything special Thursday, which was stormy but Friday was a glorious day and in the afternoon Alec got out the car and we went around delivering our presents, Alec Jr acting as messenger.

In the evening we went to the church where they had a service upstairs where I played a solo, and then later a Christmas tree downstairs for the children, each one getting a bag of candy and an apple. We got home at nine o'clock but Alec Jr had to have the Night Before Christmas before he would go to bed. After that we had to fix the things on the tree – we trimmed the tree before supper – and tacked the steamer rug up between the rooms so he wouldn't see the tree until after Christmas breakfast.

We hung all four stockings on the Christmas tree, baby's and all, and Alec and I fixed things in each others. In the morning Alec Jr just missed seeing Santa Claus. He heard him slam the door and his feet on the piazza but he got to the window too late.

Alec went out into the front room and got the stockings while I went and got the baby and we all were in bed together just as we used to do at home. The baby had a teaspoon and a clothes pin in his sock with a rattle sticking out the top, so he began by trying to get them all in his mouth at once which kept him busy while we looked at our things.

Alec Jr had some candy in the toe of his and a horn and that Santa Claus on a sleigh you sent him. He seemed to be more taken with the horn and Santa Claus than anything else for he kept going back to them all day. In mine I had a pair of bedroom slippers with a thick sole which are fine when you have to get up these cold nights with the baby and a jack-in-the-box. As Alec ordered a new party dress for me he just wanted to give me something for a surprise. I put in his stocking all wrapped in pretty paper and ribbons, a lot of things out of his drawer. In the toe, I put three new collar buttons.

After breakfast we had the tree and Alec, Jr. certainly was surprised and delighted with everything. We got him a sled and a tiny carpet sweeper and the horn. These were from Santa Claus.

But the other things were from the people who really sent them. The baby loves his big rattle from you and has it every afternoon when he sits up for an hour or two in his high chair.

I had to give him a bath and sterilize bottles and fix his milk, so Alec and I waited until he was safely on the piazza sound asleep before opening our things.

Mrs Chase[79] has a son who is working in Sheridan. He thought he could get over for Christmas and then found he couldn't and her disappointment was so great, Alec said he would go over after him for a Christmas present for her. Then the roads got bad and Alec said he would rather pay his fare on the Stanley Steamer, a car that makes a trip over and back the same day, for six dollars round trip, than have the wear and tear on the car.

She didn't want to accept but finally she was so anxious to see her boy she did and he came over Friday morning and got here at noon and stayed until Monday morning.

As we were going out for Christmas dinner, I told her she could invite any one she chose to share their Christmas dinner, for my Christmas present to her, so they asked four young men, friends of Russell's in town here, who were all away from home and had nowhere to go. We left at one o'clock for our dinner and theirs was at one thirty and as they were gone when we got home we didn't see them at all, but I know they had a good dinner and a good time from what the others said.

Ethelyn's present I can't get over. I am just crazy about it. It is a filet lace luncheon set. A stunner! Centerpiece, six plates and six tumbler doilies. The lace is in squares and has a tiny edge to go on around it. She has had trouble with her eyes and couldn't do it, so sent me the materials and it won't take any time at all. She did one to show me how. I am wild to use it. By the way did you ever have a chance at Dr. Bolters again to ask him anything about that table cloth? I guess I can kiss it goodbye in my mind.

Mother Healy sent me a lovely black leather wrist bag lined with brocade. I'm glad to have it as I haven't anything but my bead bag and I ought not to use that so common. Nellie sent a crepe de chine chemise with beautiful crochet at the top. Mary Healy gave me a pink one so I am well equipped for parties. They sent Alec gold cuff buttons with engraved monogram and socks and tie to match, and an electric lantern which pleases him much.

I liked the scarf you sent very much – I was using that long chiffon one and it was not convenient and too nice for what I needed. Thank you.

I gave Alec a smoking jacket which seems to please him immensely.

I got a lot of things which I won't stop to enumerate now. I liked Lillian's pin tree. Please read her this letter and thank her. It is standing on my bureau and looks so cute and I am always wanting those pins.

Alec, Jr. wants me to read Terrible Towser[80] to him and every time I say Towser he corrects me and says Rowdy. Alec, Jr. is much pleased with Daniel Sampson's gift and nearly drove me crazy rushing over the house with it. I think I shall put it away for DS.

The Furbers sent four presents to Alec Jr and DS. I didn't take the cute books and boxing darkies to put on the Victrola.[81] More track and tunnel and switches for the train – they were certainly very generous.

I did not take the baby up with us to dinner. He was sleeping sweetly when we left, and as long as Mrs Chase was here I thought he was better off at home.

We planned after dinner for Alec to come and get him to spend the afternoon. However after dinner they wanted to go to the picture show so I telephoned Mrs Chase not to get him ready, he was better off at home. Some people came in and the men went off after the mail so we didn't get to the show after all but the baby was better off at home. Much as I should like to have shown him off. The children got excited and noisy and he is used to quiet and placidly eating, sleeping and kicking his feet on the bed.

We got home from Mary's at 5:30. Got Alec, Jr. into bed and had just time to make a change of clothes and up to the other part of town to the Balden's for a seven o'clock dinner. Just eight of us and a jolly crowd. Jeffers, Williams, Baldens and us.

The table was lovely. A Santa Claus in a sleigh drawn by eight reindeer in the center. The bundles in the sleigh each had ribbons on which ran to each plate giving us souvenirs afterward.

Everything was red and green. First course a white maraschino sherbet with red and green cherries on top. Next white soup with pimento and green pepper garnish. Next clams steamed with melted butter. Where on earth did she get them – in the shells. Think of the distance they had to come. Next roast pig! A whole one with his head on, an apple in his mouth and a necklace of cranberries. It was as delicate as chicken. Mashed potatoes and peas, and a steamed apple which had been colored red with cinnamon drop candy. Salad of lettuce, cucumber, and radishes. Dessert pistachio ice cream with red cherries on and two birthday cakes with candles for Mr Balden and Mrs Williams whose birthday it was.

After dinner the men had their smoke and we sat and chatted awhile and then all went out and got into our autos (each couple had one) and went down to the hotel to the dance. I danced every dance from nine until twelve and I don't know when I've had such a good time. Having these dancing lessons has made a lot of difference for we are all doing things alike so it's fun to dance with each other. A dancing club was organized that night and we are to have twenty couples and meet every other Saturday night. Alec has developed into a wonderfully good dancer and can do the Hesitation beautifully and can get the most glorious "fade away" step into his reverse turn. So our Christmas lasted from 6 a.m. until 12 p.m.

I had to get up early the next morning for I had to attend to the baby and get ready to go to church and play for that Cantata.

Monday evening was that Bridge party I sent you the fine invitation I had – twelve tables. Got home at twelve o'clock.

Tuesday I rested. Yesterday was Wednesday and Mr and Mrs Van Houten had a dinner dance. Seven couples to dinner and then we danced until twelve. I don't know when I've had such a good time. It was a very cold night snowing and blowing so Mr V put the curtains up around his car and went around and collected us all. You see none of the other men wanted to take their cars out because there wasn't any shelter for them while we were at the party, and they would freeze up. Mr Van could just put his in his own garage and drain it, then when it was time for us to go home, he went out with a tea kettle of boiling water and started it up again.

Today was the History Club and I had to give the story of As You Like It and selections from it. We read out loud most of the whole play of Macbeth this afternoon.

Alec went to the sheep camp this morning. It was 2 below zero this morning when he started horseback and I hated to have him go for he had to face the wind but he said he thought he better go to the sheep camp and get rested.

Tomorrow is New Year's Eve. Mr Van Houten had to go to his camps too this morning and think I'll see if Mrs Van doesn't want to go and "look on" at the dance at the Armory.

I guess I've told you all I know and I want to get to bed early – tonight.

Isn't it wonderful that I am strong enough to do all these things and not get over tired.

Just got Flossie Thomas' wedding announcements. She has married a dentist in Fort Worth, Texas where she is living with her mother.

I was awfully surprised but now that I think it over I am glad for her if he is a nice man.

The more I realize how I feel the more anxious I am that Ethelyn get out here and see what this country would do for her. I certainly am growing fat. Alec's nickname for me now is "fatty."

I'll enclose Ethelyn's letter which I found.

I will send this letter to Waban hoping you are still there.

I'll send Aunt Caroline and Uncle Rob the money at the same time, just before my birthday.

Hope you get better and stronger soon.

Affectionately,
Edith

Edith relished in describing new and interesting foods to her mother. Edith's recipe for molded salmon with cucumber sauce was published in the St. Luke's Sunday School Ladies Auxiliary second edition of *Buffalo Cookery* in 1916. It is a show-off buffet pleaser, sure to impress guests. To make this dish in the approved Boston School of Cooking manner as Edith was taught, begin by preparing all of the ingredients in individual bowls before combining them.[82]

Buffalo Cookery
Compiled by the Ladies' Auxiliary of St. Luke's Sunday-School:

Moulded Salmon with Cucumber Sauce—Mrs. Alex Healy
1 can salmon
½ tablespoon salt
1½ tablespoons sugar
½ tablespoon flour
1 teaspoon mustard
Few grains cayenne
2 egg yolks
1½ tablespoons melted butter
¾ cup milk
¼ cup vinegar
2 tablespoons cold water
¾ tablespoon granulated gelatin

Remove salmon from can, rinse thoroughly with hot water and separate in flakes. Mix dry ingredients. Add egg yolks, butter, milk and vinegar. Cook over boiling water, stirring constantly until mixture thickens. Add gelatin soaked in cold water. Strain and add to salmon. Fill individual moulds and chill. Serve with cucumber sauce.

Cucumber Sauce
Beat one-half cup heavy cream until stiff, add one-fourth teaspoon salt, a few grains of pepper and gradually, two tablespoons vinegar. Then add one cucumber pared, chopped and squeezed hard in cheesecloth to remove all liquid.

Buffalo may fly more Wyoming flags per capita than any other town in the state.
Verna Keays, daughter of Edith and Alec's next door neighbors, designed the flag in 1916.

CHAPTER 13

WORLD GETS LARGER

1916

FRONTIER ENDS – WORLD WAR I – LEAVING BUFFALO

Edith's letter about the annual state meetings of the Daughters of the American Revolution (DAR), Colonial Dames, and Federated Women's Clubs illuminates life in a vast state with few people. Women from the three national organizations, many with the same members, met the same week in the same town, one club after another, to accomplish all of their business and deepen friendships.

In 1916, DAR selected the design for the Wyoming state flag, a white buffalo on a field of blue framed by a white border surrounded by a red border. (The young woman who submitted the winning design, Verna Keays, lived next door to the Healys in Buffalo.) During the same meeting, Edith wrote that the women also talked about how to protect the Medicine Wheel in the Big Horns, a pre-Columbian ceremonial site, which, at seventy-five feet in diameter ranks with the largest of North American Indian medicine wheels. Edith and her colleagues did not have much success with the federal government, which took more than fifty years to designate the Big Horn Medicine Wheel a National Historic Landmark.[83]

For people in Wyoming, Edith's assumption about the legislature's acceptance of the DAR's flag choice brings an "of course" shrug.[84] People in Wyoming are used to life "in a small town with a five-hundred-mile main street," which is their joking way to explain how everyone knows everyone—or knows someone who does.

This two-degrees-of-separation was even more true in 1916 than today. From 1900 to 1920, Wyoming's population grew from 92, 531 to 194,402, so more than double, but still, in 1916, the population was a mere 170,000. One major project that improved movement and increased growth was building a connecting track between the Gulf of Mexico in Texas and the Pacific Ocean in Seattle. Tycoon James J. Hill, the new owner of the Chicago, Burlington & Quincy Railroad, was willing to pay the fortune it would take to blast through the narrow granite walls of Wind River Canyon at the southern end of the Big Horn Basin to connect to the east–west tracks of the Northern Pacific in Montana. Three tunnels were blasted through granite that was about 2,500 feet high. When the work was completed in 1913, even residents of the mountain-blocked Basin, where peaks passing thirteen thousand feet rise on two sides, were connected with the rest of the state in all seasons. Eleven years later the road along the same route was completed, including an additional three tunnels blasted through granite.

Buffalo, Wyoming
Oct. 8, 1916

Dear Mother,
    I know you want to hear all about the Federation so I will begin way back on Monday morning when I started from here. It had been raining the night before and was still drizzling and I had my doubts about being able to start because it takes such a little time in this country to make the roads dangerous for automobiles.
    There is a man here who runs an auto between here and Sheridan who has just purchased a limousine.
    Of course he charges more than the jitney hire that runs a sort of bus affair, but my goodness I was glad when he called up and said Mr Healy had engaged him to take me over – that was before he left town on Saturday.

I got in the car at the house here. I was all bundled up because it was snowing a little and quite cold. I soon began shedding my wraps for the car was electrically heated and really that whole ride was a delight instead of the torture I expected.

The autumn foliage was beautiful, and the frosting of snow on those red hills exquisite. It took us about two hours and a half to make the trip and I was delivered at the hotel nice and warm and not tired a bit.

I had been invited to Mrs Gillette's for dinner and to spend the night, but the ride over generally tires you so, I thought it wise to go in the morning and rest in the afternoon before going to her house.

I took a room at the hotel and then went out to see the city for I haven't been to Sheridan more than twice this whole year.

Think of not seeing a train or a trolley for a whole year.

Funny how you never think about them at all in Buffalo and hence don't miss them as much as you would think.

I invited two girls to lunch with me. One is engaged to Jimmy Young. Then I thought I'd copy you, so I bought Good Housekeeping and rested and read all the afternoon.

At five I called a taxi (you see I've not forgotten how to behave in a city) and went to Mrs Gillette's. That gave me time to dress for dinner. Fortunately I had the right clothes for all the places I went during the week and that is saying a lot, for the pleasure correct clothes gives a woman is not easily expressed by mere words.

I wore my rose colored chiffon that is trimmed with velvet the same shade and a touch of gold at the belt. Also, my gold chain with the big topaz.

Mrs Gillette's home I love. It is so pretty and yet so homelike it is a pleasure just to be in it. It is the one house I have been in out here that has antique furniture. A table like we had in the front hall. Old fashioned gold mirror like ours. Sewing table, and the little mahogany one like your telephone stands on now, etc.

Perhaps that is one reason it all appeals so to me. Dinner was at six thirty in a most attractive dining room furnished in different shades of green with round mahogany table.

A bowl of pink roses in the center and four silver candle sticks with pink candles and no shades, made a picture in the green dining room.

Only six of us at dinner. Mr and Mrs Gillette, a Mr Dawes from Philadelphia (a Yale classmate of Mr G's) a Dr. West from Pittsburgh and Dr. Grace Hebard[85] of the State University at Laramie and yours truly.

It is still a mystery to me how I ever got in on that dinner. It is such a pleasure to hear brainy people talk, that, except for a funny story or two, I just listened with all my might.

After dinner the men smoked and we ladies went into the parlor and soon the Colonial Dames arrived and we had our annual meeting. There are only thirteen of us in the whole state and on account of bad roads (I was sorry Mrs Ed Dana couldn't get in from her ranch) we had only seven present.

We voted a twenty dollar prize to be given to the best essay on Wyoming trails by High School pupils all over the state, and twenty dollars towards a bronze tablet to mark the site of Fort Phil Kearney, which was where a terrible Indian massacre took place.

Our dues are four dollars a year so we have enough in the treasury to do these things. Then we are to join with the D.A.R. to try to get the State to preserve an Indian relic on the mountain called the Medicine Wheel. It is 70 feet across.[86]

Then we adjourned until another year.

The men joined us after this and we had a pleasant chat and then departed.

The guest room I was in was done in grey and old rose with painted grey furniture. A lovely old rose satin down quilt on the bed. A knock on the door the next morning and here was a maid with a breakfast tray which she set upon the bed. And after closing the window, departed. I was sure glad I had on my best pink crepe de chine nightie and hair ribbon. My, I think I never felt any more luxurious in my life than I did then.

It was such a complete change from a very ordinary nightie and a wet baby who has jammed himself up against the small of your back and has one leg under your arm.

I don't suppose it was proper but I ate everything on
that tray and could have eaten the dishes themselves they
were so dainty.

How pretty everything in someone else's house looks
and tastes. Anyway.

Mrs Gillette was busy with Federation affairs and I wanted
to get back to the hotel to meet Rose Dodau who was coming
over from Buffalo to play my accompaniment that night. So I
left there early.

Rose had just arrived when I got to the hotel. She came
with Mrs Whitcomb. So we all had lunch together. In the
afternoon Rose had errands and I wanted to make use of
my opportunities so I had a shampoo, a facial massage, a
manicure and a pedicure. I tell you I was "some" clean lady,
when I left that place.

On going back to the hotel I found Lily Baker had arrived.
She was a delegate and was to come over with Maggie Young
early the next morning, Wednesday, when the federation began,
but as it was still raining she didn't dare wait, but came in the
limousine as I did.

I played that evening for the State Library Association.
I wore my yellow dress, which "if I do say it as I shouldn't," is a
beauty. The things went so well that Miss Hebard, Mrs Gillette,
Mrs Baker, Whitcomb, and Van Dyke went to Mrs Morton, the
President of the Federation and asked her to put me on the
Federation Programe [*sic*] but she said the programe had been
arranged by the state committee and printed and she didn't
feel she could interfere with their work.

I didn't care a bit because Rose couldn't stay any longer
and I'd have had to risk any old accompanist and spend a lot
of time rehearsing, yet when I heard a lady say in speaking of
another, "wherever Mrs Gates goes she puts Worland on the
map," and I want to put Buffalo on the map.

The Southern part of the state has always had the best
music at the Federation and it was they who made out the
programe and by the way the President was from Cheyenne
so she was wise not to interfere in any way.

This Dr. Hebard was the bright and shining light of the whole week, of Library as well as Federation and State Regent of D.A.R.

The next morning Maggie Young arrived bringing with her four ladies from Buffalo and Mrs Rothwell and her guest came over too, so you see there was quite a Buffalo Delegation.

Rose went home the next morning so I asked Lily Baker to room with me. She was a delegate and I was an alternate with Mrs Van Dyke who was our President, so we were invited to homes but we had rather stay at the hotel. Maggie and Mrs Whitcomb were together so we four had such a good time running into each other's rooms.

I went to the Wednesday morning meeting, then all the delegates had lunch together at the Congregational Church then the afternoon meeting. At 3:30 after Miss Hebard's address, I left with her for the D.A.R. meeting at a house.

We had tea first then a very good meeting where twenty six flags were shown that were competing for the design for a State flag. A prize of twenty dollars was offered. The flag that won the prize was to be presented to the State Legislature this fall for adoption. Verna Keays had sent a design and it was by far the best, I thought. I said so to everyone I talked to. No names were on them but I knew hers. You see I had no vote but Mrs Van Dyke had. They were voted on the next morning and Verna got the prize![87]

Got back to the hotel at six. There was to be a fine musical programe that evening to begin with so I went and heard that and then came home. That made four meetings that one day so do you wonder that I woke up with a headache the next morning. I know what it was, eating so much hearty food and no exercise. I dressed and went down and got a cup of coffee then I came back and went to bed. Slept all the morning and ate soup and dry toast for lunch. Went to half a meeting in the afternoon, came back for another nap, and to curl my hair. By dinner time, I was all right again and ready and eager for the big reception and ball the Elks were giving us in their wonderful club house.

It began at nine, and I danced most every dance and

left at one. Thank goodness for my lovely yellow dress. There wasn't any prettier one in the hall. Fine music and a splendid floor. I knew quite a few of the young men and the Sheridan ladies were lovely about introducing their husbands – I found out later there was an unwritten law that no man should ask a Sheridan lady to dance until the ball was half over. That gave us a chance to meet their men.

There was a man named Theodore Diers who seemed to be running this affair. He opened the ball with Mrs Morton, the President, and closed it with me. He is very good looking and my, doesn't he know it. I was dancing with Charles Carter, Mrs Van Dyke's nephew, when this Mr Diers went strutting by us and I whispered, "My how that man hates himself," and I thought Charles would have hysterics then and there. We had to stop dancing.

We got back to the hotel at quarter past one to find the hotel cabaret in full swing. So in we four went as we all had Mrs in front of our names, we felt we didn't need a chaperone. Then we all had club sandwiches and coffee and my, I was hungry. A lot of people came in from the ball and it seemed quite gay – I only danced once. With Reuben Barkey. The man, or rather young fellow, he's about twenty four, who won most all the events at both the Sheridan and Buffalo Fairs. He is really a wonder at riding and bucking and roping steers. He won several prizes at Cheyenne last Frontier Day.

As Lily and I crawled into bed at two thirty that night we said "Cinderella tonight and back to the ash pan of life tomorrow."

Breakfast at nine the next day and then I did some shopping I had put off. Some toys for the babies and a dress for me to wear around the house mornings. I got a very good looking dark blue serge, piped with red. Paid ten dollars for it and they altered it (and it fits perfectly) for nothing.

Then I heard the end of the morning meeting and went to lunch with the crowd at the Episcopal Church. After lunch, a Mrs Ralph Denio whom I had been much attracted to, invited Mrs Bond and me to go for a spin in her runabout. She lives in

Sheridan and I liked her immensely from the minute she gave her report. She is extremely good looking in a refined way and seemed so jolly as well as capable and efficient. I was glad of the opportunity to know her better.

The meetings were too close that night. Maggie and I were sitting together and about three o'clock we decided we had had enough and we wanted to go home. We passed the word to the others. There was a meeting tea a Mrs Metz was giving and had asked all the Buffalo ladies to come to her house after the meeting. By the way this Mrs Metz was in the receiving line that night of the reception and ball, and when I got to her, she kissed me. As I have met her in my life just three times, you can imagine the shock! I am glad I had the presence of mind not to give way to my first instinct, which was to dodge.

Somewhere in this narrative I have left out a Domestic Science demonstration at the High School on cake frosting with glycerine in it. You can keep it in the ice chest a month. I wouldn't have missed that for anything. The lecture, not the frosting.

To resume. Maggie and I wanted to go home and we went. Packed in half an hour and left at four o'clock. It was a glorious afternoon, warm and lovely and we felt like two kids running away from school.

Got home at six to find the babies well and happy – the next morning I called Maggie up. All I said was" Maggie!" and she said "Edith!" in the same tone.

It was raining guns and had been all night and the wind was howling and it was cold and damp and awful!

The others left Sheridan at twelve noon and got into Buffalo at seven at night, getting stuck in the mud twice, and chilled through. I saw Lily Baker Tues morning and she said she hadn't got warmed through yet.

Here endeth the story of my meetings with Dames, Daughters and Women's Clubs.

Lovingly,
Edith

Top: Three generations of Patrick Healys: Patsy, Sr., Patrick III and Patsy, Jr.
Above: Mary Healy. This is the only known photo of Patsy, Jr.'s wife.

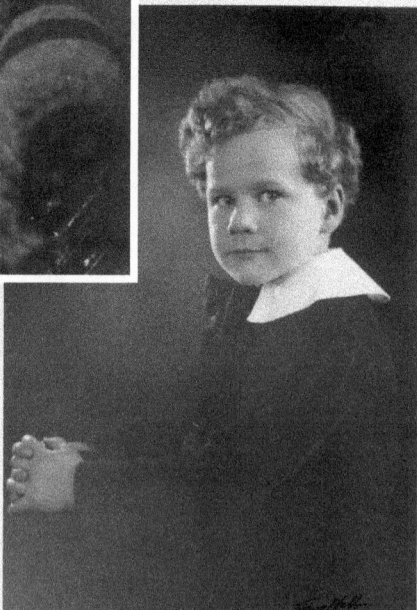

Top: Alec, Jr., 4, tolerates a velvet suit reminiscent of the one that Edith was photographed wearing as a child (see page 15). Dan, about 6, hated the Bostonian-boy clothes his mother insisted he wear, especially knickers when all he wanted was scruffy long pants like other Wyoming boys.

And so endeth the surviving letters from Edith to her mother. Six months later, Elizabeth Harmon Holden died at her Vernon Street apartment on the evening of April 2, 1917, a few hours before Edith's sixth anniversary. Edith was with her mother. She and Holden took Elizabeth's coffin by train to Portland, where she was buried next to CW in Evergreen Cemetery with generations of Harmons and Holdens.

As Edith made burial arrangements, Alec, Jr., celebrated his fifth birthday, likely in Buffalo on April 5. The following day, April 6, the United States declared war on Germany and joined the European War. After settling her mother's affairs, Edith returned to Wyoming. Never again would Boston be her home.

The West that became Edith's home was not the wide open spaces that made Patsy Healy, Sr., his fortune. Settling of the frontier accelerated in 1909 when Congress acknowledged the realities of western farming in the semi-arid prairies and doubled the size of free land for homesteaders to 320 acres.[88] In 1909, livestock operations began paying per head for summer grazing on federal forest lands, such as the Big Horn Mountains. That happened the year after Alec and Patsy, Jr., formed Healy Brothers, which was an open range sheep outfit. Ten years later when Healy Brothers dissolved their partnership, the Old West was dead. In 1919, Alec and Patsy, Jr., went their separate ways, each going into banking with an emphasis on loans to Western ranchers and farmers.

During the decade-long partnership, Healy Brothers faced the usual droughts, blizzards, and shrinking grazing lands. Unexpectedly, World War I (1914–1919) brought a boom time to the U.S. sheep business.

When Edith wrote her Christmas letter of 1915, soldiers fighting the European War had been hunkered down for more than a year in trenches that stretched from the North Sea to the Swiss border on the Western Front. They stayed until the Allies, bolstered by U.S. troops, broke through the German lines in early August 1918. The war ended about a hundred days later.

Ultimately, more than seventy million men on both sides were called up, sixty million of them Europeans. The armies needed winter uniforms made of wool, a material that keeps the soldier warm even when wet, and the armies needed meat for rations. Prices broke records. When the war first started, wool sold for twenty-five to thirty cents a pound. As the war continued, prices doubled and kept rising because of the demand—and everyone wanted to get into the sheep business. Farmers needed more acreage so they could raise sheep, too, and political pressure mounted to enable homesteaders to have enough land to raise livestock as well as crops. In 1916, Congress passed the Stock-Raising Homestead Act which doubled free acreage for homesteading to 640 acres.

The next year, with the entry of the United States into the war, the Healy wives orchestrated series of luncheons to raise money for the Red Cross war effort and to buy an ambulance for the State of Wyoming. At the end of the year, Edith played her violin for the New Year's Eve feast at the Occidental Hotel.

In 1918, the nation's mood was despairing as the Germans launched a spring offensive that brought them to within seventy-five miles of Paris and close to victory. That same dismal spring, the deadly Spanish influenza reached the United States from the battlefields in a pandemic that eventually killed between fifty and a hundred million people worldwide.

Close to home, Alec and Edith faced death, too. Alec's father's health was failing, and Edith and Alec were worried to distraction when their toddler, Dan, 2½, became "quite sick, but improving rapidly," as reported in the February 7 issue of the Buffalo *Bulletin*.

Patsy, Sr., 72, died a few months later from kidney problems at home in Ogden on May 23. His older sister, Mary Bridget Hoppenyan of Ashland, Wisconsin, and his youngest brother, Maytor, a lifelong railroader who lived in Ogden, were with him when he died.

For Healy Brothers, the death of their father ended their own stalemate. Like everyone in the sheep business, they enjoyed the high prices for wool. By spring 1918, wool hit seventy-five cents a pound, a 380 percent increase in just four years. And, like other large operators, the brothers struggled to find land to graze their animals. The work was complicated by the serious shortage of herders, since most shepherds came from Europe and were no longer available because they were fighting in the war.[89] It was an impossible business situation, and it had become impossible personally. With their father's death, the brothers launched plans to dissolve the business and separate, a turn of events that proved lucky.

Patsy, Jr.—already a director for the First National Bank of Buffalo—was named to fill his father's position as president of the Commercial National Bank of Ogden. With that announcement, he and Alec began to sell their land and livestock and split their partnership. They kept some land in the mountains and a few herds of sheep.

Prices were still high, with no end in sight for the war. "Everyone in Buffalo said they were wrong to do so," said Dan, but the brothers had had enough. They easily found buyers and liquidated rapidly. Suddenly, the Allies broke through the German lines in a hundred-day offensive, and the war was over on November 11, 1918.

Pent-up civilian demand for wool[90] kept prices relatively high through 1919, the first year of peace, especially for fine Merino-like wool from desert sheep like the Healys raised. Healy Brothers was down to only one band of sheep (about 1,200) by the summer of 1919, when sheepmen were hit with double disasters. First the extremely dry summer of 1919 left little grass heading into winter, and by the spring of 1920, "dead sheep and cattle were everywhere," said Dan, who interviewed a number of pioneering ranchers, some bankrupted by the catastrophe. The winter was often compared to the memorable winter of 1886 to 1887, made infamous by Charlie Russell's iconic watercolor, *Waiting for a Chinook,* showing an emaciated steer encircled by wolves.

Next came the wool price reckoning. During the war years, everyone was led to believe there was a shortage of wool. By July 1920, reality hit the woolgrowers' industry hard, although fine wool pricing held until January 1921. Reports said it would take woolen mills two years to use the surplus wool in storage. An estimated hundred million dollars of stored wool was warehoused. Prices dropped back to 1914 levels for all but fine wools, but even so there was no market to sell the wool.

For friends and colleagues of Patsy, Jr., and Alec, the post-World War I years were punishing, including for the man who bought their Clear Creek ranch. In February 1921, Buffalo *Bulletin* published an ad for the public sale of "the Old Healy Ranch," by owner Addison Felix, who announced that he had "decided to quit ranching." Healy Brothers had escaped the financial disaster through savvy and luck.

Perhaps the greatest gift that Patrick, Sr., gave his sons was showing them how to shift careers as circumstances changed. This was the man who climbed out of the mines and into building rails, then to railroad engineer, to sheepman, to bankrolling ranchers and farmers, and finally to banking. Along the way, he built the landmark Healy Hotel.

Both brothers moved from sheep into banking that not only specialized in loans for farmers and ranchers, but also for the retail businesses that supplied them. Family lore holds that Patsy, Jr.'s move was immediate, while Alec, the younger brother by four years, moved his family to Denver to scout for a new business opportunity. Even so, the Buffalo *Bulletin* revealed that Patsy, Jr., continued as oft-absent Buffalo City councilman for another year. It wasn't until 1923 that both brothers sold the homes they had built. Patsy, Jr., and Mary's house on six lots on North Main Street sold for $14,000; Alec and Edith's house on six lots in south Buffalo at the corner of South Lobban Avenue and East Gatchell Street sold for $2,200.

Edith continued to play the violin often for the Congregational Church's 11 a.m. services and other community events. Interestingly, the *Bulletin* makes apparent the growing strength of her leadership abilities, especially with educational women's clubs. When the Mountain Division of the Red Cross mobilized nurses and nursing aides in October 1918 as Spanish influenza spread across the country, Edith took charge of collecting the names in the Buffalo area. A year later, Edith helped found the Delphian Society in Buffalo on July 31, 1919, with a starting membership of thirty. She was elected the first president of the national group which aimed to "promote social progress, higher education and personal empowerment." Members presented lessons on topics such as the study of art and the social life of Egypt. These two examples out of many foretold Edith's rising respect as an organizational leader.

In October 1920, Alec made an extended trip to the Big Horn Basin, the only one noted by the *Bulletin*, but life continued as normal in Buffalo for Edith and their two sons, Alec, Jr., 8, and Dan, 5, but not for long. The family spent Christmas in Ogden and then traveled on to the Los Angeles area where they spent the winter. Alec and Edith were home in Buffalo for the summer of 1921, and then left for Denver at the

EDITH'S NEW HOME

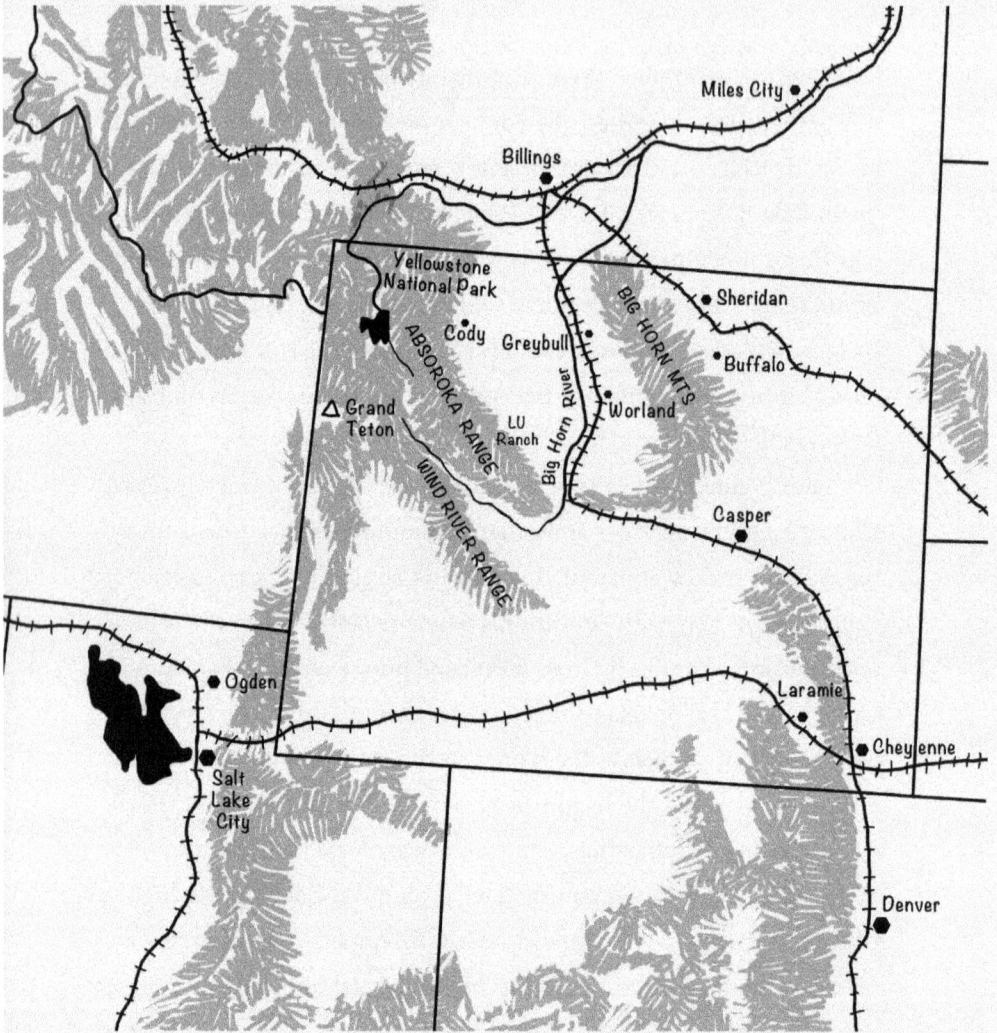

Map: Meagan Healy

end of August, in time for the boys to be enrolled in school. A young Basque woman, Celectina Arrachea, stayed in their house.

That winter in Denver, Alec invested in the First National Bank in Worland where he was named managing officer and vice president. He took over management of the bank—Worland's first bank—in late March. Before the family moved across the Big Horns to Worland, they lingered in Buffalo with their friends.

Edith and the boys returned to Buffalo on their way to Worland on June 8, 1922. They were back for the Fourth of July and drove over the mountains again in August before school started.[91] Then, they settled in their new home.

Worland is where Edith and Alec and their sons and their families would live their lives. It was a healthy move for the serious younger Healy son and his wife, who stepped out from the shade of the gregarious elder son and thrived in the Big Horn Basin, where, remarkably, the sun shines 310 days a year.

Alec's portrait for the Wyoming Legislature, taken in 1925 in Cheyenne.
The famous portraitist, Bachrach, captured Edith's flapper look.

CHAPTER 14

THE OTHER SIDE OF THE MOUNTAIN

1 9 2 4

HEALY'S MOVE TO WORLAND – FIRST IMPRESSIONS
EILEEN AND HELEN JOIN THE FAMILY

The Worland *Grit* bannered the Healys' arrival in Worland across its front page on March 30, 1922. New management and $50 thousand in new capital (about $652,000 in 2012 dollars) added to the $25 million in Worland's first bank made "the First" a strong rival to Stockgrowers State Bank, the newer bank in town. The weekly *Grit* described Alec as "one of the leading capitalists in Wyoming and Utah." Although he lived in Denver, "Mr. Healy already has farming and livestock interests in Washakie County" and planned to move his family to Worland, the county seat. As bank officer, it was Mr. Healy who would direct the First National Bank of Worland, the newspaper noted.

The other major investor, Herman B. Gates of Denver, had been a former president of First National before becoming state treasurer of Wyoming. Gates left political office for the oil business.

Alec and Edith had made their decision. They invested in Worland, in the center of the Big Horn Basin, on the dry side of the Big Horn Mountains. Where Buffalo was grassy and green with a mountain creek tumbling through the town center, Worland, thirty miles from the mountains, originally resembled a colony on the moon set beside the slow-flowing Big Horn River. Along the river lay valley lands of sage flanked by what locals call *benches*, two hundred-foot-high rises of hills that stretched into eroded badlands as beige gray and wrinkled as elephant hide. The arid lands reached the mountain ranges that ring the Basin with their prolific green pastures and creeks.

The mountains and green foothills drew the first pioneers in the Basin with their cattle and sheep, but the desert soil proved remarkably fertile when watered. Starting in 1903, a large network of canals and irrigation ditches opened the Basin to farmers, particularly sugar beet growers. The Lower Hanover Canal flowed through Worland, with hollow horsetail and snake grasses arcing along the banks.

In 1917, Utah investors built a million-dollar sugar processing factory made possible by the railroad completed in 1913. The factory attracted Mormon farmers to the area. After World War I, it attracted Volga Germans fleeing the communist revolution in Russia.[92]

Beet farmers toiled to bring in even six tons an acre in those early days (versus twenty-two tons in today's mechanized world). Fall harvest was a back-breaking time with each beet dug up by hand, topped with a long, hooked knife, and tossed into a wagon or truck to be carted to the factory, a practice that continued unmechanized into the 1950s. Wayne Voss, a Worland farmer and investor, remembers his drudgery as a teen in the sugar beet fields.

Alec, whose father had substantial interests in Utah sugar, understood the natural partnership between sugar beets, a refining factory, and livestock. From the first year that the factory processed beets, farmers around Worland began wintering sheep and cattle on the beet tops left in their fields. As an experiment that first year, farmers also tried feeding beet pulp to livestock, said John Mazet, a long-time Holly Sugar employee in Worland. Sheep and cattle put up with the woody pulp, so the practice continued, but in the mid-1950s, leftover molasses from the refining process was mixed with the pulp, and livestock gobbled it

NEW CAPITAL FOR FIRST NATIONAL

THE WORLAND GRIT

All the News—All the Time

Advertise Your Business

Watch for our Spring Edition Next Week

VOLUME XVII.   THE WORLAND GRIT, THURSDAY, MARCH 30, 1922.   Number 12.

H. B. GATES AND ALEX B. HEALY LEADING FIGURES IN ENTERPRISE

Board of Directors Composed of Well-Known Business Men and Farmers Who Will Maintain Past High Standard of Efficiency.

SUGAR BEETS OF RIVERTON FOR WORLAND

Wind River Valley Farmers Will Net $5 Per ton Beets.

PUBLIC ROADS FEATURE MEET OF ALFATEERS

Legion Washakie Club Move Put Up To Committee.

WINTER ENDS IN SPRING SHOWER OF CARD PARTIES

COAL STRIKE ON NINE THOUSAND MEN OFF THE JOB

New Pilots

KANE BANK ROBBERY ATTEMPTED BY 'GREEN' YEGGS

The weekly *Grit* headlined Alec's arrival in Worland—although it fancied up his name with a non-existent middle initial.

WORLAND, WYOMING

Top: Worland in the late 1920s. Above: Canals like this transformed the semi-arid Big Horn Basin, c. 1910. Below: Smokestacks show the sugar refinery in full operation. Credit: Washakie Museum, Wyoming Tales and Trails, and the Hampton Collection.

Piles of beet pulp will be trucked to feed livestock during the winter. The Holly Sugar factory opened in 1917. Credit: Washakie Museum.

down. Alec was still alive to watch the change. By then, 200,000 sheep were spending winters in the beet fields of the Big Horn Basin. A positive by-product of the mountains-to-farms feeding cycle was that the rangeland could recover from any overgrazing.

Worland's potential was obvious to Alec in 1922. The municipality was surrounded by five thousand sagebrush acres with access to water available for purchase. Oil and natural gas fields lay nearby with more to be discovered.

The town itself had the benefit of industrious residents who converted the dry land into an oasis of trees and gardens of vegetables and flowers. An aerial shot of Worland in 1920 shows a canopy of trees that people had planted around their homes. Worland's greenery was aided by the relatively mild winters and conferred on Worland the nickname, "Banana Belt of Wyoming."

When the school year ended in Denver in 1922, Alec moved his family into a small brick house on the corner of 10th and Grace until they could move into a clapboard and concrete bungalow, a block north on the corner of 10th and Culbertson. A wide veranda wrapped around the sunny eastern side of the bungalow where Alec hung a hammock for his summertime post-lunch naps.

The Healys' home was one of Worland's grandest at the time. One story is that the man who built it nearly went broke because of the expense. The home had a "little house" in the back which was connected to the main house by a dirt tunnel in the basement near the coal chute. The little house had room for a housekeeper downstairs as well as a sitting room and bedroom for guests upstairs. Alongside the little house stood a matching clapboard garage. By today's standards *grand* is a misnomer. 920 Culbertson Avenue had two bedrooms, one bathroom, a living room with a fireplace, a dining room, and a kitchen.

Edith's entry into the Worland community may have been more difficult than in Buffalo. By the time she moved to Worland she had been uprooted three times, twice recently, moving from Boston to Buffalo, Buffalo to Denver, and Denver to Worland. Edith may have felt lonely. During her first two years in Worland, her name appears only once in the Worland *Grit* when she played the violin at a woman's club program. This is a far cry from her full social life in Buffalo.

Only one of Edith's letters survives from this period, written on October 23, 1924. Fortunately, the letter describes what proved to be a critical turning point in her life.

In October 1924, Edith and Alec's sons were back down from the Big Horns where they spent summers helping to herd their father's sheep, but more importantly from their parents' point of view, isolated from summertime epidemics that killed or paralyzed children, such as polio. Alec, Jr., had started the eighth grade and was busy with inventions. Just like his Grandfather Holden, Alec, Jr., loved inventing. Tall and slender with wavy dark blond hair, Alec, Jr., also loved music, books, chess, and his pals. The Healy "baby," Dan was a sturdy fifth grader, practical and talented. He could repeat a piece of music after a first hearing; by high school band, he was able to learn a new instrument in a couple of weeks and fill in with whatever sounds were needed. His independent streak, however, was the bane of his piano teacher, as he played piano flat-fingered to thwart her authority.

Alec, 43, a community pillar, had just been nominated to run for his second term in the State House of Representatives by the Republicans in Washakie County.[93]

Two weeks later, Edith, 45, headed south by train to Laramie on a mission to adopt a daughter. The couple wanted more children. Edith's mother was forty-one when Edith was born, an advanced age for pregnancies then. Perhaps it was Edith's forty-third birthday celebrated during their winter in Denver that signaled how unlikely it was that Edith would give birth to another child. Perhaps the Healys knew another child was unlikely much earlier when Dan was born. Edith wrote in a 1949 letter to Cornelia Metz about not having been "properly taken care of after Dan's birth."

At some point, Edith put out the word that she and her husband were looking for a daughter, an older girl, because—as my father told me—his parents knew that everyone wants babies and that it is nearly impossible for an older child to be adopted. Mrs. Eggleston, one of Edith's friends and an Episcopalian connected with the church's Cathedral Home in Laramie, told her about a six-year-old girl there named Frances, promising, "You'll like her, she has beautiful manners."

Frances's parents had homesteaded land in the hills southwest of Sheridan and had five children—Irene, Frances, Jean, Robert, and Harry, the baby. Harry was only 3-months-old when their mother, Myrtle, died on August 13, 1923. The children's father decided he couldn't take care of them. Within a couple of days, Irene, 7, was left with a Sheridan family as a companion for their daughter of the same age, and the four younger ones were taken to the Cathedral Home. Harry died of pneumonia at the Home.

Mrs. Eggleston's daughter, Einna, and her husband, Deane Hunton, adopted Jean, as their only child. Mr. Hunton was professor of Commerce at the University of Wyoming and Einna was the principal at the Ivinson School for Girls, a boarding high school serving ranchers' daughters and others who needed to live at school.

Robert, a toddler, was adopted by Helen Turner, a young New York City woman teaching at the Home, who returned to the East Coast.[94]

Frances remained at the Home always feeling "scared to death," she said.

Irene didn't please the Sheridan girl, so the Sheridan family dispatched Irene to the orphanage in Laramie, where she and Frances were overjoyed to be together again. Frances often was punished for sneaking into Irene's bed at night to feel safe with her shy older sister, whose confidence had been crushed.

Edith and Alec arranged to divide Alec, Jr., and Dan's bedroom to make a bedroom for Frances and talked about their new sister-to-be. They planned to name her Helen after Alec's older sister; at the time, they didn't know about Irene.

Edith traveled to Laramie prepared to pick up their new daughter and take her to Denver for new clothes, a new doll, and time alone with her new mother so they could get acquainted before proceeding to Helen's new home. However, when Edith arrived in Laramie, she discovered the rejected eight-year-old Irene. As my Aunt Eileen (Irene) told me, Edith telephoned Alec long distance (rare in those days) to talk about what they should do. Alec agreed at once that they must adopt both girls. Eileen's eyes always got teary when she talked about how Alec never hesitated in his response to Edith's call, even though he'd never met her. Aunt Eileen's eyes laughed when she talked about how even though her father was a very formal man, he could be warm and fun, like when he would dance Edith and the girls around the kitchen.

Packing the girls to take them away was simple. They left with the clothes on their backs, says Aunt Helen. That suited Helen, who marvels now that she remembers absolutely nothing of their leaving. Her memories begin after she and her sister "escaped" the institution, and they were safely on the train with their new mother.

Helen confessed to some fearful moments after she and Eileen became Healys but never doubted the essential mother–daughter bond. "Mother drilled us and drilled us on calling her Mother. I knew she wouldn't have done that if she hadn't meant it."

Worland, Wyo.
Oct. 23, 1924

My dear Mrs. Eggleston,

I just returned to Worland last night but I know how anxious you are to hear all about everything so am starting this letter immediately as it's going to be a long one to get in every detail and will have to be written in several sittings.

After we left you and Mrs. Whitehead and got settled in the train, I began telling them about the brothers and what their names were and what kind of bedroom they were going to have, just opening off mine etc. and told them as long as they were to stay with me I wanted to call them the names I liked best, which were Eileen and Helen.[95] We made a game of it, anyone saying Irene, Frances or Mrs. Healy were to get a cross under their names on a paper and anyone saying Eileen, Helen, and Mother got a star. We played it all the way to Denver and by the time we got there they were about letter perfect.

We went directly to Daniels & Fisher[96] and had lunch and then went to the toy department for the dolls. I led them up to this huge electrically lighted show case and told them they could have any doll they wanted. I know they will never have a thrill like that again. I know it was recklessly extravagant on my part but you only have a chance like that once in a lifetime. They went right to the ones they wanted and hugged them tight. Helen chose one with light bobbed hair the shade of her own and Eileen dark hair like hers. Both dolls go to sleep, say mama and walk. You will be interested in knowing the price. Helen's was $5.00 and Eileen's was $10.00. When I found E's was more I was afraid H would see the difference in hers when she got it home so I asked her to look again and offered her several others and she shook her head and still clung to that one, so I said no more.

Then we went to the Junior Department and I got a hold of Mrs. Weems, who is the regular shopper, for she and her assistant Miss Walch have done so much shopping for me through the mails. I told them the circumstances and they were so interested they turned the stock inside out to find things. Mrs. Bosworth, my friend, and I sat in comfortable easy chairs in Mrs. W's office and she and Miss Walsh dressed the children and sent them out like models in their new dresses.

Eileen was easier to find things for. I got her a dark blue crepe made so simply with a little bright embroidery on it and a touch of moiré ribbon. Also a dark blue serge trimmed in bands of old rose and a challis that was lighter with an allover figure on it and orange ruffle around the neck and sleeves and long orange ribbon ends hanging from one shoulder.

Helen looked darling in a sage green jersey cloth made with bloomers and trimmed with lavender and green embroidery. Also a gray, trimmed with cerise bands around neck and sleeves and a little cerise embroidery, oh just a touch. I got also for school little hunter green pleated skirts and pongee middies just alike. Tan colored sweaters and Helen a tan hat and Eileen a black hat. It was hard to find hats to match the sweaters that were becoming to both girls and that they could give me the two sizes. Brown shoes and stockings and the most adorable coats and hats alike for best. Brown camelhair coats with dark fur collars. Looks like mole but it isn't as fragile a fur. Had to go everywhere for hats to match but got darling ones. The crowns are fur cloth that matches the coat and the brims are dark fur that matches the collar. I am going to take a Kodak picture of them in these coats because I know you'll be crazy about them. I went to that store you told me of, but they had very few in stock their sizes, and I thought I'd let them wear the middie costumes to school, as I got three blouses apiece and the other dresses for best were enough.

I got them union suits and waists and combs and toothbrushes, rubbers and overshoes and their pictures taken. Maybe you don't think I hustled. We didn't go to a fancy place as I just wanted little informal pictures and couldn't bother with

someone taking too much time. They had on, Eileen her dark
blue crepe and Helen that adorable shade of green.
The photographer couldn't make her smile to save his life.

We finished with the children's things Tuesday noon and
took them home to Mrs. Bosworth's to play with her little six
year old girl and she and I started down town to lunch and
had the afternoon for me. We went to a new place, whose card
I enclose. A most attractive place but I didn't find anything.
Finally ended up at Gano's and I got both my dress and a hat
there. The dress a black Bengaline made straight without any
belt and just a touch of two shades of old blue at the neck and
sleeves. My beads, earrings and comb go with it wonderfully.
A peach of a dress and fitted as though it were made for me,
only having to have the sleeves made a little shorter.

I got a stone gray camel's hair coat which comes high in
the neck and I can wear my neck piece with it. Nothing to do
that I also went to Broadhurst's and got 2 pairs of shoes, winter
ladies and bought 2 sets of doilies for everyday use. Went to the
Denver got more trying to match my set and four salt cellars
for the children shaped like ducks, went to Neusteter's and got
a new handbag and some artificial flowers for my living room
and fancy candles and a pair of overshoes. Was through by four
o'clock. Time to go back to Mrs. Bosworth, pack my bag and lie
down a half an hour before taking the 6 o'clock train. And oh you
think I am "some shopper!" I'm satisfied with everything I got,
too, and didn't get anything just because I was pressed for time.

I couldn't have done it without the wonderful cooperation
of those clerks at D&F and Mrs. Bosworth who is with me
every minute neglecting her own affairs and drive me about in
her car helping me with decisions. We always shop for clothes
together. She had a committee meeting at her house and I
heard her call a member and tell them they were welcome to
come to the house, she wouldn't be able to be there and for the
secretary to leave the minutes of the meeting for her to read,
and tell her what they wanted her to do on a slip of paper. That
is the kind of friend she is to me. And yet when I was leaving
and tried to thank her, she said, "for goodness sake Edith, the

obligation is on my side, I've had the time of my life. I wouldn't have missed it for anything."

The 1st night we went to her house. She has a large 1 and 3 children, the youngest 6. At the table that night you never saw such perfect table manners by my two. Even when Eileen had to use her handkerchief, she turned away her head and blew gently. Mrs. Bosworth just marveled at it and said she thought she would have to send her 3 to the Cathedral home for intensive training. I certainly was proud of them. Mrs. B. called several of my friends and told them I was to be there with my daughters and they came over during and after supper to see them. Those children entered the room and behaved as if they were used to all this sort of thing all their lives. I think their good clothes helped them, for they instinctively felt they looked well and it gave them confidence. They certainly did look adorable. I wish you could see that lovely shade of green on Helen. 2 of my friends begged to go up and put them to bed and I was so glad I had brought home some lovely pink pajamas so they look like little soft pink rosebuds in them. I could only get one pair, so those Mrs. W gave me will do for every day, and these for special occasions.

The next afternoon the children had the time of their lives playing in Mrs. B's little girls' play room, wood doll furniture and dollhouse, little chairs and tables and dishes for a tea party. You can imagine we were all pretty worn out when we landed on the train. They love sleeping in an upper berth and each had a dollie cuddled tight.

The next day we spent a lot of it in the observation car. There was a lady in the seat opposite who took so much interest in us. She asked if my husband was light complected or rather said, "I suppose your husband is light" and I thought that the queerest remark, until she added, "the oldest one looks so much like you, and I suppose the youngest one takes after him." That certainly did amuse me. As Mr. Healy is light with blue eyes, it is rather a joke. Helen and my Dan have hair and eyes exactly the same, only Dan's is curly.

Mr. Healy and the boys were down to meet us and I know just what an impression we made. The boys were turned terrible embarrassed and Mr. Healy tried not to stare too hard to embarrass the girls. Alex Jr., the older one, lagged way behind him. When I asked him what he thought, he said, "I didn't expect them to have nice clothes on, or be so nice looking." Dan asked me the next day if I found them in rags. On the idea of poor Orphan Annie[97] I suppose. Mr. Healy was awfully busy at the bank so he could only drive us home and go right back, so you can imagine how pleased I was when a friend of mine dropped in later and told me she met him downtown and asked him if I'd come and he said, "yes, and those are two mighty fine girls at the house, you'd better go up and see them, Mrs. Hake." That tickled me to death because 1st impressions mean so much.

My 1st 2 callers were 2 people that I didn't know very well but who adopted children. They came to tell me how glad they were and they knew I would never regret it, which I thought nice of them. One was a man and in a little while later his wife called up. The other was a lady and she couldn't say enough about how much her little girl meant to her. From then on the telephone has been busy.

Mr. Healy had to go to a political meeting but I was tired and went to bed. In the morning he was telling me about it and I said, "did anyone say anything about the girls and he said, "everyone did". That's the small town of it and I think it's fine. I don't think anything has stirred up a town more than this. People I hardly know tell me how fine they think it is, and I don't doubt that it has made people think and I hope it may make others follow the example.

It was amusing last night. There was a Parent Teachers meeting and as I had had charge of the program I felt I had to go. Mr. Healy had a headache so it was his turn to go to bed and let me go out. When they called the roll of grades, that is when a Grade is called the parents with children in that grade stand and they find out which grade has most interested parents, everyone smiled when I stood for the 1st, 2nd, 5th and 8th grades.

Well to go back. The house was a sight when we came in. I expected it to be bad but it was far worse. Rolls of dust and dirt everywhere and so untidy. Eileen said at once, "give me a broom and I'll sweep these floors, I love to sweep." So I tied aprons on them and it would've tickled you, as it did me, to see Helen going off at the dining room table, rubbing with all her might to get sticky spots off. We did wonders in an hour. After supper or rather dinner as we have called it at night, Eileen came over and sat beside me and said "I've been watching and I can do everything she, the high school girl helping me out, does and now you won't have to keep a servant anymore. You've got me." It made tears come to my eyes it was so sweet and I thought to myself how that willingness to help might have been abused in some families.

I forgot to tell you in Daniels & Fisher one of the saleswomen came to me and said "those are the sweetest children. I was pinning up a dress for one of them and I hadn't said a word and the oldest one burst out with, "we're from the Cathedral home and we just got adopted this morning. We've got new dollies and new names and everything." And the other little one piped up and said "oh my gracious, I've forgotten my name!" Those girls in D&F couldn't do enough for them.

After supper the 1st night, oh I must tell you right now how my oldest boy insisted on taking them to school the 1st day. He begged so hard I thought it would give him the feeling of responsibility so I let him. He, who up to this time had thought of girls as merely cluttering up an otherwise perfectly good Earth, rushes home from school as fast as he can run. With other boys out playing football on the front lawn he sits inside on the piano stool[98] with Helen, playing every roll she wants to hear and singing the songs, and he can't sing at all.

Dan is more bashful and it will take more time for him to get used to them. The 1st afternoon we're home, he came in bringing 3 marigolds that had escaped the Frost. He gave me one and said, "you suppose the little girls would like one," and I said, "you might ask them". So he presented them each with a flower.

I notice they both wait to walk to school with them each time, so they are proud of them and I am so glad. They are

The Healy Home

920 Culbertson Avenue: Hollyhocks and sunny yellow paint make
Edith and Alec's home still appealing today. Credit: Dave Huber.

good girls and the prospect of becoming appropriately close is also a great asset.

Every night after supper we read to the children, Mr. Healy in his chair with Helen on his lap and me on the couch with the other 3 children, makes a family group I want you to hold in your minds whenever you think of us.

Yours Sincerely,
Edith Sampson Healy

This letter is written in different settings as you will realize as you read it. The proofs of the pictures have come. Helen's are lovely but Eileen's is awful. I'll have to take it because they can't sit over. However, I'll take a Kodak picture and may have better luck. I'm so sorry though about Eileen's.

The Family Is Complete

Christmas card picture 1924: Alec, Edith, Alec and Dan (in their loathed knickers), Eileen, and Helen. The headless dog to the left may have been the "mean Airedale." Later they had springer spaniels, all named "Angus." Credit: Washakie Museum.

Alec, Jr. could have posed for the new Wyoming license design in 1936, when
Wyoming first put the Bucking Horse and Rider on its plates. Alec mounted this
"stuffed bronc" in a tourist studio near Cody. Credit: Washakie Museum.

CHAPTER 15

INTERLUDE

1924 – 1944

ROARIN' 20S – GREAT DEPRESSION – WORLD WAR II

Of all of the hundreds of Christmas snapshots and letters that Edith must have sent during the next twenty-five years, only one letter remains in the collection, her December 1949 Christmas note to Alec, Jr.'s in-laws in Vermont (see Chapter 16). This chapter fills in the gap between Edith's 1924 letter about the adoption trip and her 1944 letter from Mexico City about changes she disliked being adopted by her fellow directors on the National Girl Scout Council.

Edith's Christmas letter of 1924 must have been filled with the fun of a Christmas with four children and Alec's recent election to the legislature. She may or may not have bothered to write about the funerals, high school musicals, and local entertainments she played for.

By the next Christmas, her friends and family glimpsed the beginnings of Edith's new calling. Scouting for girls started in Worland in 1925, with one troop led by Miss Gwendolyn Hill, a grade school teacher. Naturally Edith enrolled Eileen and Helen in Scouts. Edith valued self-sufficiency in the outdoors, self-confidence, and generosity of character, and she found every opportunity to organize clubs for women and girls to learn together and to socialize. Under Edith's salesmanship, Worland soon had three troops of Girl Scouts.[99]

Alec was defeated for re-election in 1926, a year when he, like many Republicans in Wyoming, lost by about the same number of votes that they had won by two years before. Edith probably didn't mention the loss in her Christmas letters because Alec had more important news. He and his partners sold First National Bank to Farmers State Bank, and Alec opened his own banking enterprise called Washakie Livestock Loan Company. His two-room office was in the Farmers State Bank building and he shared it with Frank Dent, a sheep broker, whose wife Dorothy was one of Edith's close friends.

News during the late 1920s included summer vacations with the family to the Washington and Oregon coast and a 1929 sailing adventure to Hawaii. No doubt Christmas letters were filled with stories about the children growing up and Edith's climb in the Girl Scout hierarchy as she began organizing troops for other Big Horn Basin communities, and yet, for some of those years, she felt fatigued and unwell. At some point after the adoption, no one is quite sure when, Edith traveled to Denver where she spent several months under the care of a nutrition-minded physician, Dr. John H. Tilden, who ran a sanitarium known as the Tilden Health School. She returned home restored. (In a 1949 letter, Edith described her treatment; see Chapter 17.)

Despite Worland's isolated location—a highway through the Wind River Canyon wasn't completed until 1924—the Healys held strong connections to the outside world. These connections were not through Boston but through the Federal Reserve Board and Girl Scouting. Alec's cousin, Roy Young, the son of his father's sister, Julia Healy Young, was chairman of the Federal Reserve Board from 1927 to 1929 under President Herbert Hoover. Edith later met Mrs. Hoover through their mutual work in the Girl Scouts. Alec's banking ties to Washington DC resumed in 1934 when President Franklin Delano Roosevelt appointed Marriner Eccles as chairman of the Federal Reserve Board. Eccles's father, David, a Scotsman, had moved to Ogden about the same time as Alec's father and the two had been involved in business.

In 1929, Alec watched the gyrations of the stock market as the

LU Ranch

Top: Alec meets with LU ranch manager George Bain, left, and an unidentified herder.
Above: LU's prized Rambouillets are herded into sorting corrals, c. 1938.

Mrs. Herbert (Lou Henry) Hoover, second from the right,
visited Edith and Alec at their home and mountain cabin in 1943.
The first woman to graduate in geology in the United States, Lou Henry Hoover
wanted girls to join the Scouts to strengthen their bodies and minds. Edith and
Mrs. Hoover served together on the National Girl Scout Board. Cornelia Metz,
Edith's close friend, stands next to Mrs. Hoover on the far right.

decade neared an end and, ever cautious, concluded that holding money in stocks had become too risky. He sold all of his stocks before the market crashed in October 1929 and thus had money to lend during the Great Depression.[100] The economic shocks panicked the nation. The new decade brought an emotional shock to the Healys, too, when Alec's beloved sister, Helen, had a heart attack and died in Ogden in August 1930. She was only fifty-one and already widowed, her husband, John, having died two years earlier.

Helen had named Alec the trustee for her only child, Jack Lynch, 23. A Dartmouth graduate with a rah-rah raccoon coat, a Packard convertible—the fastest, luxury car on the market—income from a trust fund and an irresistible cocky streak, Jack moved to Worland to become an instant legend. A handsome young man with wavy hair and Irish blue eyes, Jack looked like he could have been his cousins' blonder older brother. Jack's influence on their sons was worrisome to Edith and Alec, especially when Alec, Jr., 19, arrived home from college for vacation and Jack still hadn't settled into gainful employment. And again the next summer. And the next. One summer morning when Jack and Alec, Jr. ,were sleeping off a late night in the little house, an exasperated Alec, who customarily arose before 6 a.m., strode into their room and, with his cane., whacked the soles of the feet in the twin bed on the left, whacked the soles of the feet in the twin bed on the right, left again, right again, whack, whack, whack while he snapped, "Only two kinds of people make money in bed and one of them's a banker. You're neither. Now get up."

The boisterous boys were no longer boys and irresponsible habits can become fixed, the couple feared. Then like in a movie, out of the East rode Edith's nephew, Dr. Holden Furber, to the rescue. The unsuspecting historian was taking time off from his teaching at Harvard to travel to dusty archives in the far reaches of the British Colonial Empire researching his second book. Holden stopped in Worland en route to catching his ship in California.[101] He arrived with his notebooks and he left with Jack Lynch. An odder pair cannot be imagined, and no one thought it was funnier than Holden, who in his later life delighted my cousin Tim and me with outrageous stories from their journey. Stories like the time Jack went swimming in shark-infested Sydney Bay or how he always arrived at the dock with a passel of pretty girls hanging onto him just as the gangplank was about to be raised.

Worland's population doubled during the Depression. Local historians like John Davis report that Worland was spared the worst of the troubles, and the town looked different from the forlorn places dotting the nation. However, many Worlanders did not escape financial crisis, especially in agriculture. Sheep, for example, were worth only half of the value of the loans Alec was carrying on them.

One story to come out of the Washakie Livestock Loan Company office on 7th Street during that time is reported by Tim.

> My father, [Alec, Jr.], was taking a nap in the back room on that old leather couch when he heard a farmer or rancher come into the room. Grandfather was sitting at his roll-top desk. The man approached and threw down a piece of paper on the top of the desk and said, "Well, it's all yours. I can't make it." Grandfather picked up the paper and handed it back to him and said, "What are you, a quitter?" The man expressed genuine surprise but relief and left with a reprieve on his loan. My father said this was an event often repeated in those years. I heard later, as we [Tim and his family] were living up in Shell in the 1970s, that Grandfather had held the notes for a lot of the ranches in the Big Horn Basin but hadn't foreclosed when he could have and allowed many ranchers to survive those awful years.

Dan said that this willingness to absorb those non-producing loans "kind of broke Father's heart," meaning caused a heart attack.

When Alec recovered, he decided to leave banking and return to ranching. The inheritance he received after the death of his mother in 1934 may have helped him make the shift.

By 1936, Alec had liquidated the Washakie Livestock Loan Company and purchased majority holdings in the LU Sheep Company from the heirs of Dave Dickie, a Scotsman who established and incorporated the LU in 1899 with starting herds of 8,500 sheep. LU also ran the first registered Angus herd in the state, but decades passed before the LU Sheep Company was allowed to join the Wyoming Cattlemen's Association.

Dave Dickie expanded his ranch until his forest permits reached within seventeen miles of Dubois, far south of the Big Horn Basin, and included ownership of five creeks in the jagged eastern foothills of the Absarokas on the other side from Jackson Hole. (The LU holdings at that time included 250,000 acres, many with leased national forest, U.S. Department of Interior, and state lands. However, a quarter of a million acres is a deceptive number. For one thing, the LU Ranch covered far more land because of the way ranches were surveyed. Land area was calculated by drawing one-mile squares (640 acres per square) on a map as though the rugged mountains and steep valleys were flat. Also, to put the LU's acreage into perspective, it can take as many as a hundred Wyoming acres to feed one cow and twenty acres to feed one sheep. Wyoming ranchers need a lot of land.

Dickie's sheep were Rambouillets, a specialty offspring of the fine-wooled Merinos, but taller, stronger, and tasting better. The Rambouillets have short hair on their faces, so they don't get blinded by blizzards freezing snow on woollier faces, like other breeds. Alec worked to improve the herds, and woolen mills on the East Coast ranked LU wool as exceptionally fine and used it to blend with courser "fine wools" to weave material for summer wool suits.

Dave Dickie located his LU headquarters—The Dickie—on Gooseberry Creek, about five miles into the Absarokas off the Meeteetse–Thermopolis highway. The Dickie included a dusty general store for herders and cowboys and still had a hitching post out front next to the hand-cranked gas pump. It even had its own official U.S. post office next to the shelves stacked with canned goods.

Alec and Edith's children didn't enjoy childhood days on the LU like my cousins and me.[102] By the time Alec returned to ranching and Edith was expanding her role in Girl Scouts, their children had grown up.

In the world of Wyoming banking and ranching, the Healys had money, but they knew their world was different from the broader world. In the broader world, they were not counted among the wealthy families. When Alec and Edith sent their sons to the University of Pennsylvania, an Ivy League school, Dan was required to hold part-time jobs and pay for his own room and board. Moreover, Alec made it quite clear to his sons that they were at Penn because of the Wharton School of Business. He told them they could take any courses they wanted as long as they majored in banking. Alec, Jr., became fascinated with film and jazz music[103] and could not wait to get to New York. Dan spent most of his spare time playing the piano in the Alpha Tau Omega fraternity house where Alec, Jr., had opened the way for his shyer brother.

New York proved to be a Siren's call not only for Alec, Jr., but also for his cousin, Stuart, three months older and his buddy since their Buffalo days. While Stuart, who had attended Amherst, went to work in a brokerage house, Alec, Jr., flexed his artistic flair—his Harmon heritage—and joined the Amateur Film League at its headquarters. At the time, experimentation in film was considered the province of amateurs, and the League was dedicated to helping amateurs make movies. It published how-to books and a magazine and ran film contests.

Back home, Eileen feared that she would be forced to go in a Boston suburb, but persuaded her parents to let her go to Oregon State University and study interior design. The major suited her need to be in beautiful, orderly environments.

Helen, a pretty, petite tomboy, was the first to wed. She and Buren Bonine, the handsomest boy at Worland High School, began their sixty-four-year marriage in 1934. Buren, bright, popular, and caring, matched Helen's meticulousness. He went to work at Read's Drug Store, where students liked to stop by the soda fountain for banana splits from the ice cream machine. Lyle Read encouraged Buren to go to Denver to take the intensive training program at the Capitol College of Pharmacy. When he graduated with his license, Buren returned to work as a pharmacist at Read's.

While her three oldest children were away at college, Edith's Scout work began drawing national attention. In 1936 and 1937, Region 11 (Wyoming, Montana, Idaho, Utah, and Nevada) held the record for most Girl Scout campers per capita in the country, and Edith, along with Cornelia Metz from Basin and her Buffalo neighbor, Verna Keyes, were attending regional conferences. In Worland, Edith was known for organizing the Girl Scouts' Wednesday evening dance classes that burnished the social graces of the *volunteer* boys.

In 1937, Dan received his bachelor's degree from Penn. His parents offered him a trip to Europe as a graduation present, expecting him to find a travel friend from school. Instead, he asked Edith to go with him, and Alec, Jr., joined them. As well as the usual destinations, Edith devised an itinerary that encompassed two Girl Scouting stops (Scotland for the International Girl Scout camp and the Netherlands for the World Scout Conference) and included, by chance, an unnerving Nazi rally in Germany.

Edith's 1937 Christmas letters must have been long. Not only had she gone to Europe, but upon their return, Dan had moved to Ogden to work for the Eccles's First Security Bank and was living at the Healy Hotel. There was the news about the marriage of Alec, Jr., to his fellow New Yorker newcomer, Lorraine Cooney, the tall, dramatic, and high-spirited daughter of an Irish–American dentist in Burlington, Vermont. And, of course, Edith's Christmas letter was surely filled with the delights and charms of their one-year-old grandchild, Kay, who lived nearby in Worland.

The next year, it was Eileen's turn. Her graduation gift was a trip to Hawaii with her parents, where they visited Jack Lynch who was married to a Hawaiian. When they returned home, Eileen got a sales job in a woman's shop.

Down in Ogden, Dan quickly decided he didn't want to be a banker—his father's sheepherders were making more than he was as a teller, the Wharton grad said. Besides, he enjoyed the sheep business and returned to Worland to consider his future at the same time that Buren and Helen decided they wanted to ranch, too, and the three began to look for property to buy. They found a spread in the prairie country of eastern Montana, south of Miles City, and Edith staked them to the ranch.

Alec, Jr., and Lorraine returned to Worland in 1939 with the birth of their first child, Diana. With his return, he became involved in sheep raising, too.

At some point when Dan was still home, a friend of his, Jim Horn, spotted Eileen striding into the movie theatre, her high cheek bones as distinct as a magazine model's. "Who's THAT?!" he asked. "My sister," said Dan. "Do you want to meet her?"

Eileen and Jim married. Eileen was the only one of Alec and Edith's children who didn't at some point go into ranching. Jim's father owned a furniture store in Worland, where Jim worked. The elder Horn believed that Greybull, forty miles north, offered more opportunity, so he closed the Worland store and re-opened in Greybull, where Jim's salesmanship and Eileen's decorating advice attracted a following. When they did well enough to retire young, Jim, a dashing outdoorsman, invested in a ski area in the Big Horns. He raced cars but could slow down and fly fish as well as Eileen. Eileen was a master fly fisher with a knack for casting her rod precisely on target, just as her father had taught her.

As for Dan, he reconnected with Martha Omenson, a friend from the neighboring town of Thermopolis whose parents, William "Bill" and Catherine Parr Omenson, owned the Plaza and the Carter, the two hotels in the Hot Springs State Park. Martha, a graduate from Cornell University's famous School of Hotel Management, had come home from California on holiday. Known for her looks and her loveliness, Martha had represented her home state as Miss Wyoming at the 1939 World's Fair in San Francisco. Dan and Martha soon married, with Eileen and Jim standing up for them.

The Healys gathered in Worland at Christmas and when possible Thanksgiving and the Fourth of July, too. Edith and Alec's family reunions in those days included four children, four spouses, and three grandchildren—Kay and Dick Bonine, and Diana Healy, Alec, Jr.'s daughter.

The December 7th Japanese attack on Pearl Harbor found the Healys as shocked as the rest of the world. With Edith's well-known efficiency, her 1941 Christmas letters probably were already written. Did she tear them up and start over? Add postscripts? Wait to address the changing world in later letters after learning what would happen to her children? Abandon Christmas cards altogether and concentrate on maintaining a calm shelter for her family during the holidays?

1920s

Christmas card, 1929: Helen, Eileen,
Dan (they were about six months apart in age), Alec, Jr., Edith and Alec.

Summer 1929: The Healys vacationed
in Hawaii where they devoured fresh
pineapple and Alec, Jr. (above) learned
the ukulele. Edith and Alec, draped in
leis, were sorry to leave.

The Healys deeply enjoyed their retreat in the Big Horns near Deer Haven. A Swedish carpenter built the cozy cabin with four small bedrooms in c. 1928. Dan, left, Alec, Jr. sitting, and their cousin, Jack Lynch, help with the construction.

1930s

This passport, properly visaed, is valid for travel in all countries unless otherwise specified.

This passport, unless limited to a shorter period, is valid for two years from its date of issue and may be renewed for an additional period of two years.

Limitations

This passport not valid for travel in SPAIN

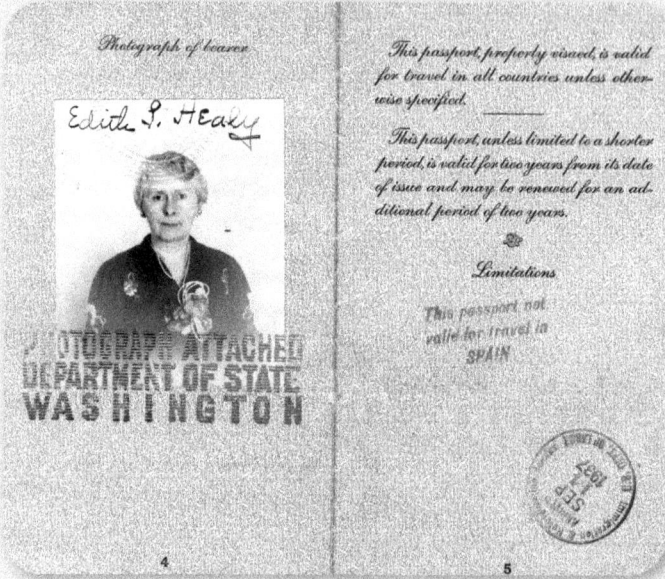

1937: Edith returned to Europe when Dan invited her along on his college graduation trip.

All roads led to UPenn: Alec, Jr. waits for the CB&Q at the Worland Railroad Station (left) while Dan (sitting on car) and his best friend from Buffalo, George Knepper, drove an old jalopy back to school and sold it at a profit for $15.

Edith's nephew Holden Furber, left, graduated with a Ph.D. from Harvard. Alec relaxes with a book.

Eileen, left, graduated from Oregon State in 1938, while Helen opted for a family, pictured here with Dick, Buren and their daughter Kay.

Christmas 1940: The Healys had to send two family photos since their children
and grandchildren were split between Worland and the ranch in Montana.
Top: Edith, Eileen, Alec, Jim Horn, Alec, Jr., Lorraine, and Diana.
Below: Buren, Kay, Helen, Dick on the horse, Martha, and Dan.

World War II: An ROTC graduate, Dan was called up immediately after Pearl Harbor. On Christmas Day 1942, he shipped out for Italy where he spent the war.

Dan, who had served in the Reserve Officer Training Corps (ROTC) at Penn, at once sent a telegram to his commanding officer to find out where he should report. He and Martha were in Belle Fourche, South Dakota, near the eastern Wyoming border where Dan was running sheep. Dan left, and Alec drove to South Dakota immediately to sell the livestock.

Dan spent the next year being transferred around the country to various Army Air Force bases. Martha followed when she could. I was born in Wenatchee, Washington, three weeks late and ten months after Pearl Harbor. (Do the math!) A few months later, my father was transferred again and my mother took me home to her parents' hotels in Thermopolis. When I was a one-year-old, my mother took me to Salt Lake City to see my father just before he shipped out on Christmas Day 1943—across an Atlantic treacherous with Nazi submarines—for Italy's war zone.

Eileen's husband, Jim Horn, enlisted in the army and was honorably discharged shortly after with a back injury. Alec and Edith's other children and spouses learned—particularly Buren to his disappointment—that if employed in the livestock business you were considered necessary to the home front, so you couldn't enlist, especially Buren, who was one of the few men left in the Miles City area with medical knowledge.

Patsy, Jr., and Mary's daughter, Patricia, married an army captain she met in Ogden. Patsy, Jr., and Mary's son, Patrick III, joined the navy, and their younger son, Stuart, who had married a Casper girl, joined the army. Stuart's jeep flipped over and killed him in Ogden on April 3, 1944, the only Healy to die during World War II. His death can be counted among the life-changing events that seem to cluster for the Healys in the first days of April. Stuart died on Edith and Alec's thirty-third wedding anniversary, which was also the seventh birthday of Patrick IV, his nephew, and two days before the thirty-second birthday of his cousin and close friend, Alec, Jr. When loss, like Stuart's death, lands so close to joyous occasions, they become more fixed on the calendar then they might otherwise.

With the war dragging on in the Pacific, Alec, Jr., volunteered to join the army. Before he was mustered, Japan surrendered.

Alec's nephew, Jack Lynch, a married man, spent the war in Honolulu. Not long after the war ended, he divorced and sailed to Tahiti, where he remarried and settled for life. Jack Lynch is such an irresistible character that it is difficult not to get lost with Alice down the rabbit hole telling story after story, but hence the purpose of chapter notes![104-107]

Edith's nephew, Holden Furber, also married, used his prodigious vocabulary for the Office of Strategic Services (OSS), the World War II forerunner of the CIA. Holden and his wife, Elizabeth, moved to Washington DC where he rephrased translations of coded messages as a further firewall to protect the codes. Holden also advised the OSS on the British Commonwealth, particularly the Indian subcontinent and shipping lanes used by the European colonial powers since the sixteenth century. Dr. Furber became an eminent professor of history at the University of Pennsylvania.[108]

After the war and after the Bonines and Dan Healys sold their Montana ranch, Buren, Helen, Kay, and Dick remained in Miles City, where Buren returned to pharmacy. In 1956, he and Helen established Western Pharmacy, which they continued to operate together until about 1975, when they sold it. They returned home to Worland for summers, but spent winters in Phoenix with other Wyoming and Montana snowbirds, including Dan and Martha.

First, a roomette and dining car on the overnight CB&Q to Denver, then on to the world, c. 1938. After the war, Edith and Alec shifted to cars and airplanes.

CHAPTER 16

WILD BLUE YONDER

1944 – 1949

Edith and Alec were settled, a distinguished and formal couple. For decades they had called one another "Mother" and "Father" which sounds terribly unromantic. Could they have changed so very much? Happily, Edith's letters from the 1940s were scrawled with the same hurry of discovery and romance as her honeymoon letters.

This chapter includes a travel letter describing Edith and Alec catching the last Pan Am flight out of Costa Rica with the revolutionaries' tanks (or pickups with gunmen) rolling down the side of the runway.[109] Edith's letters in this chapter mostly are to Cornelia Metz, whose family gave her Girl Scout letters and a scrapbook to Dan to add to the Healy archives. In the 1940s, Cornelia was chairman of the Rocky Mountain Regional Board, and Edith was one of the two representatives of the region on the National Girl Scout Board of Directors.

Edith's letters to Cornelia give more insight into what it meant to recruit and organize more than one thousand girls and their leaders into an ongoing and coordinated Girl Scout program in the Big Horn Basin. Edith's achievement to attract so many leaders and enroll so many girls in a sparsely populated region like the Big Horn Basin was an incredible achievement. Edith went after one leader at a time.

The first letter reveals Edith's reaction to the National Girl Scout Board changing the boundaries of the regions.

Mexico City
March 10, 44

Dear Cornelia, –
    Mrs. Terrell's and Mrs. Means[110] letter has just arrived. Well that letter certainly was a shock, even if we knew it was coming sometime.
    It is like a death, when a person is very ill you think you are prepared, but when it comes, you never are. I feel this is like a death, the death of the Rocky Mountain Region and it is! It's been alive for about twenty years or at least as long as I have been a Scout, fifteen years and this Fall it will be no more.
    Mrs. Hoover's dying works into it too. She was such a vital part of our Regional conferences, like at Butte.
    Well, it's the end of a phase of our Scout work. But the Scout work is too big for us to let our part of it die, so we'll start our second phase as members of the Covered Wagon Region.
    I can't help wondering what the future in that Region holds. There are fine women in all the Regions and as Mrs. Means says, we can look forward to making new friends while keeping the old.
    I wrote Mrs Means a few minutes ago. Among other things, I said I thought you and I were about the only ones in our State that would be deeply affected by this change. The others had not attended the Regional meetings and made such good friendships as we had.
    I shall miss seeing Mrs. Porter, Irvine, Rushmer and Bintz, but I shall miss even more our contact with the Billings group. We were closer to them than to Casper and we didn't know anyone in Cheyenne, at least I didn't.
    I did hope they would let us keep our three states, Utah, Montana and Wyoming, and I really thought they would, for some time yet, so this certainly is a shock to me. After reading the two letters (Newell and Means) I can see we were thinking locally, and they, nationally. Their viewpoint is bigger than ours. We are like children and they the parents. They know what is best for the family and we are just concerned

with ourselves and our small scope activities. So I told Helen Means I would bow to the inevitable, knowing they knew best what was right to do for the good of the organization as a whole. That I could "take it" and although I wouldn't "like it," that they needn't be afraid of my attitude, because no one in the Covered Wagon Region would ever know but what I was pleased over the new setup.

This will relieve you in a very graceful way of being Regional Chairman without your having to put in a resignation and have people refuse to accept it etc. etc. etc –

Now about me. The thought has come to me that although I was publicly elected by the 700 delegates of the National Convention at Cleveland last Fall to serve on the National Board for the next four years, I was elected to represent the Rocky Mountain Region. If there is no Rocky Mountain Region there is no need of me. Mrs. Aldrich also has two more years to serve. Looks like we should pass out of the picture along with the Region.

Each Region has two Board members. The Covered Wagon Region naturally has its two. So that is that.

Looks like you and I just vanish into space. Well, it was fun while it lasted.

Alec and I leave Mexico City Monday Feb 13th. We stay two days in Dallas. Alec comes home from Denver but I have to stay in Denver for more dental work. There has been a mix up over my appointments so I am not sure the day I'll get home. Alec will be home the 21st and I think I will be on the 26th but I am not sure.

We must get together as soon as we possibly can. So much to talk about.

Lovingly
Edith

——

Worland, Wyo.
April 16, '45

Dear Cornelia, –

Here is our money. I am so glad I don't have to go to Powell today, although it is a nice day. That 8th Grade dinner party of six courses, 18 people (15 girls and 2 leaders and me – one table with 10 in the dining room and 8 in the living room.) is looming high in the horizon and I think I shall stay in bed this morning and read Lloyd Douglas's "The Robe."[111]

Wasn't it awful about Baird McClellan.[112] That strikes pretty close to home. He was one of Dan's best friends and Helen's and Buren's too. His wife is going to have a baby in June and have been so ill throughout her pregnancy one can't help fearing what this shock will do.

Hope you are being sensible too. I have hopes of us turning out to be quite sensible people in time.

If Rowena[113] is going to continue to stay away from Basin so long, she isn't going to be of much use for general Scouting. She can do things with her group in the summer, but when we need her is in the winter.

Hope to see you soon –
Love E.S.H.

——

Dan Healy, a captain in the Army Air Corps, arrived home safely from Italy in June 1945. When Dan sailed away, the war in Europe was still going on, but by May 8, the Italians and Germans had surrendered and Dan ended up on the next troop ship that landed in the United States. Edith had had a hunch that Dan would be on the ship, she told Martha, who received his phone call as soon after he docked as was possible to get to a phone. At first it was only temporary good news—Dan had been shipped home early to go on to the war in the Pacific, where fighting was still intense. Then suddenly, the atom bombs were dropped, the Japanese surrendered, and Dan was released from active duty.

Summer 1945. Dan temporarily home from war. With him, from left: Martha, Cathy riding a broom, Eileen, Jim, Alec, Edith and Diana, the daughter of Alec, Jr. and Lorraine. The Sheltie was Dan and Martha's dog, Fella.

World War II was over.

After the first Christmas with all of their children and grandchildren gathered in Worland in years,[114] the Healys left in January 1946 for the warm Brazilian sun. Sailing with Wyoming friends on a freighter from New Orleans, Alec and Edith stopped at coastal cities en route, ending up in Río de Janeiro.

They returned to Worland as winter was drawing to an end and time was nearing for shearing and lambing at the LU Ranch. They brought back suitcases full of gifts, most memorably, native-garbed dolls for their three (then) granddaughters. They also brought back big, beautiful aquamarines from the famous H. Stern store, whose jewelry stores still dazzle. Even Alec bought an 8.8 carat aquamarine ring for himself, which he probably hid in a drawer because the ring is too gigantic, flashy, fun, and peculiar for a Wyoming man to be seen wearing. I wear the ring when I want to feel like a glamorous girl from Ipanema, and my doll collection has been displayed in almost every home I've had.

Although we grandchildren remember Edith and Alec confidently setting off for exotic winters in the tropics, Edith was apparently nervous before she left for Brazil. Or, perhaps she was following that old Maine adage, "When you travel, leave like you're preparing to die." In January 1946, a few days before she and Alec left home, Edith wrote a collection of letters, each sealed in an envelope labeled: To Be Opened After My Death. We grandchildren didn't know about the letters until I discovered the ones that my father had saved in the LU Ranch office. They were zipped in a pine-colored, 6½ x 8½ inch Stockgrowers State Bank deposit bag and tucked away in a fireproof file cabinet where we keep the family archives.

In the following letter about distribution of property, Edith mentions adopting the system that Alec's father used to guarantee fairness when dividing up bands of sheep with buyers. The envelope was labeled: To Be Opened After My Death.

Worland, Wyo.
Jan 6, 1946

Dear Children, –

I have tried to think of a wise way to divide up the things and after much deliberation have arrived at this decision.

I would like to have the large Sheffield silver tray with handles go to my son Alex Jr to use with the silver service that was his great uncle George Harmon's wedding silver, date 1860.

I would like to have my mother's wedding silver, date 1863, and the tray that goes with it, which was a wedding present to Father and me, go to my son Dan.

The things that were handed down to me by my parents, all the rest of the silver and jewelry, I want to be divided between my two sons Alex, Jr and Dan. One boy and his wife making the division. The other boy and his wife having first choice. After the choice is made if you want to trade some of the things back and forth it is all right with me.

Now for all the rest of the things. One of the sons and one of the daughters divide them as equally as possible into four parts. The other son and daughter having first choice—drawing lots to see who will be first and second the other two drawing lots to see who will be third and fourth.

In this case if you want to trade some of your things with someone else it is all right with me.

If you can think of some better way to divide the things that are allotted to you four and it meets the approval of all of you, it is all right with me. All I want is to have you all good friends, because after all what are a few material things beside a family united, who stand by each other through thick and thin. That's what I want more than anything else in the world.

    You are all four good children and I love you dearly. I love my daughters-in-law and my sons-in-law too and my five grandchildren.

    I have been very much blessed in my life and I appreciate it.

God bless you all,

Mother

———

Edith and Alec didn't venture as far afield in the winter of 1947. Instead, they chose the warm and relatively tame destinations of Florida and Jamaica, where her letters to Cornelia chatted about scouting and neighbors, Neiman Marcus, decorating, flowers, dinner dresses, and looking out at the Caribbean. Lorraine joked that Edith would arrive back in Worland from a trip exclaiming, "I'm so glad to be home . . . now where am I going to go next?"

Hotel Casa Blanca
Montego Bay
Jamaica, B. W. I.
March 9, 1947

My dear Cornelia,–

    You don't know how often I have thought about you and the things I wanted to talk over with you but as I wanted to write a fairly long letter, the opportunity has never presented itself until now.

    It seems to me the less you have to do the less you do. That is why you enjoy a vacation I guess, just relax.

    I know just how Maurine feels about scouting. We all get that way and get over it. I don't think I ever was so "Fed up" as I was when I left home. From the time of that Thermop meeting in the summer when the Ex. Sec idea was started, I have had it full blast, including Colorado Springs and national board in Chicago.

I can see your point about Cappy. It is unfortunate that she wants it so badly and you are neighbors. However that will straighten itself out in time but in the meantime it is definitely awkward for us all. What will I do if she comes to me to recommend her?

My blood turns cold at the thought.

As for Powell, they make me tired too. As you say "who doesn't want a little house".[115] We and Greybull raised their money with that in mind.

What is bothering me is who is going to succeed Maurine. I doubt if we should have a Powell gal although that is open to much thought. Is there anyone in Cody that would be good. What is the latest on Ann.

I wonder how Worland came out in their drive. The last I heard they didn't raise but half of what they wanted—guess Greybull came out fine. I have a letter from Eileen. After that drive she was through, absolutely through, with scouting. She couldn't take another thing. That was 2 weeks ago. Yesterday a letter mentioning having a Council meeting at her house next week and plans for a Juliette Lowe tea. She also told me (not to be repeated) that Mrs. M[116] was their treasurer. She left for 5 weeks (when they started their drive) and later Eileen wanted to check with the bank and asked her [Mrs. M's] daughter to get her scout bankbook and the account book. The account book was a blank and the bank book had nothing deposited for 6 months. They were all having a fit and decided no matter what it costs after this they were going to have their books audited every January 1.

She talks so big (quoting Eileen) and bosses everyone around and then the important things she never gets done. We have met others like her haven't we? This scouting certainly shows up people's characters, doesn't it.

A letter from Rowena busy with fixing up a home. Does my heart good to think of her at last buying carpets, wallpapers and drapes. Even if they cost unmercifully. Also a little touch that interested me, [she was] so worried because Jerry had to go to Pittsburgh for three days and flew. I am so glad she is in

Tulsa where they can start making new friends together, and in a climate that isn't cold. She minds cold much more than he.

She begs us to come home by way of Tulsa and even though it means giving up Neiman Marcus we are going to do it. I told her that was real friendship on my part. I will be glad to see her new home and be able to tell you all about how things are with her.

As for us this has been and is now, a wonderfully satisfying trip. Congenial companionship as well as exotic tropical scenery. Who could ask for more.

We loved Bluebeard's, but I'm glad we went there first because this is along the same line of scenery and interesting native life but this hotel is run superlatively and the bathing beach is at our door.

The food here is wonderful, almost as good as the Gloria in Rio and the service perfect. Black boys everywhere to do things for you. Even standing around to get a card table and cards for you. The dining room has just a roof over it, otherwise all outdoors. Soft breezes. We wear thin clothes and haven't had a coat on. All the tables have flowers on them and last night (Sat) each table had masses of red bougainvillea over the top and even little bunches sitting up on the napkins. The effect of red and white was stunning. They dress for dinner here and especially on Wednesday and Saturday at their dinner dances.

My one long evening dress is getting overworked. I have two short ones that will do for other nights. It's fun to see such lovely clothes on people. Half the people here are Americans, the other half British. British money is hard to get used to.

Alec and I are in a cottage on the main street a little way from the hotel. We have the 2nd floor which has a broad veranda all around. Tables, couch, chairs on the veranda and we are hanging over the railing most of the time watching the native life go by. Across from the rather narrow street are the waters of the bay with sailboats and native dugouts and fishing boats to watch on water that is the most gorgeous color you ever saw. Right now there are three shades, light green, bright blue and deep blue. From here the shore is so clear you can see the bottom where I sit on the porch.

I am thoroughly enjoying every minute of this trip.

Lovingly Edith

Expect to be with Rowena about April 6 and home about the 10th.

———

A constant accolade given my grandmother was that she was a great organizer. The comment was made so frequently that it started to fly by unheard and unrecognized. "She organized the Worland Community Concerts." "She organized the Current Events Club for the wives of her sons' friends when they returned from War." "She organized the Girl Scouts in the Big Horn Basin." I had never witnessed Edith-the-Persuader in action, however, until my sister, Debbie, read the next letter aloud while I proofed the transcription. My sister and I could not stop giggling over her oil derrick idea for the Nielsons[117] and admired Mrs. Nielson's tact in resisting the force of nature that was Edith.

Worland, Wyo
June 29, 1947
(feels like January)

My dear Cornelia,–

What are you planning for the Fourth. If you feel like coming to the cabin we would be delighted to have you.[118] Bring your own plates, cups, knives and forks, etc. (so we won't have to wash dishes). Chicken enough for you and Percy and Louise if she'd like to come and some kind of jam and a bottle of pickles. If you want to decide at the last minute, do it. You don't have to let me know. Come if you can–

Maurine and I had an interesting time at Elk Basin[119] but most people would have been pretty discouraged at the outlook. She had written to two people (both of whom she had seen at the Rally) asking if it would be convenient to have us to come and see them on Monday, the 23rd of June. No answer. (Which makes you feel so welcome.)

We met at 9:30 as planned at Eileen's just the same, as they didn't tell us not to come and Maurine called up Mrs. Austen from there. She said she was leaving that noon on the plane (didn't sound too downhearted about not seeing us either) but she thought Mrs. Peterson was back in town and she'd let her know. We said we'd eat in Powell and get to Mrs. Peterson's at 1:30. Which we did and Mrs. Peterson was delighted apparently to see us, but she was one of those who had received the letter and done nothing about it. She then started calling people and got four others to come over.

When we had a chance to get at them, our enthusiasm was evidently contagious because before we left we had two of them lined up as intermediate leaders and two senior leaders (They have no Brownies) and one for chairman of committee and all raring to go.

We left at 5 o'clock feeling our time had been well spent as now they understood what it was all about and where they fitted into the picture.

We got to Cody at 6. Mrs. Nielson was to have dinner with us and had followed the day before that she was to go to Denver and wasn't sure she'd get back. She didn't. We had dinner, an excellent one at the Burlington Inn and stayed all night there. We went to a Humphrey Bogart picture (killings etc.) and were so fascinated we sat through it twice to be sure who killed who.[120]

The next morning before starting home I suggested trying to find Mrs. Nielson as it would be a wonderful chance to see her new house. We went out. She wasn't there but we went through the house just the same, as the workmen were willing we should.

Then we went and interviewed a Miss Corrigan who has looms and hand weaves Wyo. wool. Maurine is Vice Pres. of the Wyoming wool growers auxiliary and Mrs. Quaely who is president, asked her to. Had lunch with Miss Corrigan. Then we went to where Mrs. Nielson is living in town, to be told she had returned from Denver and had gone out to the new house. Out there we went again, found her and asked her to be one of the directors of the Big Horn Basin Council Inc. When we have the articles of incorporation drawn up, Stanley Davis the lawyer, said we had to have three directors. We thought of you and I and had added Maurine and then felt it might look too cut and dried and maybe we better have someone from another town in the North.

She accepted thank goodness and between you and Maurine and me, we decided on the way home to ask her to have the B. H. Basin Council meeting at her home in the spring. She gets into her house in Sept. and someone said Basin was having the Fall meeting. Everyone will be dying to see her house which should make for a well attended meeting.

She took us through the house again, so happy to show us all the extras we had missed. In Mr. Nielson's office which is on the first floor there is a fireplace that is all faced with the stone cores out of oil wells. They are lovely, imagine, and full of color!

We suggested that they have the drapes at the window bordered with oil derricks with a pipe in between with the exhaust flare on it and have Ms. Corrigan get the design made and she weave it.

Room was knotty pine—have turquoise curtains with brown derricks and brown pipes with yellow and red exhaust flame. Have Grigwire make the design and she could put it on with yarn and weave it. Wyo. wool etc.

We thought it a wonderful idea and stopped in and told Miss C. to go ahead and make a sample and submit it. Mrs. Nielson said she had her drapes for that room picked out but thought it worth looking into.

Then we looked down and saw Paul Stock's house and
Mrs. Nielson offered to drive down with us and take us through it.
We went and he was there and so pleased to show it all to us.

When I got home I told Alec our living room looked just as
big as a peanut but nevertheless I liked it best.

So you see we had a wonderful time and accomplished
two things, Elk Basin and the B.H.B. Director.

I enclose a Council Fire, Girl Scout International Paper,
which always gives me great inspiration. And if I can find it, a
letter from Mrs. Hagler from Great Falls. I wrote and asked her
what she knew about the Alcan Highway (it starts there) and
in answer she reported it is not ready for tourist travel yet. Alec
wanted to go on it.

I was so amused at the party Mrs. Bishop gave. At the
people she asked. Mrs. Muirhead and Lucille Hake and Lorraine
and Martha, the latter did not go, she hardly knows her, Mrs.
Flynn—how does she know her? Anyway I got a kick out of
reading the guest list and wondering why she wanted to go to
so much trouble to entertain that group.

People are funny aren't they.

Rowena was evidently much pleased over the telephone
call. Did you note Dotty is not coming to live with them. (Thank
goodness.)

Have to stop now. Love
Edith

————

Edith wrote this letter after a National Girl Scout Board meeting.

Beverly-Wilshire
Nov. 9, 1947

My dear Cornelia,–

Well you have at last accomplished the thing you have
been working towards for several years. Our executive for the
Big Horn basin. You are to be congratulated—I wanted it too,

but not the way you did, that meant to dig in and work for it. When Miss Crowe said in Thermop it would take $5000 or $6000 I just knew we couldn't get it. But we did.

I don't take any credit for it at all. It is all yours. I helped, yes, but the faith and performance was yours and I am so happy for you. Now it's up to the local Scout organizations to make it work.

I'm just going to tell you one thing more in this letter than leave the rest until we are together.

When I got to this hotel Friday night I certainly was impressed with it. A beautiful place, more like a movie set for beauty. A great many clear glass partitions in the lobby, tall windows, high ceiling, soft carpets, indirect lighting, azure pool and terraces outside, just beautiful. What disappointed me was the people. All day yesterday I looked at them in the lobby, in the restaurants, at the pool, they looked so sort of ordinary— well-dressed but uninteresting. I wondered why there wasn't even one face that I'd really like to know better.

Then all of a sudden, last evening when I was sitting there watching people, it suddenly dawned on me. It wasn't the people that were different, it was me and my viewpoint. For a week I had been associating with people who have dedicated themselves to service, who knew what they were doing and why, and were going places with eagerness and keen interest. It wasn't that they were any better looking but there was an inner spark that I had missed in the groups passing through this hotel.

If there ever was an argument for adults doing a scouting job, this is one. It even changes the looks on your face—isn't that something!

Mrs. Means and Mrs. Mudd[121] asked after you very particularly.

I get home Saturday next. Leave here at 8 AM and am in Worland at 3. Isn't that wonderful–

Lots of love
Edith

By 1948, the Healys again were ready for high adventure, which turned out to be far more adventure than they anticipated. With their good friends from Worland, Dr. W. O. Gray and his wife, Mary, they decided to caravan in their own cars to New Orleans, then fly to Guatemala, El Salvador, and Costa Rica, and from there travel on to Peru for a month. Edith and Alec, as usual, had been reading everything they could find about the countries to learn and determine what sights they wanted to visit on tours that they arranged themselves.

Edith wrote letters to the National Girl Scouts and Girl Guide board members in the countries they planned to visit. Everyone looked forward to greeting and hosting their Wyoming visitors.

The Grays' only child, Georgia, begged to come, too. A junior at the University of Maryland, Georgia had fallen in love with a young man from Worland, Ken St. Clair. They planned to marry in September 1948 and Georgia, 20, thought this might be her only chance to ever take a long foreign trip. She was invited along.[122] She remembers:

> Everyone said to me, "Why do you want to go on a trip with those old folks?" but they were more fun to travel with. They read everything they could get their hands on before we went. We didn't go on tours. These were all privately planned to do what they wanted. It made it so nice.
>
> They wanted to see everything. Mr. Healy and my father together were the most curious men in the world. They could get us into the oddest places. Like, we spent a day of all places at this dairy out of Lima—we thought if we'd survive the taxi ride we'd get to the dairy.
>
> The Healys knew how to travel. Things were done when they wanted to do it. Or not, if they just wanted to take it easy for a few days. Mrs. Healy would pick out the place to stay. Always. She'd say she'd scan the horizon and pick out the tallest building because that would be the latest and the best.

Edith and Alec played off each other. Both of them had eyes that twinkled and they would make each other's eyes twinkle better than anyone in the world. We'd go to dinner and she'd say, "Now Father, don't forget to tip the waiter—in front of the waiter—and of course, he always tipped the waiter. Then the night we were going out to dinner in New Orleans and Mr. Healy said, "Mother, you did go get some money for the dinner, didn't you?" like he was going to put it on her ticket. And when the waiter came, he said, "Now Mother, do not forget to tip the waiter." And she just giggled.[123]

On the Healy side of the younger generation, Dan, 32, was still recovering from World War II. He wanted out of the Montana ranch to do whatever he wanted to do next. This was a painful sale for the Bonines who had lived on the ranch for several years and didn't want to leave.

As for Dan, he returned from war "restless and angry," as he said in an oral history interview with the Washakie Museum and Cultural Center. He was especially angry that the taxes on his share of the ranch sale totaled more than he had been paid by the U.S. government for risking his life for four years. Dan decided to buy a ranch somewhere in Latin America—in the pampas of Argentina or the llanos of Venezuela or Colombia or the grasslands of southern Brazil—and move us south. This was not my mother's dream and, as it transpired, it wasn't my father's either, as he learned firsthand.

In January 1948, about the time that Edith, Alec, and the Grays set out on their journey, Dan and a bachelor friend from Worland, Jim Kelly, also flew south.[124] As it turned out, Latin America's poverty, its hungry children, and its corruption reminded Dan strongly of his aversion to wartime Italy. He returned home ready to settle down.

Edith's letter to Dan and Jim from the Hotel Astoria in San Salvador was rushed. Punctuation and some words went missing, but the pressure of the moment was sharp. She addressed their letter in care of Pan American Airlines, Buenos Aires, Argentina.

Feb. 13, 1948

My dear Dan, – and Jim.

Received your cable and will send this to Argentina. We are quite disturbed about conditions in Costa Rica. You told us to check and Father and Doc have gone to Pan American this morning for information.

If it is possible for us to get reservations, think we will pass up Costa Rica and go directly to Lima and take in Costa Rica on our way back. I'll hold this letter open until I know exactly what we are going to do.

Grays had a letter from home that said Brookings have sold the store to a Sheridan man and are going to California. That Dr. Anderson performed two difficult operations and they did him up so, that he and his family have gone to California so he can rest.

Georgia is having a wonderful time. Most of the drivers we get for these auto trips of several days are young, so she has a partner for dancing in the evening and someone her age to talk to. Each place we go she wants to stay longer. Same here, the boy was educated in the States. He wants to take her to a Spanish wedding Sunday and naturally she's crazy to stay.

Yesterday we looked down into the crater of a volcano. It hasn't gone off for thirty years but might of course any time. This country is full of volcanoes.

Coffee coffee everywhere. They are picking and processing it in million dollar mills. We went to a huge plantation yesterday. As we drove up the side of the volcano yesterday people were picking the berries and having themselves a wonderful time.

We were at a lake a few days lovely and I went in bathing every day.

We liked Guatemala better than Salvador. This is such an over populated poor country.

Be sure and have a meal, preferably lunch at Gloria Hotel in Rio that is where we stayed.

Love Mother -

Later. In checking with Pan American they say things are under control and it's all right to go there. The Salvador papers say the same. The Miami paper says the President in power is not the one running for office for re-election, it is another and the President is putting down any disturbances with the army. So we have decided to go tomorrow. We can always leave if we don't like it, or go to the beach. We are going three days ahead of time because there isn't any more for us to see here. Salvador is one of the most densely populated countries in the world, hence poor. Guatemala was so much more colorful and interesting. We're anxious to move on.

We were at Lake Coatepeque when your wire came and the hotel phoned it down to us. Good service, I'll say. I waited to know our plans before writing that is why you didn't hear sooner — aren't we all having fun.

Love, Mother

I'll write in a few days and tell you how things are in Costa Rica. In looking at the itinerary you gave me there is no address for Buenos Aires so I will send in care of Pan American. Our best to both you boys.

———

Gran Hotel Costa Rica
San Jose, Costa Rica

America Central
Feb 20, 1948

My dear Cornelia, –
I can't help wondering how you are getting along. Write to me at Hotel Bolivar Lima, Peru and say on it, "Hold until Arrival." We'll get there about March 6th. We are having a wonderful time.

I want you and Percy to plan a trip sometime to Guatemala. We liked it the best of these Central American countries. You could see all you want to in two weeks there. Fly down to New Orleans and from there to Guatemala City (6 1/2 hours) so if Percy didn't feel he could be away more than three weeks that would give you plenty of time – It is so much cleaner than Mexico, food is better, and it is more picturesque.

Hope the pictures we took come out all right so I can prove it to you.

Had a birthday Tuesday and was I thrilled when Alec brought me a bunch of orchids. Three sprays with nine blossoms on a spray. I have worn a spray on my dress every day since. And a large bottle of Chanel No 5. I wondered how he ever knew what kind of perfume to buy and he said he had heard me and the girls talking about it once. He hears more than I give him credit for, and remembers.

Be sure in your letter to tell me the latest on our favorite topic, Mary Grace and what is Marjorie Smith (bless her dear little heart (?) doing. Bet Bill got a shock when she didn't fit into his plans. Not her. She'd rather hang around the neck of poor Lois.

Plan to see Rowena on the way home. We land in New Orleans March 31.

We went to a club in San Salvador one Saturday night with guest tickets given us by the manager of the hotel. Two men in white uniforms guarded the door. We showed our cards and they bowed us in. An attendant took the men's hats and poured forth a stream of Spanish. I smiled and said "Cena" (dinner). He showed us the elevator. To the elevator boy again I said, "Cena." He bowed and took us to the roof where there was a dance floor surrounded by tables and a 12-piece orchestra at one end.

To the head waiter I said "Cena." He showed us a menu —a table d'Hotel affair I noted. We bowed our heads yes. A wonderful time was had by all and all we needed was one word of Spanish.

Having fun.
Love Edith

Despite what the Pan Am office told them, Costa Rica was not safe. As they watched more and more shouting gunmen circling around in pickups and threatening crowds in the central plaza, Alec and Dr. Gray changed the plane tickets while the women packed.

The hotel called for two taxis, but only one arrived. Georgia said, "At first my dad and Mr. Healy said, 'We'll wait for a second taxi to get the rest of our things,' but the man told us, 'There won't be another taxi,' so we all squeezed into one, with our baggage tied to a support on the back of the cab."

The taxi raced to the airport which they found crowded with more gunmen in pickups. "Everyone had a gun," said Georgia, but she never saw or heard any shooting. The Worland five caught the last Pan Am flight out of the country for a couple of weeks. As they lifted off, they looked out the windows and saw pickups with gunmen chasing down the runway after them..

Costa Rica's revolution entered their lives again during the month they stayed in Peru. Georgia recalled that she was "sitting down in the lobby and this gal came in wearing the most beautiful jewelry you've ever seen in your life. We were kind of visiting, and I told her, 'I've been admiring your jewelry.'" The woman thanked Georgia and told her that her husband was the president of Costa Rica.[125] She explained that you put your money in jewels there, so when an uprising starts, you put the jewelry on and get out. "This is all we have," she told Georgia.

The next letter to Rowena and Jerry Coons includes what is probably my favorite all time line from Edith. She briefly mentions the close escape from revolutionary forces in Costa Rica, then says she, "wouldn't have missed it for the world."

Gran Hotel Bolivar
Lima, Peru
March 7, 48

My dear Rowena & Jerry [Coons], –
    I have a trip all planned for you to go to Guatamala [*sic*]
some day and you can do it nicely, flying from Tulsa on a two
week vacation – just how you are to spend your time to see the
most and where to stay. You'll love it.
    It won't be long now before we see you. We land in New
Orleans March 31 and will figure how long it will take us and
will wire time of arrival.
    This hotel reminds me a lot of the Gloria [in Rio de
Janeiro] only it's not so handsome inside. The dining room is
the same type. High ceiling with the high windows and the
same colored drapes and flowers on each table – and the
headwaiter translating the menu.
    Speaking of Rio I got a note from Adele Lynch yesterday
forwarded from Worland. She is coming to New York for some
Western Hemisphere Girl Scout Conference and hopes to see
me. Sorry I won't be there.
    I don't know where the Aldriches are. Just before they
were to leave their daughter, Mary Virginia got pneumonia.
While she was convalescing she was to go to Arizona and they
were starting out to find a place to be with her. They found it in
Phoenix. They were supposed to be in Guatamala [*sic*] City Feb
2 but they weren't. I don't know what happened.
    All these winter trips are different. This is thrilling and
interesting but none has been as glamorous as the one to Rio.
    Last I heard from Dan he was in Buenos Aires. I gave him
Maybrook's address and told him when he was in Rio to be sure
and have a meal at the Gloria and think of us. Preferably lunch,
so he could see the Buffet Froid and be impressed, as we were.
    A letter from Cornelia. She is getting along all right and
has a housekeeper, thank goodness.
    Hope you will have the latest on our favorite topic, Mary Grace.
    Instead of getting into a Revolution in Rio we got into one

in Costa Rica. Were on the last Pan American plane to leave there. Some excitement. Wouldn't have missed it for the world but don't want any more. Whew!!!!!!!

Love
Edith.
Did you know Lee Simonson of the Northern Hotel in Billings died in Phoenix this winter.

Alec has on his white suit and shoes. Looks like he did in Rio. Very elegant. This is summer.

———

March 8, 1948.
Lima Peru

Dear Cornelia, –

I thought of you real hard tonight. What do you think! I saw that picture of Grace Moore's "One Night of Love"[126] that we showed in Worland to our friends with a tea at my house afterward, at least twenty years ago!! Imagine! It was fun to see. Such funny clothes, but it was still a good show.

Glad to get your letter and know how things were with you and that you had help in the house.

We will land in New Orleans March 31 so our trip is nearing its end. We are still having a wonderful time -

Lots of love
Edith

———

Hotel Bolivar
Lima Peru
March 27, 1948

My dear Cornelia, –

Well I am lying down after a final orgy of shopping. I am so happy over the things we have bought that I just glow all over when I think of the fun of taking them home. Do hope you and Helen[127] will like what I am bringing you this time.

Had a long letter from Rowena. She enclosed one just received from you in which you said how well you were getting along. I was certainly glad to hear that. Also about the news of Louise going to live in Tulsa. How strange life often is, as it moves a person around from place to place.

I will not say anything to anyone of what you said in the letter about Louise's future plans because plans so often change.

I am so happy for her and for you and Percy that she has found someone so fine. She deserves the best.

We start our homeward journey tomorrow night. A night flight this time. The pilots say the night flight from Lima to Panama is "super" especially when there is a moon. We have one. We leave at 10 p.m. and get in at 6:45 a.m. with only one stop, at Guayaquil Ecuador.

We had planned to go to Quito but changed our mind on account of high flying over mountains and Quito itself is over 9,000 altitude.

We went on a trip into the interior of Peru that was "super." Llamas grazing everywhere and yesterday went 138 miles up the coast to a hacienda. Had lunch there and back in the afternoon. A man who used to live in Wyoming, John Neal by name, took us. A treat.

Shall see you before long.

Lots of love,
Edith

———

Georgia added,

Mrs. Healy liked the shop. I think the happiest couple of days of her life were when we were in Lima and she was buying silver. She wanted to buy four tea sets, three for her children and one for herself. Mr. Healy said, "Now Mother, you have nothing for Dan." "Well, he can have my set when I'm gone," she said. "You may live to be 120 years old," he said.

Edith went ahead and bought only four sets, and the Grays bought one. "The shop bundled up the sets and each of us carried a set on the plane."

When Edith and Alec distributed their gifts, it probably never occurred to them how deeply their trips affected some of their grand-children. Kay always thought of how Edith handled new places when Phillips Petroleum transferred her husband to Europe with only a week or two notice. Alec, Jr.'s daughter, the late Diana Healy Hor-vath, majored in Spanish and Portuguese at Georgetown University, and his late son, Alex III, married a British girl and moved to a village near Cambridge University where he found and sold antiques. Tim, the youngest, received his master's degree in classical guitar from the New England Conservatory of Music. He then founded and directs the International Conservatory of Music in Washington DC. The conser-vatory is now beginning the twentieth year of Marlow Guitar Services, which brings world-renowned classical guitarists to perform in DC. I became editor of *Amèricas Magazine*, published by the Organization of American States (OAS), before working as a writer and editor for the National Geographic Society.

Like Alec, his grandsons, Dick Bonine and Mike Healy, focused on ranching. Along the way, Dick became an exceptional horseman, and Mike won many awards for his conservation and breeding achieve-ments at the LU Ranch.

Edith wrote this letter to Cornelia after a National Girl Scout Board meeting.

The Waldorf-Astoria
Saturday eve.
Oct 30, 1948

Dear Cornelia, –

When my friend from Portland Maine, who had come to Boston to be with me for a few days, said, "Edith, I think you ought to invest in some new luggage," I decided I'd better do something about it.

I wish you'd see what I bought yesterday with the assistance of my New York shopper who knows where to go and what to buy. Blue nylon with white leather edging and initials and white leather baggage tags. Light as a feather.

Got large case, one for hats and shoes, and one for cosmetics and overnight (small square one with handle on top.) So I am all set and ready for my next trip. Am thrilled with it. Walked down Fifth Ave today window shopping and ended up at the Plaza Palm Room for lunch. Did I love every minute of it.

Having fun!

———

Edith was a networker more than a half century before the word existed, not for business gain but for the experiences. She arranged her travels to take advantage of her contacts, including childhood friends, friends of friends, and connections through her volunteer organizations. She maintained her connections and made visiting arrangements writing letters with paper, pen, and stamps—not the Internet.

Edith explained her networking system for developing international friendships to the PEO Sisterhood's Worland chapter, which she helped found. Kay Bonine Johnson shared this copy of our grandmother's 1948 PEO program.[128]

International Friendship

Each time I go to a foreign country I try to make the acquaintance of some of its citizens to promote, in my small way, International Friendship.

I am a member of the Regional Board of the Girl Scouts as well as being a P.E.O., and it is through the Girl Scouts I make contacts. If there were P.E.O.s there I would look them up, too.

This year, 1948, I found myself in Guatemala City and got in touch with the Girl Guides. Every country except the United States calls their Scouts, Guides. I found some very fine women in charge, two of whom could speak English. So they interpreted for me when I wanted to talk to the others.

Such interesting things as they had been doing. Among other things they had gone to orphanages at Christmas taking presents and singing carols. Then to my amazement I learned they had gone to the Leper colony, also at Christmas, with presents and carols. The girls had been met with so much enthusiasm, they decided they would go there four times a year, instead of one.

Another remarkable thing they had done was for three leaders to learn Braille and then bring that blessing to sixty blind people who otherwise would not have any such help.

During 1942, there was a revolution and the Guides had performed such outstanding service in carrying messages and helping take care of the wounded and sick, that their grateful government had presented them with a large lot in the best part of the city for a swimming pool. (The lot today is valued at $20,000.) The girls raised $2,000.00 themselves and helped in the excavation of the dirt for the pool. A little house to change their clothes in, stands beside this very lovely pool. They are planning landscaping it and putting in flower gardens, which they will take care of themselves.

Just before I left I received a silver Guatemala Girl Guide pin, with their best wishes, so I in turn pinned my United States Girl Scout pin upon the leader who had done much for me, coming to see me several times and bringing me flowers.

They are a fine group of women doing their best to make good citizens of their little girls.

In San Jose, Costa Rica, I again looked up the Guides. I found there, too, a fine group of women but they were working under the handicap of poverty. They only had twelve handbooks to serve two hundred girls. They did not have any pins. Everything they did, the money angle had to be considered first. In spite of it they had accomplished much in the way of training in cooking, homemaking and arts and crafts.

As a revolution was starting when we left, things are not going to be any easier for them and I am sorry. They were so eager to hear all about the United States and our girls and when I said good bye they wanted me to give the best wishes for a successful future to our girls from the Girl Guides of Costa Rica.

These experiences have given me new friends and good neighbors. I feel it is my small contribution toward International Friendship.

Edith S. Healy
Chapter AA, P.E.O.
Worland, Wyoming

———

Back home life took a tragic turn. On June 4, 1948, Alec, Jr., and Lorraine had their fourth and last child, Melinda, who died from respiratory problems an hour or so after her birth.

Although Edith had written her after-my-death letters with instructions about how to distribute family heirlooms in 1946, it wasn't until Melinda's death that the Healys bought a family lot with eight plots in Worland's Riverside Cemetery, an expanse of green lawn irrigated by the Big Horn Canal and separated from the grasslands, sage, and prickly pear cactus by a barbed wire fence. Worland Court records show that Alec bought the lot from the city; his son Dan, then the mayor of Worland, signed the deed, along with L. C. Sheppard, the deputy clerk.

They were to need the lot again far sooner than they had imagined.

FOUR NEPHEWS AND A NIECE

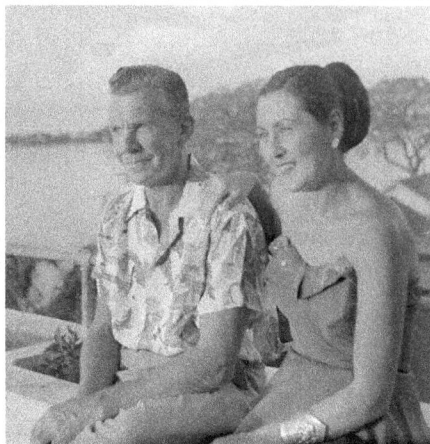

Above: Holden and Elizabeth Furber visit at the cabin in the Big Horns. Right: Jack at home in Papeete with his Tahitian wife, Suzanne. Credit: National Library of New Zealand.

Patsy, Jr. and Mary's three children: Stuart and Martha Healy (Stuart died in 1944), Patrick III as president of his fraternity at Amherst College, and Patricia, a glamorous woman whose "children" were her niece, nephews and cousins' children.

Unbeknowst at the time, this would be Edith's final portrait, c. 1948, taken by Carl Schmidt, a Florida-based photographer who was northern Wyoming's leading portraitist well into the 1970s.

CHAPTER 17

LIVING AND DYING

1 9 4 9 – 1 9 5 0

HEALTH ROUTINE – PREPARING GRANDDAUGHTER FOR HIGH SCHOOL
THOUGHTS ON DYING – STORY OF A GRUB

Something was wrong. Edith sensed it, but the whole world was upended and who was to know what was the result of strain from worry and what was a real health problem? In her 1948 Christmas letter, Edith didn't need to mention the Healys' disappointment that Harry Truman, a Democrat, was re-elected president. Her bedside copy of *Wake Up and Live!*—a primer on optimism by Dorothea Brande—was increasingly well-thumbed.

As Worland rang in New Year's Eve 1949, there was little peace on earth. Wrath raged in Biblical lands, where a Jewish state was declared in May 1948 on lands Arabs considered their own and so triggered the 1948–1949 war. A shaky ceasefire was achieved in January 1949, and Israel gained admittance to the United Nations that May.

Most of the world's eyes watched the expanding communist nations and their belief that history foretold that communism would destroy capitalism and take over the world. It looked like they might be right. Clearly Mao Zedong's Chinese Communists were winning their civil war. By January 22, they had taken over Beijing and less than eight months later, on October 1, 1949, Zedong declared the People's Republic of China. Joseph Stalin's Union of Soviet Socialist Republics was pressuring its captured Eastern European nations to conform to the Soviet way, citizens in the Baltic were deported to Russia, the Hungarians held show trials against "traitors," and in August, the Soviets tested their first atomic bomb.

The United States had countered in April by forming the North Atlantic Treaty Organization (NATO), a mutual defense agreement to protect the rest of Europe from the Soviets. And, European colonies began fighting for independence, led by Indonesia, who gained their independence before the end of the year.

In Worland, such threats felt close. North Korea's insistence on "liberating," South Korea was real peril. Dan had been promoted to major in the U.S. Army Reserves and would be called back to service immediately if war broke out in Korea.

Even so, Edith's focus was her health. Her long May 14 letter to Cornelia details the Healy's beliefs about diet and recovery from sickness that they had been practicing since the mid-1920s, an approach that required far more fresh vegetables than was usual in their Wyoming culture. Figuring that Alec, Jr., was famished after a dinner consisting of a serving bowl of salad and fresh buttered asparagus on toast, his pal, Jack Howell, used to sneak Alec, Jr., home with him for potatoes and gravy and meat.

Worland Wyoming
May 14, 1949

Dear Cornelia, –

I know you want to know just what the situation here is with me and as I have "time on my hands" I thought I'd write it to you.

All winter I have been conscious of being short of breath when I was doing things. At first when it came I noticed I had so much gas and figured it was gas pressing against the heart which was what Alec had, especially when the gas left, that shortness of breath left.

Well I tried my best to control that gas. At first I could and then I couldn't. Gas means fermentation inside. When we were

in Phoenix I thought I'd consult Dr. Gray about it but I knew
he had no apparatus for testing hearts or blood pressure, so
decided to say nothing until I got home and he got home and
really could tell what was going on. It wasn't so bad, so I went
on doing things until last week when I realized I had to sit down
in the middle of getting a meal and then I said to myself, now
it's time to do something.

I knew what I had to do.

You have been at Tilden's[129] and seen the type of place
it was and Alec and I had been restored to health by him
and have seen so many wonderful cures he accomplished,
especially me in the six months I was there twenty years ago.

But to others his theories are just plain crazy, so we
don't talk about them because we are just misunderstood.
We learned that long ago.

His theory is that all disease starts from toxemia, that
is fermentation of feeds pent up in the body and putrefying,
sending their poisons through the body. Whatever is your
weakest point the poison concentrates these—and you have
kidney trouble or lungs (tuberculosis), etc. etc. etc.

So what he does for everyone when they go in there, is
to put them on a fast of a week or even as much as two weeks,
to get rid of that fermentation and leave the body completely
cleared out. Sounds like common sense to me to get at the
cause of the trouble.

After that a light diet until the patient is back to normal
and it generally takes care of most all but the most stubborn
cases—when I was there six months it was because I was not
properly taken care of after Dan's birth. The result of my staying
so long has given me fine health ever since, something I never
had before.

Alec and I both have had the fasts several times and after
Dr Tilden died I had to give it to him here at home. I do not know
what I would have done if it hadn't been for Dorothy Dent[130] who
as you know is a trained nurse, and who believes in this Tilden
way, as she worked under a doctor who had similar ideas.

With Alec we just went ahead and did what both Alec and

I remembered of Tilden's methods. I felt it worked once with Alec and why shouldn't it the second time and I'd rather trust to that, than risk what a doctor might do. But of course the children couldn't understand why I wouldn't have a doctor, so I had to follow the dictates of my own conscience and go ahead. And you see the results.

When you go without food, all the poisons in the body pour into the stomach. It makes you feel awful! But that is where the stomach pump comes in. It is rather a siphon than pump. You pour water in and siphon it out.

So every morning you have to have a stomach wash, an enema and a warm bath. A cup of hot, hot water at meal times. It would not be wise or safe for a person to take this fast at home if they could not use a stomach tube or if they didn't have someone to check on the pulse. Dorothy came over twice a day to do that for me.

Well to go back to last week when I decided I must do something. I thought if I can get someone to take my woman's club programe (I was to do Lohengrin) and someone to take my Current Events programe I'll go to bed right now and start on that fast.

As you probably know, I got Mrs. Fred McGee to give her travelogue on Japan and Hawaii and you to do the other, and to bed I went last Friday.

It is bad enough to go without food in a hospital room where you can't get at anything anyway, but to do it where there is an ice chest full of it across the hall, is something else again. Alec is an expert on giving the stomach wash and we both know what symptoms I should have, so they don't worry us.

I started my fast Friday noon and when you were here Thursday night I hadn't had a thing to eat for six and half days!

We know too when to stop a Fast. It is when the saliva comes freely in your mouth from under your tongue. That happened to me, so I could finish mine in a week, which was yesterday Friday noon, just seven days.

I know you will be interested to know what you have when you break your Fast. A large combination salad, dressed with

Wesson oil, lemon and salt. You can imagine how that first bite tasted after seven days of hot water only.

Last night I had apple sauce and celery. This morning what we call 50-50 which is half hot milk, half hot water. The hot water breaks up the curds in the milk and makes it more easily digested. This noon I had the same big combinations salad and a dish of peas with salt and no butter, tonight tomato soup and celery, tomorrow breakfast 50-50 and orange juice, tomorrow noon a couple of lamb chops and an extra large salad, etc etc. We know what to do from experience.

Whether this will clear up my condition in a month's time as it did Alec's I don't know. Alec's, it seems to me, was worse than mine. His pulse was very irregular and skipped beats and wasn't too strong. Mine is strong, regular but gets rapid when I stir around and do much that calls for physical exertion. Mine is perfectly normal when I lie in bed.

Dr Gray will be home next Tuesday and Dorothy and I both think he should give me the once over and see exactly what the condition is. After I check with him I shall be able to tell the children something definite and that is why I haven't done it before.

They think, like most people, this fasting is foolish and would have a town doctor in here in a hurry. That is why Alec, Dorothy and I have kept our own council.

I know I've done the right thing but no one knows how much will power it took with plenty of food so handy. Alec trusted me and I wasn't letting him or myself down. Thank heaven it is behind me. How I look forward to every meal and lick the platter clean.

Incidentally I lost ten pounds in those seven days which Dorothy says is the best of all, as it takes the fat from around my heart—and think what all that hot water did to clear out my kidneys especially when there was nothing going in. Gave them a good rest. Then of course there were exercises I had to take night and morning lying on my bed. The strenuous ones I did gently and checked pulse before and after and there was no difference.

So that is the situation at present. Tilden would never take anyone who would not stay a month, so I shall try to lie around myself for that length of time. I don't mind a bit, even though all the nicest parties have come this week and next I think.

I have a lot I want to tell you of the Cody situation and what I went through up there with Mrs. Nielson beside me and Mrs. Bushnell opposite but that can wait until we have a chance to get in a real visit.

This is certainly a book but I knew you were concerned about me as I always am about you when you are sick, so I thought I'd tell all.

Lovingly
Edith.

P.S. I don't mind if you read this letter to Percy as long as you don't say what's the matter with me until after Wednesday when I'll talk things over with the children.

———

Early in the summer of 1949, Edith traveled to Denver to have a full physical examination and received a clean bill of health. The fact was that even then she was dying from colon cancer. Dan never trusted physicals again.

Safely back home, Edith's mind was on her eldest grandchild, Kay Bonine, who was about to enter high school. Edith invited Kay into her bedroom, sat her in the rocking chair across from the bed and read aloud the following essay, then gave it to her. Kay said that when she and her daughter, Dr. Lyn Johnson, read it again recently, they found themselves agreeing that much of the advice remains useful today.

You are about to enter High School, a different world from the one you have been living in. Here you will be a young lady and a lot will be expected of you, sometimes more than you will be able to give, because you have had no experience to handle difficult situations when they come up. It is to help you over some of these situations

Spring 1949: Ready to celebrate, Kay Bonine wore graduation white for her eighth-grade ceremonies in Miles City, Montana.

that I, who have had to learn the hard way, am writing these suggestions, hoping you will find them helpful.

One of the biggest of your difficulties will be the contacts you will make with boys of all kinds. These suggestions for handling your associations with both boys and girls, are for your four years of high school life, not only for the Freshman year. Some of the situations that I will mention may not come for a year or two yet, but if you know in advance what to do, you can handle situations when they come up and this advance knowledge will give you peace of mind.

First before we talk about the boys we should talk about you. Everybody wants to be liked by their friends, neighbors, and acquaintances. As with all things worthwhile, that has to be earned. Just remember in order to have friends you must be friendly, in order to be loved you must be lovable. Your face is what you are most often judged by. If your face is blank, without a sign of interest on it, who is going to want to know you. People will just turn away and go seek someone who shows some signs of life and interest in them. Make yourself look interested in what is going on around you. You can acquire this alert look, if you try. Notice the girls that are popular at dances. They are the ones who look alive, who look at another person as though they were really interested in them (and that can be acquired if you try. You can make yourself look interested and then later you will be surprised to find you really are.)

Personality is a word that stands for a lot, especially in popularity, and the foundation of personality is being interested in people and in what is going on about you. You may think now you don't want to be bothered, that you'll find later on when you are left out of the "things" you're dying to go to, you'll wish you had bothered.

The four years in high school are unique in your life. They stand out as a lot of carefree good times and often a place where you meet your future lifelong friends. If you don't start in with the right attitude of making yourself agreeable, easy to get acquainted with, and fun to know, those four years will be those of frustration and heartache.

I knew a girl once who was lovely to look at, had beautiful clothes and a fine home to entertain in. She did nothing to make herself inside a person worth knowing. She seemed to feel because she was lovely to look at, that was enough. At dances, especially in a town where people didn't know her, the boys flocked around her for dances, and just look at her, she was so pretty. After one dance the boys seldom came back for another, all the burden of conversation was on them.

Speaking of conversation, you do not have to be a brilliant conversationalist to get along. In fact people like you better if you will let them do the talking. All they ask of you is to be interested in what they are saying. Even if you are not, you can make yourself look that way. You can start the conversation with a question. When they finish answering it you make some comment on what they have said, or start on another topic. Don't let the conversation die with you.

Generally boys like to talk about games. A good starter for conversation with the boy you don't know very well is to ask them what kind of games he liked when he was little. Make yourself easy to talk to by helping in the conversation. It really should be a fifty-fifty proposition but of course there are some people who need only to get started on a favorite topic and all you have to do is be an interested listener.

When you go to a party, go in a party mood, all ready to have a good time. Some girls go with the attitude that they defy their hostess to interest them in anything. Who is the person not invited the next time. Be ready and glad to play the games suggested. It is rude to say, "I don't feel like that game, let's play something else." Play the game and put all you have into it! Feel when you go to a party your hostess is depending on you to help put the party over, which she is. The hostess can't do it alone.

When you're older, you will go to dinner parties. You will have a young man on your right and one on your left. You are supposed to go in with the one on your right, so you talk to him first, then after a while and when you've reached a good place in your conversation to stop, you turn and start talking with the young man on your other side.

To go back to you again. I want to emphasize good grooming as a valuable asset. Have your hair neat and becoming at all times. Your nails clean, your dress without spots and be careful to take enough baths and use a deodorant so you will never have the least hint of a body odor. Be what someone called, "lettuce fresh." Use an antiseptic mouthwash if your breath is bad.

Be careful in your conversation not to brag. No one likes to listen to that. When anyone asks how much something you have cost, and you don't want to tell her, just answer, "plenty" and change the subject. Don't talk about money or dwell on your health or the state of your feelings. Few people are interested.

Be on time. Don't make people wait for you. It shows you are a selfish person and very careless with other people's time, if you're constantly making them wait for you.

Later on in your life, in a city you may have a date to go to the theater or some public place. You go in first, except when going to your seat. He precedes you and hands the seat checks to the usher. The man follows in a restaurant, you precede. About ordering your meal. If you feel your escort has plenty of money with him and he asks you what you want and you know what you want, you tell him and he gives both yours and his order to the waiter. If you don't know how much money he can afford, ask him to suggest something for you, or wait until he makes up his mind and then say that's what you'd like too.

Should you take some friends out to lunch in a restaurant you will have to leave a tip and that should be reckoned as 10% of your bill. If your bill is small, say $2.20, $.20 would be a bit small so make it $.25 or $.30. If you happen to be left to tip the porter who brings up the bags in a hotel room, give him a quarter.

Now about introductions. Remember to always present the boy to the girl, or the younger person to an older and don't forget to smile when you say to the person who is being introduced to you, "I am very glad to know you," and say it as though you really meant it. The style of shaking hands when you are introduced changes every now and then. If you see the person is about to shake hands you put out your hand too, but if they don't, you don't.

When a date takes you to a movie go into the lobby of the theater to wait for him but be where you can see him and make it easy for him to find you when he has the tickets. This goes the same when you are in a city at a theater.

After a boy takes you on a date, when you get home, say simply and directly how much you enjoyed it and you hope you can have some more good times together, then leave the rest up to the boy. But during the evening show him you are having a good time by acting so.

Never make up your face in public. Never chew gum in public or out on a date.

It isn't wise to go about much with boys a lot older than you are. Their ideas are different, you are expected to know more than you do, and in the long run it does not work out well.

Now about the big event in high school, the "prom" or any formal dance! 1st place, First place, the corsage. Be sure you thank the boy enthusiastically for it. It has cost him a lot and he has probably sacrificed something he really wanted to get it for you and you should be duly appreciative.

I will never forget one time I happened to be at the home of a friend when her daughter was about to go to her first prom. Her date arrived, with a broad smile, he handed her the corsage. She barely thanked him (how his smile disappeared) and rushed into the bedroom to pin it on. When she came out she had her coat over her shoulders and said in a matter-of-fact way, "Come on, let's go." I never wanted to shake a girl until her teeth rattled, as I did that girl. I thought to myself, if I were that boy I'd never give her another thing if I lived to be a hundred– and that was her first corsage. But you see she didn't know how to act and was afraid of doing the wrong thing, which she certainly did.

In dressing for a dance be sure the back of your hair is pleasing. Most people do not realize at a dance your back is the most in evidence. One evening I saw a girl be

318   An Improbable Pioneer

unusually popular because she had a band of fresh flowers across the back of her head and she had a very tricky bow with long streamers, in bright color on a pale pink dress. That bright color attracted the onlookers' eyes as she danced and the boys standing in the doorway noticed her and asked for dances, when ordinarily they never would have noticed her.

Never walk across the ballroom floor alone. Either go with your partner or if not him get another girl or don't go.

Be sure you never, never, never chew gum at a dance. No matter how lovely you look, you look cheap and common chewing gum in a formal. Loud talk and loud laughter are out of place in a public place.

If some boy cuts in on a dance, say some pleasant remark to your partner who is leaving you, and give a friendly greeting to the cutter in. At the end of the dance, smile at your partner and say something like, "I enjoyed that so much."

At a dance and at all times be sincere, kind, courteous and enthusiastic when enthusiasm is looked for. As for instance when a boy gives you a corsage, say how pretty it is, and really mean it. Ask his advice about where you should pin it on, and show you appreciate his giving it to you.

All through life you will meet problems you do not know how to handle. Just remember your mother is your best friend and shall stand behind you through thick and thin. Your father too. But sometimes your mother isn't around when you have to make a decision. In that case just run through your Girl Scout Laws in your mind and some one of those will tell you what is the right thing to do.

To end this chat with you, I would like to leave this thought in your mind. Try to be the kind of girl, the kind of boy you'll like to marry, would be attracted to, and you come out all right.

Sincerely,
Edith S. Healy

———

In December, Edith returned to Denver for more medical tests. Lorraine Healy, Alec, Jr.'s wife, went with her. The following Christmas letter was sent to Lorraine's parents in Burlington, Vermont.

> **Worland, Wyo.**
> **Dec 17, 1949**
>
> **My dear Cooney Family,–**
>   **I am sure you will be glad to see such a good picture of your daughter and her family.**
>   **How are you these days –**
>   **We are getting ready to go to South Africa Jan. 12.**
>   **Lorraine was with me when I was checking with the Doctor in Denver and I don't know what I would have done without her. She was a pillar of strength to lean on when I didn't know what was wrong with me and naturally feared the worst.**
>
> **Merry Xmas to you and a Happy New Year**
> **From The Healy Family**
>
> ─────

The doctors didn't mince words. Edith had five to six months to live. She and Alec canceled their African exploration and began to investigate alternative treatments. While they made plans, Edith continued to write. Her letters are about what it might mean to die, why she set up her will as she did, and her hopes that she would recover. A woman that the Healys knew in Basin, a town about thirty miles north, had a friend who had had alternative cancer treatments at a clinic in the Los Angeles area. Alec began making arrangements to take Edith there.

Edith read this undated essay to her children and their spouses before she left for California. As my Aunt Eileen was nearing her own death in 2010, she talked with me about her mother's view of life after death—she particularly remembered the dragonfly story—and Eileen said this gave her courage.

Edith's Thoughts on Dying

I have had you come down here so we could talk over the subject of death, which is uppermost in our minds just now. No one who has died has ever come back to tell us what sort of a place our spirit goes to when we die, so naturally we wonder.

Death is always accompanied by people feeling badly and crying. They are crying and feeling badly for themselves. How they will miss the person that is gone. They don't feel badly for the person who has gone because how do they know but what that person is better off than they were here with us. They just don't know.

This is the way it could be. I don't say it is, but it could be.

I am going to tell you a story I read not long ago that made me feel much better about death. The story spoke of a beautiful valley where there was a deep pond. In this pond there were hundreds of little grubs swimming around. Grubbs live under the water, they don't even come up to breathe. All these grubs were swimming around having a fine time when a few of them got together and were talking things over. They said, "Have you noticed every now and then one of us climbs up on a reed, and finally disappears and never comes back. Let us make a pledge that the next one that climbs up on a reed be sure and come back and tell us what it's like up there."

So they all took a solemn vow they would do that very thing. One day they discovered one of their number was missing and they said to each other "Now we're going to know what it is like up there for he took the vow to come back and tell us."

They waited and waited and waited, and he didn't come back. They just couldn't understand it because he had always been so good and always kept his promises.

One day this little grub who is telling the story felt the urge to climb up the reed. He had always wanted to break through the top of the water but his spirit had never been strong enough. This time it was different. He felt a big urge or a feeling of great strength and as he climbed higher and higher he got stronger and stronger and he went right through the top of the water. As he did so his spirit came out of his body, which floated back down under the water, and he was surprised to find he had wings. He was a dragonfly! (You can see them any time over the water.) With these wings he could fly anywhere he wanted to. The sky was blue with big white fleecy clouds, the breezes soft, the flowers pretty colors. Such a beautiful place to be. How happy he was.

Then he thought of the promise he had made to go back and tell the others how lovely it was up here. When he tried to go down under the water he couldn't on account of his wings. The other dragonflies came and they said how badly they had wanted to go back and how dreadfully they had felt they couldn't keep their promise that it just could not be done. That if only their parents and friends could know how beautiful it was in this other life they wouldn't grieve for them anymore.

So that is the way we should think about death. As the release of the spirit into a happy place. Our friends who have died have just gone ahead of us and will be waiting for us when it is our turn to go.

––––

In between comforting her family and reassuring herself, Edith hurried to get the final details of her life in order, including the money that she had inherited and invested. Edith wrote on the envelope of this letter, "To Be Opened After My Death."

ESH
920 Culbertson Avenue
Worland, Wyoming
Feb. 23, 1950

Dear Boys and Girls, Daughters-in-law and Sons-in-law, –
This is to suggest that you do not tell your children of the contents of this will, until they have to be told. Most children know they are to get what their parents have on their death, but this making it sure might destroy their initiative to make their own way.

The part in the will about re-marriage doesn't mean I
don't want you to re-marry. I do. In the case of the girls the
new husband would want to support you, and in the case of the
boys they would want to support the new wife. This is to protect
the children. Suppose you re-married and died soon after, the
children would be dependent on a step-mother or step-father
which I have seen happen, and the children came out with
practically nothing. So this is just to protect the children.

Father and I have put lots of time ad thought on both wills
and hope we have done them satisfactorily to you all—at least
you will know we tried.

Lovingly
Mother –

————

In late February, Dr. Lial Anderson, a Worland physician, asked a surgeon to come up from Denver to operate on Edith. "The surgeon said
after he opened her up, that the cancer was so widespread he couldn't
do her any good," remembered Helen. Dorothy Dent nursed her back
to some strength to make the journey to the Los Angeles clinic. They
drove there, arriving in late March.

My Grandmother Healy was still in the hospital when I saw her
for the last time. I remember her long, white hair combed up and off
her face, as usual, but her skin was as white as the sheets and blue veins
showed in her hands. She was so thin, so delicate, so quiet, not sitting
up even, not like my usual busy grandmother. I was only in the second
grade and I don't remember feeling anything, but I already was grieving. Only a couple weeks before, my Grandmother Omenson, who
had helped raise me during the war,[131] had died suddenly from a heart
attack. She was buried on Valentine's Day.

So while I last visited my Grandmother Healy, I didn't realize
this would be our final time together when I kissed her good-bye on

the cheek. My parents were extremely protective about what children should know. And I was excited about the trip Mother, Dad, my brother, Mike, 3, and I were taking to Mexico. I was about to have my own tropical adventure.

In September 2011, I was researching the family archives at the LU Ranch office. I was sitting at the desk I claim when at home and my brother Mike was at his when I came across a thin unopened airmail envelope addressed with Edith's now familiar writing. I carefully slit the envelope. "Look at this," I called over to Mike and handed the letter to him with my heart racing. I didn't know that Edith had ever written to me or to Mike. The letter was postmarked from the Beverly Wilshire in Los Angeles to the Hotel Reforma in Mexico City after her arrival for treatment. The letter had been forwarded a number of times before reaching Worland.

I suspect when the letter arrived at home, Edith already had died and my parents felt too sad to open it. The right time just never came.

In these next letters, Edith sends hope and humor, and takes care of business, all with that same infectious zest and love that she showed in her honeymoon letters.

Beverly Wilshire
Beverly Hills, California
Crestview 5-4282
Friday afternoon
March 24, [19]50

My dear Martha & Dan and Cathy and Mike–
We keep wondering where you are which brings forth many guesses. We hope you are having a good time and know you are.
Now about us.
Lorraine was able to get Kimmey, the Japanese girl that

worked for her at one time, and she was delirious with joy. (she, Lorraine). Lorraine realized Kim was pretty young to leave but Max[132] was going to keep an eye on her and any sickness question she and Kim couldn't answer they would ask Dorothy Dent. The children are crazy about her as she plays games with them, etc. Lorraine said when she came Monday night they made as big a fuss over her as they do about Alec and her when they return from a trip.

We started out Tuesday morning. Went from Lander over South Pass between high banks of snow that had just been cleared by snowplows. Cut off 100 miles that way but was slow going. Got to Evanston the first night. Cedar City, Utah on the second night. Barstow last night and here about 1 o'clock.

I sat or laid down on the back seat most of the way and was really very comfortable. I am surprised how well I stood the trip.

This morning at Barstow the office called and said the newspaper boy's car had rolled down the hill and banged into our car. He had put on the break but it was not in gear. We had our car parked, as lots of the guests did, on the curving driveway! Its stove in the back left door very badly and jammed the front door, so neither would open.

It was a Mexican boy, scared to death, his car and he with a wife and two babies. No insurance.

Lorraine said Father was wonderful. Did not lose his temper and was so nice to the tearful boy. I guess Father admired his honesty, as I did, for going in and telling it was he who had done it.

The only rooms we could get today here are those in a suite. We have to take them just for today until something else is vacated. Martha, you can imagine how Lorraine and I are eating this up. A beautiful sitting room, radio, etc. Beautiful suite! I feel like a movie star.

At noon at lunch today a woman took off her coat and revealed a strapless gown. Very low in front. And this at noon. Father said he was ashamed to look, but just the same I think he got a kick out of it. He said under his breath, "city of crazy acting people."

As tomorrow is Saturday and generally a half day with most people ,I won't look up the doctor until Monday. I feel good. Better than when I left home.

Love,
Mother

———

The next set of letters were sent to Edith's nephew, Holden, and his wife, Elizabeth,[133] to their home in Glen Mills, Pennsylvania, on the outskirts of Philadelphia, where he commuted into the city to teach his classes at the University of Pennsylvania. On the back of the envelope from this April 8 letter, Alec had written the address of the medical facility—734 S. Sycamore Ave. in Los Angeles—and his phone number in Worland—Tel: Wyoming 9803. Even today, when Wyoming is the most sparsely populated state in the country, it is astonishing that Wyoming residents had a four-digit, statewide, long-distance telephone number. In 1950, there were 290,529 people in the state and most, apparently, never had made a long distance call.

April 8, 1950

Dear Holden & Elizabeth, -
    Alec just brought the papers to sign and your letter, over to me tonight. I am staying in a sort of nursing home where I can get the diet required and care, when Alec goes back to Worland for the shearing. He will not be here the weekend of the 22nd. He won't get back here until about May 15th. Will that be too late for you.
    I hope not.
    I am enjoying being out here and I am well taken care of. I take a walk every morning and afternoon and love the balmy air of Southern California.
    My best to Elizabeth and to you.

Sweethearts: Edith and Alec found ways to laugh
as life slipped away.

Lovingly
Aunt Edith
I hope you can come when Alec is here but if it is not possible
come at a time that suits you best.

Reports Meritious Bank of Jacksonville instead of St. Pete.
You or the bank can correct this error. AH

———

The next day, before Alec mailed her note, Edith received a letter from Holden and Elizabeth. She immediately wrote a response and included it in the envelope, along with a photo of Edith and Alec clowning around.

734 S. Sycamore Ave.
Los Angeles Cal
April 9th 1950

My dear Holden & Elizabeth, -
Such a pleasant surprise to receive from you an Easter Greeting.
Thanks so much!
It rained all night and so disappointed the 30,000 people who were planning a sunrise service attendance at the Hollywood Bowl.
Now the sun is shining so all the ladies and girls can wear their Easter hats to church.
Just a word of warning Holden before you see me. I look like "something the cat dragged in." – It always surprises me to look in the mirror and see my face when I feel real good inside. I am asked not to use any makeup. So many of them have lanolin as their base and that is from sheep. I am not to have any animal fat in any form. I find I can have some cosmetics put up by a Chicago firm, so I am sending for some. I hope they include rouge and lipstick to help my morale when I look in the mirror.

I hope for your sake they get here before you come.

Alec Jr[134] and Lorraine drove with us, Alex, Jr doing most of the driving. They put me on the back seat with a pillow and a car robe so I could either sit or lie down. We took 4 1/2 days to it, so I didn't get over tired.

Another thing I only weigh 104 after having weighed around 135 for years this is quite a change. Alec and Lorraine stayed awhile, going home by plane. They were gone from home just two weeks.

About the same time Dan, Martha and children took off for Mexico. Drove to Denver, then decided to fly to Mexico City. After being there a few days they hired a car and driver and went to Acapulco, stopping at Cuernavaca and Taxco on the way. They relaxed and rested on the Acapulco beaches, then flew home. They were only gone 2 1/2 weeks, and my, they saw a lot.

They were both very tired and needed a rest and change. Martha's mother died after only four days of serious illness, an awful shock to Martha.

Am looking forward to seeing you Holden. Only sorry I am so far away.

Lovingly
Aunt Edith

———

Edith's April 11 letter to Holden and Elizabeth included a clipping (no date) from the Northern Wyoming *Daily News* in Worland, announcing that Edith had been nominated for the 1950 Wyoming's Distinguished Service Award by the Business and Professional Women's Club (see Appendix B).

734 S. Sycamore Ave
Los Angeles
California
April 11, 1950

Dear Holden and Elizabeth, -
    Just a hasty line to tell you Alec got your letter. By this
time you got mine telling you he would be back by May 15th.
So if you could make it the weekend of May 16th that would be
swell. There will be quite a few things to talk over about Beaver
Block[135] I imagine in case you are gone a long time.
    Shall be so glad to see you.

Affectionately
Aunt Edith.

———

734 S. Sycamore Ave.
Los Angeles Cal.
April 27, 1950

My dear Cornelia, –
    Thanks so much for your letter about your trip. It was
especially interesting because we had just come over that
route.
    The first report came from the doctor a few days ago. I
mean a blood check up after three weeks of treatment. He said
I was responding to it and wrote on my chart "improving" which
made me happy, as you can imagine.
    I don't know whether I told you that the vaginal condition
I had badly when I arrived and have had for some time. This
doctor cured me in 2 1/2 weeks, which gave me confidence in
him as a doctor.
    Rowena said a friend of hers had it for four years and
Mrs. Hamilton in whose house I stay, had it for two years, a long
time ago.
    Another thing. Last week Ollie Webster, Bud Webster's
brother in Cody, came. He has had a cold for four months and

coughed badly the whole four months. He's only been here a week, his cough is gone and he said he couldn't imagine anyone getting such quick relief as he had. The doctor pronounced it asthma and gave him treatments and put him on a strict diet.

Poor man has spinal arthritis which is really why he came I guess. He hadn't heard from the x-rays yet. That is bad medicine. Wasn't that what Will Metz had? I remember your telling me what a serious operation he had.

These two things make me feel the doctor knows what he is doing, so I am hoping for the best along the other line of disease.

I saw Rowena twice. The last time I sure laid her out much to the amusement of her sister and Alec. She said she needed someone to talk to her like that. (I'm a good one to talk). She and Alice had come to California to see an old aunt, 87 years old. Jerry had taken one week of his three weeks yearly vacation, as he was tired from a convention just held in Tulsa.

Well it isn't so long since Rowena was in a hospital in Chicago and what does she do. Chase from one end of California to the other. On Jerry's arrival they, with Lois who had a vacation, drive down to Mexico, then back here. The morning they were here, Rowena said they were taking him to La Brea pits, to Hollywood Bowl, to the Rose Bowl up the mountain to Griffith Observatory, etc. etc. etc.

I said that day when I was giving her the talk that's a fine vacation for a tired man. What you should have done was go to a good beach hotel with a pool (ocean too cold now). Let him put on shorts and sit around the pool and bask in the sun and take it easy. As for you, why didn't you go see the aunts and then concentrate on one of two other places or people you wanted to see, and stay there.

This chasing down into Mexico then up to San Francisco and back again to Los Angeles. What has it got you but tired nerves.

She had confessed to me she was never so tired in her life. And it seems so silly to me, when she needs to build up reserve, instead of exhausting it.

Talked to her last summer. Told her to take Jerry up to

Paint Rock Lakes and both of them rest. What did they do but go up to Canada or somewhere. If I keep on trying maybe I'll make an impression sometime if nature doesn't slap her down with a great big slap.

Say she was in La Jolla when the Aldriches were, at the same hotel. That evening Helen Phelps breezed in and sat with them all at dinner. Next day, Mrs. Aldrich told me Helen Phelps came into the hotel and went up to Mrs. Aldrich and said, "How does she do it?" Rowena I mean. How does she get two such good looking men. What has she got that I haven't got:

Mrs. Aldrich said she nearly died laughing inside. I said, "Too bad you didn't answer her and say, "Plenty." Isn't that rich. What a good opinion some people have of themselves.

My nephew Holden flew out from Philadelphia to see me last week. He was here three days. He is going to Europe in June and may be an exchange professor to India. He is in line for it. If so he won't come back to this county in September but go from Paris to India which means he would be gone at least a year from September.

Alec left for home the same day he left.

A special delivery letter Sunday from him telling of his safe arrival and in ending said, "I think my visit with you both was just perfect." Which made me glad.

I am glad of the good reports of Louise. I knew with her good common sense, her sense of values and her standing with her two feet planted firmly on the ground, it wouldn't take her as long as most, to find herself.

Alec was feeling fine when he left for home. He always gets so tired at shearing time. I am glad he had plenty of reserve to call on.

Martha wrote that Dan was driving a sheepwagon up to the L.U. so Alec could sleep right at the pens and not have to go back and forth to Worland as he has been doing. A 60-mile ride.

Rowena wrote that a letter from Katherine Meloney told about Jay Walker. A person never knows where trouble is going to hit next. I'm so sorry for Olive and Doc. Parents take things happening to their children even harder than the children do.

My hair is all falling out. Really it's awful! I hope I shan't be entirely bald. Wouldn't that be something.

I am certainly very fortunate to be here. Mrs. Hamilton is so jolly and pleasant. Nothing is too much trouble to do for me. Even washes out my underclothes and night gowns so have fresh ones every day. Clean sheets and pillow cases on the bed each day too. Have been having corn on the cob from Imperial Valley, artichokes, egg plant, zucchini, beet greens, fresh strawberries and pineapple. She's a good cook and makes things attractive.

Will you send this letter to Maureen. I'll write her soon.

Love, Edith
Best to Percy, Adleen and Fred.

———

May 26, 1950
734 S. Sycamore Ave.
Los Angeles Cal
May 26, 1950

Dear Cornelia, –

What a fine write up that was in the Cody paper!

The picture looked like him only I never saw him with that very judicial expression on. But then after all I have never been sentenced by him to life imprisonment, so how do I know but what he can look like that. But I am glad he doesn't look at me like that.

I'm getting letters from P.E.O's in Worland still saying what a wonderful party you had.

I had some good news the other day. The doctor told Alec when he got here, that in a month from then (May 15th) I could go home for a month! He said by that time I would need a month's rest from the treatments. He never said a truer thing.

Dan called me up the other night and said, "Are you gaining strength every day like you did here? " and I said "No" —"Are you gaining weight?" and I said "No." Well then why don't you come home, and how do you know you are getting along all right." I said "Because the doctor says so and he knows from the blood count I have taken every Monday. "

Well, I got to thinking, no one knows at home what is going on down here with me, and its time they knew why I don't gain in weight and strength. So I sat me down and wrote a long letter telling it in all details. Took up nine sheets of typewritten paper on both sides. It is to go to Alec Jr, Dan, Eileen, Helen, Dorothy Dent, you and Maureen and Doc Gray. I don't mind if you read it to Helen Brome and Adleen and Fred after you've read it to Percy. I know they are interested.

I had thought of including Kitty but I am not sure how much discretion she has about telling others and as I went into such detail and it so so personal, I'd rather not have it broadcasted.

Rowena went through a clinic in Tulsa. They told her nothing organically wrong. Just nerves—which must have been a relief to her.

Our Martha is to have another baby[136] I am so glad. They are making fine parents for a family. The first store I've been into since I came was last week when Mrs. Hamilton drove me to the Page Boy Shop and I got some lovely maternity clothes for Martha. Three dresses and a sort of box like jacket in white pique, she can wear with two of them. The third has a jacket. They were darling and how I enjoyed buying them. One of those deluxe California stores. Flower and plants everywhere in it. So artistic.

Yesterday was the first time we've seen the sun for a month. Sunny California, my eye!

Alec flew out on Saturday, getting in late, to be with me Sunday for Mother's Day. I was watching for him out the window in the morning Sunday. Here he came in a new suit, with a cellophane box containing an orchid under his arm. "Gay Lochinvar come out of the West."[137]

Well my dear I hope all is well with you and I'll see you before long. Won't that be fine.

Lovingly,
E

I am just about bald. These temperatures I get twice a week make my hair come out in big handfuls. I have only a few wisps left.

———

Edith died in Los Angeles on June 17, 1950; Alec was with her. As soon as he telephoned their children, they left for Los Angeles to help. Alec, Jr., Dan, and Eileen flew from Worland, and Helen and Buren flew from Miles City, Montana. Once there, they moved quickly.

Dan and Buren drove the car back to Worland, a journey of about twelve hundred miles before there were interstate highways. Eileen and Helen took the plane back to Worland with their father, while Alec, Jr., brought his mother's coffin home by train. Jim Horn, Lorraine, and Martha greeted each arrival.

Crowds filled the Worland Methodist Church for the funeral in the largest house of worship in town. Edith was buried in her Girl Scout leader's suit, next to the plot with her granddaughter, Melinda.

To eastern eyes, Worland's Riverside Cemetery must have looked barren with irrigated lawn and some fairly young trees. Alec and Edith had four Engelmann spruces brought down from the LU Ranch and planted so as to mark the edges of the central family plot, before buying nearby lots in case more plots were needed. Bonines and Horns are buried there.

The spruce at the southwest corner died, but the others tower now, their dense branches creating a small, deeply shaded glen that is very different from the rest of the cemetery. The Healys' protective spruces echo the multitude of trees in the Evergreen Cemetery in Portland, Maine, where Edith's parents, grandparents, some of her great-grandparents, and many family members are buried. Evergreen

Cemetery is a huge, 239-acre parkland, established in 1854 with "winding carriage paths, ponds, footbridges, gardens, chapel, funerary art and sculpture . . . [and] extensive wooded wetlands," according to City of Portland information.

No wonder Edith thrived in the Big Horn Mountains with the beauty of wildflowers, grasses, lodgepole pine, spruce, fir, and aspen. These mountains are now a 1.1 million acre national forest. No wonder Edith and Alec spent many summer days in their log cabin in the Big Horns, and no wonder that when the end still seemed far off, Alec made sure that Edith would always be sheltered by evergreens and a sense of home.

Today, Edith and Alec's children and their spouses lie in the family plots, with the exception of Helen Healy Bonine, who remains healthy and lives in Powell near one of her grandsons and his family. Helen's gravestone is carved and waiting next to her husband's, Buren Bonine.

Two grave spaces remain under the evergreens.

"With You Always"

Sometime soon thereafter or perhaps much later, Alec read Edith's final letter to him. It lay in the archives, opened, carefully re-inserted into the envelope, and saved.

Father

To be opened after my death

E.S.H. Worland, Wyo. Jan 8, 1946
    Sweetheart, - We have had a wonderful life together haven't we. No one could have had a finer husband than you have been and I do appreciate everything you have done. I've had a glorious and interesting life and enjoyed it to the utmost.
    When you get lonesome talk things over with me, either out loud or in your mind, as we always used to talk things over, together. I am sure it would help. No one has ever come back from "the hereafter" so it is all a mystery but if a spirit can be near a mortal, I'll be near you and listening when you talk things over with me.
    Don't grieve too much for me. When you feel that way do something nice for one of the children and grandchildren and that will take your mind along a different channel, and I know it will help.

My love is with you always, Edith.

When Alec adjusted the brim of his hat and smiled for the camera, he was a happily married 68-year-old looking forward to wintering in the in the summer warmth of South Africa. A year later, still energetic, still attractive, he was a widower.

CHAPTER 19

ALEC'S LIFE CONTINUES

Edith recognized that Alec was the sort of man who needed a wife. Several times before she died they talked about him remarrying, as he later told Cornelia Metz. He confessed to being very lonely and sheepishly admitted to feeling like an old goat. By then he had proposed to his high school sweetheart, a widow who lived in Salt Lake City.

When Alec showed up at the doorstep of Verna Harris's home at 98 U Street carrying a bouquet of flowers, he was a recent widower, however, his worry and grief were not newly felt. By the fall of 1950, Edith was sick and Alec had cared for her for nearly two years before she passed away.

Edith had urged her sixty-nine-year-old husband to live and for Alec, going back home to find a bride made good sense. As two among the thirty-two seniors about to graduate in the Ogden High School Class of 1899, he and Virginia May (Verna) Barrows had planned to marry. Verna's granddaughter, Terrell Harris Dougan, said that the young couple got into an argument their senior year, and Verna ended both the argument and the engagement by throwing her engagement ring at Alec.

Verna became a lifelong teacher. An early photo shows an attractive brunette with an exceedingly narrow waist, serious brown eyes, and a shy smile. She worshiped words, loved flowers and nature walks, and despised wasting money and time.

Joel Harris entered Verna's life as a teacher at Ogden High School in Verna's senior year. Joel soon became a principal in the Ogden schools. They married in 1905. Eventually Joel, Verna, and their two sons, Robert and Richmond Terrell moved to Salt Lake City where Joel received his master's degree in Science from the University of Utah.

VERNA

Verna Barrows, above, and her husband, Joel Harris. Both were English teachers who became school principals. Right: Verna when Alec re-entered her life, reading to her granddaughter, Irene.

All along, Joel continued to be a principal and Verna a teacher and then a principal, too. By the time Joel died in 1945, the couple had shared more than forty years as educators. They also shared a philosophy about living frugally and a passion for knowledge. Verna pasted a poem into her scrapbook that ended with "Thoughts rule the world."[138]

Robert Harris, called Bob, went off to sea and eventually moved his wife, Meryl, and daughter, Robin, to Washington DC.

Richmond Terrell Harris, called Dick, stayed in Salt Lake City. He founded a successful advertising agency and had two daughters, Terrell and Irene, who still live in Salt Lake City. Terrell told their story in *That Went Well: Adventures in Caring for My Sister*.[139]

When Alec entered Verna's life again, Terrell remembers that "their romance rocked the walls with gales of giggles." In a few months, Terrell, 12, was Verna's bridesmaid at the wedding at the Little Church of the West in Las Vegas.

I remember when Grandfather telephoned from Las Vegas to tell my father and mother the news. There was dismayed silence at the stiff announcement from my father that "your Grandfather has gotten married." My parents' distress had the same feeling as attending a funeral. My mother said then and repeated many times over the years that she had observed that a man who truly loved his wife often remarried quickly because he couldn't imagine living without her.

If Alec and Verna had married when they were young, it would have seemed a perfect selection. Verna was someone from his town, from his life, from his culture. Edith was the unexpected choice; someone bringing a different energy and worldliness than Verna and entering wholeheartedly into Alec's ranching interests and Wyoming life. Alec was an introvert who by following in the slipstream of an extroverted woman did new things and met new people. When Verna married Joel, she found a helpmate whose values and interest in teaching matched her own. The old friends were devoted to each other, but Verna's and Alec's worlds had become quite different. "They got on big time," said Terrell, "until they didn't."

Alec was most enthusiastic in his last few decades using the expertise he had gathered over a lifetime to help people who borrowed money from his livestock loan bank save their farms or ranches and make their properties a success. He liked working with livestock. A curious man, he enjoyed spending his time keeping up on financial news and politics.

Verna wasn't at all interested in livestock and while she liked the idea of travel, she had never left the country. A honeymoon cruise to Hawaii when it was still a U.S. territory thrilled her, but there were no foreign journeys in her future. She was a city homebody who never felt at home in a small town like Worland. A voracious reader and wordsmith, she missed her Ladies' Literary Club and Neighborly Circle.

Alec and Verna spent most of their time in Salt Lake City. This wasn't a problem for Alec, because he had turned over daily management of the LU Ranch to Dan. Contentment, however, eluded Alec and Verna. Verna developed chronic pain that proved impossible to diagnose and required continual medication. Verna died July 14, 1955, at 74. She was buried in the immense Salt Lake City cemetery next to Joel J. Harris.

Alec returned to Worland, worn out.

The Worland home in Edith's name had been left to their daughters, Eileen and Helen. A few weeks after Alec's return to Worland, they sold it for him. All four children and their spouses gathered to divide the belongings according to Edith's instructions. Years later, my dad still remembered the sadness: "Closing down a home is one of the hardest things you'll ever do," he would say.

After his home was sold, Alec divided his time between the houses of his sons in Worland, interspersed with long trips to see friends, especially during the winter months when he enjoyed southern California. He spent three months with Alec, Jr., and Lorraine and their three children and three months with my parents and we three kids.

Alec, Jr.'s only surviving child, Tim, still remembers how much they looked forward to Grandfather's living with them and the funny things they would do to make Alec laugh—they loved to hear him laugh. We loved to hear him laugh, too—he was so serious. Debbie, a toddler then and his youngest grandchild, won his heart with her mispronunciations of words like *spaghetti.*

In January 1958, Alec flew to Seattle to see an old girlfriend, also from Ogden. This time he told his children and this time his children had a different reaction. Helen remembers how pleased she and Buren were. "He needed someone," she said.

Alec's plan that winter was to spend a few more days in Seattle, then fly down to San Francisco to see Terrell, a freshman at Stanford. Instead, as midnight approached marking the end of his seventy-seventh birthday, Alec had a heart attack in his hotel room and died. The hotel called Alec, Jr., very early the next morning, and he woke his brother and sisters with the news.

Three days later, the Northern Wyoming *Daily News* carried Alec's obituary on page one. In the afternoon of January 15, 1958, after a small service officiated by an Episcopal minister at Veile Mortuary in Worland, Alec was buried at Riverside Cemetery.

It was a Wednesday, and I was dismissed for the funeral from Washakie County High School where I was a sophomore. I remember it was a clear day. The sky was the pale blue we see in Wyoming on frigid, sunny days when twilight is less than two hours away. I remember patches of snow blown by the wind, the frozen brown grass crunching underfoot, and the clods of dirt piled on the north side of the grave, jackhammered out of the three-foot permafrost the night before. I huddled next to Tim, twenty-three months younger and an eighth grader at Worland Junior High. I remember the pallbearers lowering our grandfather's coffin into the icy dark hole.

For decades I arranged my vacations so that I could visit the cemetery with my mother and father and sometimes Debbie and Mike to bring fresh lilacs and irises from our yard to the graves on Memorial Day, a time of year when lawns are greening up and the flowers beginning to blossom. Some years later I visited the cemetery with my mother, sister, and brother on Memorial Day, and now, I visit occasionally—sometimes, like last year, on Memorial Day, but never in the winter.

Always when I visit, I think about how Alec and Edith are again side by side, under the spruces. Each has a simple headstone of granite brought down from the Big Horns. Tall, taciturn, and loving, Alec lies on Edith's sunny side.

Alexander Healy   Edith Sampson Healy
1881 – 1957   1879 – 1950

Touchstones: This Victorian chair from the Harmons probably belonged to Edith's grandparents, James and Harriet, and her great-grandparents before. The trunk was one of five that Edith's Great-Uncle George R. Sampson brought home from Shanghai filled with silks for his Boston fianceé in 1836. Alec's surveyor equipment cost $8,100 in today's money—far more than he paid for his honeymoon trip. Credit: Dave Huber

Acknowledgments

This is the next morning and I am sitting under a cottonwood tree on the bank of Clear Creek, which is rushing by me, and straight in front of me are the most wonderful mountains, all snow-capped. I haven't gotten over the surprise in their beauty yet . . . Imagine what it will be to be up among them this summer.

– Edith, April 26, 1911

My grandmother was nurtured by the frontier generosity of the people of Wyoming to grow into her best self. She resonated to the beauty of Wyoming and its can-do approach to life. The people of Wyoming figure any problem can be solved by gathering together a few folks and giving it their attention.

Likewise for me, Edith's namesake, the Wyoming embrace made all the difference for *An Improbable Pioneer*. In the final days of editing, friends and acquaintances from Worland, like Wayne Voss, whose sister was a classmate, Mike Bies, and John Davis, dropped what they were doing to analyze facts and nuances to assure this book's accuracy. It may take a village to raise a child, but this book took a *Gone with the Wind*-sized cast that worked hard, unselfishly, and lovingly to make *An Improbable Pioneer* a reality we can all be proud of. Any errors are, of course, sadly mine alone.

I have a world of thanks, but my first must go to Elizabeth Holden, who saved her daughters letters. After her mother's death in 1916, Edith preserved the letters. After Edith's death in 1950, two of her children, Dan Healy, my father, and Helen Healy Bonine, my aunt, chose the letters as part of their inheritance during the round-robin distribution method Edith arranged.

I never paid much attention to the letters—they were hard to read and I was busy building a writing career and squeezing in vacation time to explore the world and come home to Worland. Twenty-one years ago, when I was home from my job in Washington DC, my father and I decided to make it our project to type the letters so they could be more easily read by future generations. Family history had become urgent. My father had terminal bone marrow cancer. Aunt Helen, who also lived in Worland, brought her letters from 1911 over so we could have the full collection. Our letter project changed from a convenience for others to a jumping off point for my father's reminiscences. For a week he read and recollected and explained, and I typed. We couldn't have spent a more satisfying time together.[140]

Dad and I thought that someday I would clean up the typos and put a booklet together with plastic spiral binding for the extended family. With my retirement, *someday* arrived along with easier access to superior print-on-demand technology and significant advances in self-publishing and distribution. I decided the time was right for a published book that told Edith's story through her letters.

By good fortune, this decision coincided with the ascension of the Washakie Museum and Cultural Center in Worland, Wyoming.[141] The museum moved into an extraordinary multimillion dollar complex and expanded its exhibits and outreach under the leadership of Cheryl Reichelt, executive director. A natural development for the museum is to create its own imprint as a publisher. I am proud that *An Improbable Pioneer* is this imprint's first book and pleased about the museum's plans to launch the book with a special collections exhibit as one example of what people can do with their family achieves. It was Cheryl's idea to create a traveling mini-exhibit to go with the book. Cheryl and her staff—Leah Stabenow, Robyn Goforth, Bob Stottler, Cheri Shelp, Sherryl Ferguson,

Brian Bower, Dalene Hill, and Loren Martinez—are making this happen in an intelligent, accurate, and gifted way.

Family Gifts

At heart, *An Improbable Pioneer* is a love story with Edith and Alec Healy's honeymoon months at its core. But the story of Edith and Alec is also the life and times of two adventurous spirits. I wanted that fuller story of Edith and Alec's life together to be told. The essays, letters, and photographs resurrected and contributed by Aunt Helen, six of nine surviving grandchildren, some of their children, second-cousins once removed, and a step-cousin form a substantial portion of this part of the story. Individually and together, Healy descendants researched outside sources, located and contacted experts, and talked together to compare stories and memories.

These conversations were not always easy. At times, we were reviving connections and memories that had lain dormant for many years. In every family, descendants tell different versions of the classic narratives from their mutual histories, and these differences sometimes harbor unresolved tensions. When one of the descendants decides to write a family history, these feelings get stirred up.[142] I thank my extended Healy family for continuing to help from beginning to end. My heartfelt thanks goes to Edith and Alec Healy's daughter, Helen Healy Bonine; and their surviving grandchildren, Kay Bonine Johnson, Dick Bonine, Tim Healy, Mike Healy, and Debbie Healy Hammons; and their great-nephews, Pat Healy IV, Ed Healy, and Stuart Healy, Jr.; and great-nieces, Patsy Healy and Nan Healy Schwanfelder.

Let me give special thanks to the Healys I worked with most closely:

My aunt, Helen Healy Bonine, who is blessed with an enviable memory and the patience to sort through her recollections. She told me she treasures these letters and very much wants to share them. Fortunately, Helen made it through diphtheria in 1928 and lives to tell the tales.

My dad, Dan Healy (1915–1993), who compiled a history of the family in a binder booklet. I often referred to his collection of timeline, oral histories, and newspaper clippings for details and context.

My late cousin Diana's daughter, Tara Horvath, who was never too pressed to dig out the most obscure facts despite her own very pressing deadlines as an epidemiology researcher at the University of California, San Francisco Medical School. She and I built a friendship as we picked through details looking for patterns that explained the whys and wherefores of the Healys.

My sister, Debbie Healy Hammons, who cheerfully scrambled to find essential information while commuting monthly from Worland to take a highly competitive master's program in applied positive psychology at the University of Pennsylvania. For several years, Debbie and her husband, Greg, produced historical documentaries about Wyoming. Debbie holds a wealth of knowledge about Wyoming and gave precious time to make a meticulous review of the manuscript.

My cousin, Kay, who shared the letters she received from her mother as well as stories, facts, feelings, and photos. She is the oldest grandchild and knew our grandparents better than any of us—she is the one who shared Edith's love of scouting. Kay copyedited with an eagle eye.

My brother, Mike, who cheerfully shared his grasp of ranching and tracked down rich details, like what kind of evergreens the Healys brought down from the LU to plant around their gravesites. **His wife Sarah** pitched in to track down important, obscure items like the photos of building the Healy cabin in the Big Horns, which Sarah's family has owned and loved for many years.

My second-cousin, once-removed, Patrick Healy IV (the son of my Dad's cousin), who has painstakingly built a Healy family tree in ancestry.com. I am beholden to his family tree and to his cheerful, "Hey, Cath!" whenever I called wanting more. I could always count on his answers.

Tim Healy, my first-cousin, not removed, who, in addition to supplying essential details and corrections, supported my work with his delightful stories. Tim was raised with me in Worland and is, hands down, the consummate storyteller in our family. We both live in DC, and Tim is my close family support. More of Tim's family stories will appear on the website—www.improbable-pioneer.org—like the one about the hot summer day that he and his older brother, Alec, III, were fighting in the car and their dad stopped and made them get out and find enough rocks to build a small tower, a sheepherder's monument to mark where they had stopped fighting.

Meagan Healy, Tim and Susan's daughter, a graphic designer who created the wonderfully evocative maps of Edith's world.

Terrell Harris Dougan, Alec's step-granddaughter, who worked with me to understand and express the relationship between her grandmother and my grandfather. A fellow writer, Terrell made me laugh about her adventures with 120-plus cousins of varying degrees while writing her current book about her great-grandparents.

The late Alex III, and Janet's daughter, Madeleine Healy, who loves the letters and cheered the project on.

Backstage Heroes

Without my editor, **Susan Simmons** (Simmons Writing and Editing, Madison, Wisconsin), *An Improbable Pioneer* wouldn't exist. Edith and Alec's transcribed letters would still be a nagging item on the should-do list. Susan met with me via Skype at least once a week through the entire process, week after week. Even when I was making lots of excuses about having too many other things to do (true), she kept the faith that this book would get done and it would be both interesting and worthwhile. Susan made my writing gleam and the points clear.

The fresh and insightful appearance of the book is due to **Marty Ittner**'s cover art and layout design (m-Art, Takoma Park, Maryland). I appreciated her experience, creativity, and willingness to argue with me even when my mind was (sort of mostly) made up and to endure my dithering when I loved all the choices. She and I had worked together on National Geographic projects.

No one could have been more willing to share his expertise on printing than Tim's brother-in-law, **Jim Rose,** founder and president of Quaker Heron Press. Jim is an expert on print-on-demand and electronic books. Thanks to Jim, a retired senior computer programmer at the Hubble Space Telescope, readers of *An Improbable Pioneer* have options for how they want to read this book.

Digging for Details

Many historical and regional experts responded to my requests and helped support this book's accuracy. Along the way they pointed me towards additional riches and so helped infuse this book with interesting detail. I wish to thank them for their good humor, expertise, and willingness to go the extra distance in search of a fact:

Nancy Jennings, local history and genealogy expert at Johnson County Library in Buffalo. Nancy delivered through snow, sleet, and hail, even going out to the Buffalo graveyard with her camera to track down and photograph the grave of Patsy, Jr., and Mary Healy's son who died at birth, so we had accurate dates. With Nancy, facts become feelings from real lives.

John W. Davis of Worland, Wyoming, attorney and author of *Wyoming Range War: The Infamous Invasion of Johnson County* (2010), *Goodbye, Judge Lynch: The End of the Lawless Era in Wyoming's Big Horn Basin* (2006), and *A Vast Amount of Trouble: A History of the Spring Creek Raid* (2005). A schoolmate and long-time friend, John knows the broad sweep of local history as well as the characters and the telling details. His wife, **Celia Davis**, added her editor's eye to the process, too.

Jerry D. Sanders of Buffalo, Wyoming, educator, outdoor expert, and author of *Bighorn Country: An Introductory Guide* (1987). Jerry knows the Big Horns and loves maps, an unbeatable combination of talents when trying to figure out which trails lead where in the mountains. His late wife, Peggy Sanders, my graduate school housemate, pitched in to help. In one of our last conversations, Peggy pushed me to hurry up and get that book published. I did, but not in time.

David Veile of Veile Mortuary, Worland, Wyoming. David is the third-generation of Veile morticians in Worland, and his father graduated from high school with my father. His family's records span generations of my family. David found answers to all of my questions, even going over to the Washakie County Courthouse Records Office for additional details.

Dennis Koch, circulation manager of Northern Wyoming *Daily News*. Dennis and I spent hours one day reading the Buffalo *Bulletin* online archives, searching for mentions of Edith and Alec. Thanks to Dennis teaching me how to use this resource, I discovered that Edith's mother actually did arrive in Buffalo for a visit. I never knew.

The correctness of detail also is due to **Christine Windheuser**, retired director of World Bank Research, who can look at old mystery photographs and determine dates by the style of the clothing, among her other gifts to this book; **Mary Murray,** freelance genealogist in Salt Lake City; **Greg Nickerson,** WyoFile.com, journalist, and American Studies historian, who was raised in Big Horn, Wyoming, and has studied Wyoming history in depth; **Jim O'Connor,** Worland historian; **Pearl Pearson,** Johnson County abstractor; **Liz Howell,** founder and executive director of the Wyoming Wilderness Society, who knows the Big Horns and whose family were Worland pioneers and friends; and **Jim Magagna,** third-generation sheep rancher in Wyoming's Red Desert and executive vice president of Wyoming Stock Growers Association.

Thanks to **Sam and Phyllis Hampton**, owners of the Hampton Sheep Company, for contributing photos from their family archives.

I called a number of organizations hoping to find someone to help hunt down some stray bit of information. I am awed at the rapid response to my inquiries by: **Sylvia Bruner**, archivist at the Jim Gatchell Museum, Buffalo, Wyoming; **Shaun A. Hayes, Emmett D. Chisum,** and **Burmma L. Hardy,** librarians at American Heritage Collection of the University of Wyoming; **Shelley Spence,** branch manager of First American Title, Worland, Wyoming, who discovered that it was Edith who privately bought the Worland house, not Alec; **Betty Marie Daniels** of the Cody, Wyoming, Girl Scouts, who was good enough to send me one of her few remaining copies of the book she authored, *Something for the Girls in Wyoming* (1977); **Karling Abernathy,** cataloging librarian, Buffalo Bill Historical Center, another graduate school housemate; **Judy Oski,** research librarian at Gloucester Public Library; **Sarah Langsdon**, associate curator of Special Collections, Weber State University; **Nora Murphy** and Myles Cowley, reference staff at Massachusetts Institute of Technology; **Bridget Carr,** archivist for the Boston Symphony Orchestra; **Dr. Metro Voloshin,** curator of music at the Boston Public Library; **Jamie Kingman Rice** of the Maine Historical Society; and freelance historian Andre Grumard in Portland, Maine.

My final thanks goes to **Tom and Mary Mercer** of Hyattville, Wyoming, who helped me track down Karma Feldman of North Barrington, Illinois. Karma Feldman kindly gave permission to use her great-grandmother's oral history archived at the Johnson County Library. Mrs. Jannette Mercer Webb's account of her Fourth of July parties attended by Edith and Alec adds texture to this book's portrait of ranch life during the early 1900s.

Edith and Alec's gifts

In closing, this book has been a goal of mine ever since my dad and I spent those days transcribing the letters left in his and Aunt Helen's care. The lives revealed in Edith's letters captured my interest, and I became fascinated about how a properly-raised Bostonian woman like Edith came to the decision to link her fortunes with Alec, relocate to the West of 1911, and live the life of a rancher's wife. Their choices and lives seem so very much their own.

Edith and Alec lived ordinary lives in an extraordinary way. They worked to make a living, raise a family, and participate in their community. *And* they made vibrant and unique choices along the way. Seeking a degree from MIT and studying to be a violin virtuoso were uncommon, settling in the West rather than Boston was the daring choice, taking on national leadership roles and running for political office show highly active community involvement, adopting when to outsiders their family seemed complete, and traveling for pleasure to uncommon locations for the times all paint a landscape of thoughtful, considered choices made by two people living determinedly uncharted lives.

I see so much of my grandparents in their children and their children's children—wonderful people who live lives of choice rather than default. I end this book very proud of them and proud of this book. Thank you to all who made it possible.

Edith and Alec relax with their son, Dan, on the sunning rock
outside their cabin in the Big Horns, c. 1939.

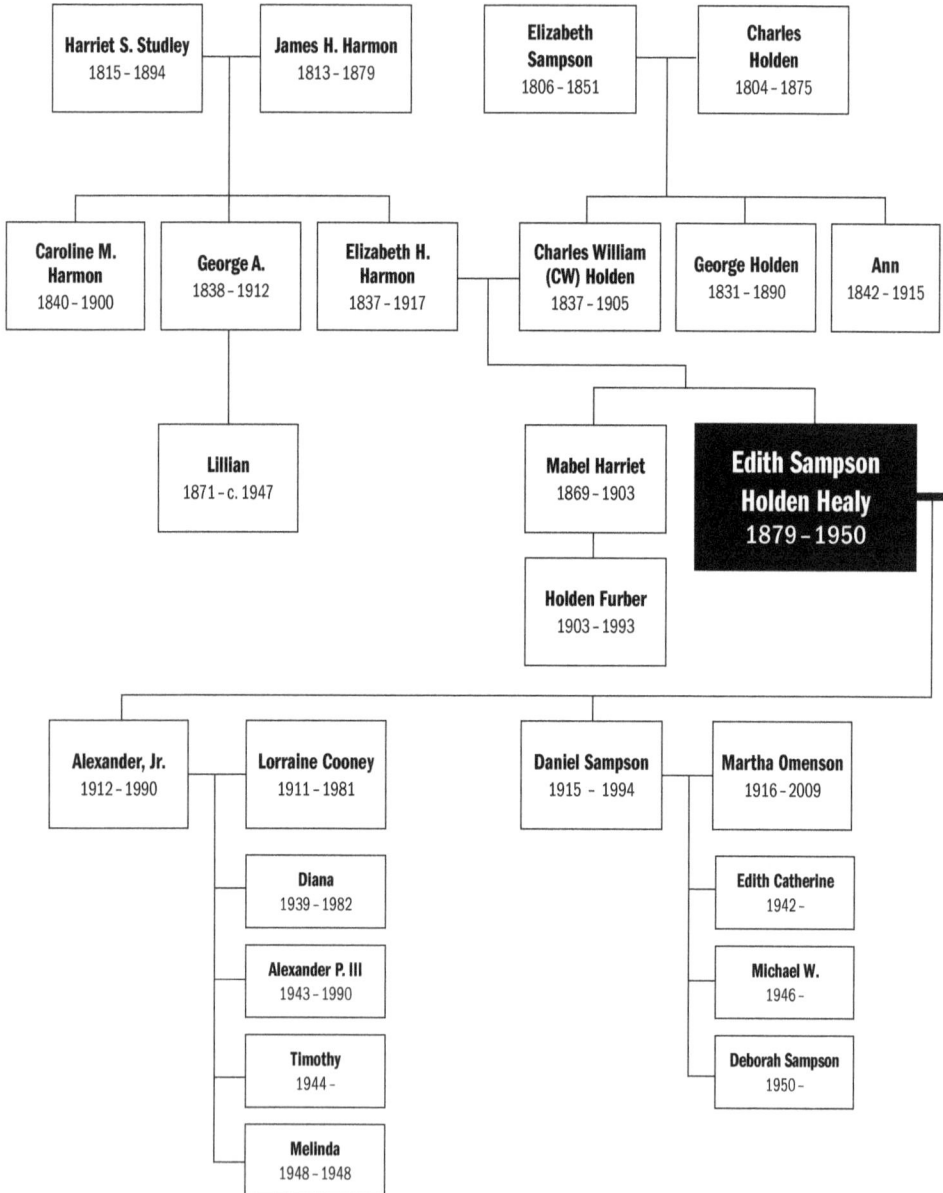

APPENDIX A

```
┌─────────────────┐   ┌─────────────────┐        ┌─────────────────┐   ┌─────────────────┐
│ Harriet S. Studley│   │ James H. Harmon │        │    Elizabeth    │   │     Charles     │
│   1815 – 1894    │   │   1813 – 1879   │        │     Sampson     │   │      Holden     │
│                  │   │                 │        │   1806 – 1851   │   │   1804 – 1875   │
└─────────────────┘   └─────────────────┘        └─────────────────┘   └─────────────────┘
```

| Caroline M. Harmon 1840 – 1900 | George A. 1838 – 1912 | Elizabeth H. Harmon 1837 – 1917 | Charles William (CW) Holden 1837 – 1905 | George Holden 1831 – 1890 | Ann 1842 – 1915 |

| Lillian 1871 – c. 1947 | | Mabel Harriet 1869 – 1903 | **Edith Sampson Holden Healy 1879 – 1950** |

| Holden Furber 1903 – 1993 |

| Alexander, Jr. 1912 – 1990 | Lorraine Cooney 1911 – 1981 | Daniel Sampson 1915 – 1994 | Martha Omenson 1916 – 2009 |

| Diana 1939 – 1982 | Edith Catherine 1942 – |

| Alexander P. III 1943 – 1990 | Michael W. 1946 – |

| Timothy 1944 – | Deborah Sampson 1950 – |

| Melinda 1948 – 1948 |

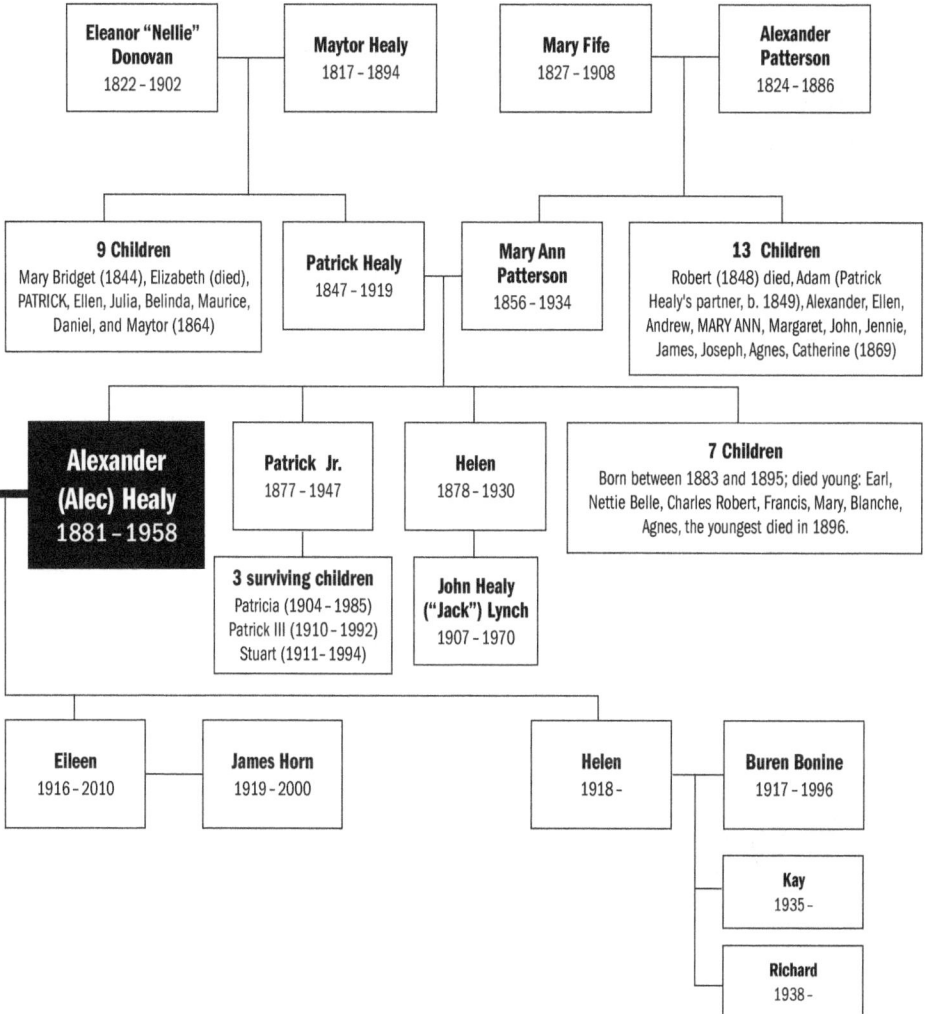

FAMILY TREE

| Eleanor "Nellie" Donovan 1822 - 1902 | Maytor Healy 1817 - 1894 | | Mary Fife 1827 - 1908 | Alexander Patterson 1824 - 1886 |

9 Children
Mary Bridget (1844), Elizabeth (died), PATRICK, Ellen, Julia, Belinda, Maurice, Daniel, and Maytor (1864)

Patrick Healy
1847 - 1919

Mary Ann Patterson
1856 - 1934

13 Children
Robert (1848) died, Adam (Patrick Healy's partner, b. 1849), Alexander, Ellen, Andrew, MARY ANN, Margaret, John, Jennie, James, Joseph, Agnes, Catherine (1869)

Alexander (Alec) Healy
1881 - 1958

Patrick Jr.
1877 - 1947

Helen
1878 - 1930

7 Children
Born between 1883 and 1895; died young: Earl, Nettie Belle, Charles Robert, Francis, Mary, Blanche, Agnes, the youngest died in 1896.

3 surviving children
Patricia (1904 - 1985)
Patrick III (1910 - 1992)
Stuart (1911 - 1994)

John Healy ("Jack") Lynch
1907 - 1970

Eileen
1916 - 2010

James Horn
1919 - 2000

Helen
1918 -

Buren Bonine
1917 - 1996

Kay
1935 -

Richard
1938 -

Edith S. Healy Little House

Top: Alec Healy's memorial gift to the Worland Girl Scouts enabled them
to build a meeting place for their activities. Setting up "Little Houses"
throughout the Big Horn Basin had driven Edith's scouting efforts
throughout the 1940s. Above: City officials, Boy and Girl scouts, and the
Healy family participate in dedication ceremonies April 10, 1952.
Credit: Dave Huber, Washakie Museum.

Appendix B

PETITION FOR WYOMING KIWANIAN
DISTINGUISHED SERVICE AWARD

Mrs. Healy as born and educated in Boston and came west to Buffalo, Wyo., in 1911. In 1922 Mr. and Mrs. Healy moved to Worland, where they have since resided.

For 15 years she was a member of Chapter J, P.E.O. at Buffalo, and is a charter member of Chapter AA, P.E.O. in Worland.

She is a member of the Wyoming Colonial Dames and was formerly the state historian of that organization and is now the state vice president.

She is a member of the Wyoming Wool Growers auxiliary, and has served on the state committee for the "Make It Yourself With Wool" contest, sponsored annually by the association.

Mrs. Healy has traveled extensively and has shared her experiences by giving talks, illustrated with colored films, at many clubs and meetings throughout the Big Horn basin.

She is an active member of the Senior Women's club of Worland. She belongs to the Unitarian church, which has no congregation here, but has given generously of her support to the other churches in the community.

A talented violinist, though out the years she has donated her services on numerous occasions, including the Corn Show Follies for five years. She served on the first Worland Community Concert committee and is still a member of that committee.

The Worland Commercial club in 1941 gave Mrs. Healy its Outstanding Citizen award.

Mrs. Healy's greatest service has been to the girls of the community, state, nation and to other countries through her activities in the Girl Scouts. She has been active in the Girl Scouts since 1925 when the first troop was organized here. She served on the committee that year and has been a member since. She has been given a life membership in the Big Horn basin council of Girl Scouts and is the "Juliette Lowe" of the Big Horn basin. She was first a member of the Rocky Mountain region council until the regions were redivided and when Wyoming was placed in the Covered Wagon Region—which comprises eight states—became director of that region. She has served the allotted two terms, eight years, as director on the national Girl Scout board. In 1937 she attended the International Girl Scout camp in Scotland, and the World Council meeting that year as well.

Mrs. Healy has been presented with honor pins by the Girl Scouts of Guatemala, Brazil and Switzerland and the Girl Guides of Great Britain. She has written a handbook which has been published for the training of leaders of Girl Scouts and Brownies.

Mrs. Healy's activities have not been confined to organizations alone. She has displayed a consistent attitude of interest and helpfulness for individuals which expresses itself in many acts of kindness and encouragement. In addition to all of her outside activities, she and Mr. Healy have raised a family of two boys and two girls and have been all the while actively engaged in the ranching and stock business.

Due to a recent illness she is now retiring from active participation in many of her activities.

Chapter Notes

1   Professor Damian McManus, chairman of Early Irish at Trinity University in Dublin,
     explained by e-mail that Healy in Irish is "Ó hÉilidhe (Ó hÉili and hÉalaí in modern
     spelling). In these the É is pronounced to rhyme with English hail, pale, scale, etc. The
     anglicized pronunciation however is Healy with ea rhyming with peel, real, feel, etc." This
     is not unusual at all, McManus continued. "Some popular Irish names (first or Christian
     names and surnames) are far removed from their original Irish pronunciations because
     they were seen in traditional spelling and pronounced as if they were English… This is
     happening again today in America, where Irish Caitlín (pronounced Catleen in Ireland)
     is pronounced Katelin."
         According to Eugene Haley, Ph.D. in Celtic Studies from Harvard, the Gaelic spell-
     ing is o'Healaighthe. He pronounced it Haley and spelled it Haley. Dr. Haley was with the
     New England Conservatory of Music. Some Healys changed the spelling of their name
     to Haley to match the pronunciation. A studio portrait of Patsy, Sr., taken in Ashland,
     Wisconsin, where his widowed mother lived with his sister, Mary Bridget, and her family,
     had his name written on the back of the print as Patrick Haley. He continued, however, to
     spell his last name the traditional way.

2   Family names can be quite tangled. Alec's older sister, Helen Healy Lynch, born May
     Ellen, was called "Nellie," after her father's mother, Eleanor "Nellie" Healy. However,
     by the time she married, Helen had switched names, perhaps calling herself after her
     mother's mother, Helen Fife, who had immigrated to Utah from Scotland with the Fifes
     and the Pattersons. In her letters, Edith always referred to her sister-in-law as "Helen" and
     she and Alec named their adopted daughter Helen after her.

3   Professor Holden Furber's specialty was the history of the British Empire in the Orient,
     especially the empire's sway in eighteenth century India. It was from these studies that
     Holden developed his pioneering thesis that the expanding frontier of European culture
     interacted similarly with the people of the North American continent and the people of
     the Indian subcontinent.

4   Massachusetts' early settlers often moved to the northern frontier of the state, which
     now is Maine.

5   Edith's grandchildren were raised knowing that the Holdens had been early and strong
     abolitionists against slavery. However, until researching this book, I didn't realize that the
     two Sampson sisters living in Portland, Maine—one was Edith's grandmother—had two
     brothers, Daniel and Henry, who had moved from Boston to Mobile, Alabama, as traders
     in the 1820s. The city on the Gulf of Mexico was booming then, as virgin lands through-
     out Mississippi and Alabama were cultivated with the help of slave labor. Products were
     transported by river to Mobile and hence traded throughout the world. The Sampson
     sisters probably continued to have contact with their brothers, even though Daniel Samp-
     son's last known visit to Boston was in 1840 while their parents were still alive.
         This new information makes the Civil War more personally complex for the Hold-
     ens in Maine than before realized. Daniel and Henry Sampson married in Mobile, raised
     their families there, and remained. In 1865, during the Civil War, the author of *Sampson
     Family in America, From the Arrival of the Mayflower in 1620, to the Present Time*, John Ad-
     ams Vinton, wrote, "There is no reason to doubt his [Daniel] loyalty to the Union and to
     the 'Star-spangled Banner;' while he has always contended for what the Southern people

have regarded as their rights under the Federal Constitution."

This reads: Confederate to me.

Also, I have noticed that neither of Charles and Elizabeth Sampson Holden's sons fought in the war. However, Elizabeth's nephew, Augustus Sampson (George's son and CW's cousin and close friend) joined the Massachusetts Volunteers six weeks after shots were fired in 1861 on Fort Sumter in South Carolina, signaling the start of the Civil War. Augustus served for about eighteen months. He returned home an honorably discharged second lieutenant and disabled by disease.

6   The Holdens in particular were late to marry. CW's grandparents married in 1800 at ages twenty-five and twenty-six (his grandmother was older) and in 1830, his parents married at twenty-six and twenty-four (his mother was younger).

The Holdens also were slow to have babies. Mabel was born born nearly ten years after CW and Elizabeth married when they were 31; Edith was born ten years later.

By the time Edith married Alec, she had only one cousin from either side of her family, Lillian Harmon, whose brother had died before 1911. Likewise, the six children of her father's older brother, George Holden, had died by then. CW's younger sister, Miss Ann Sampson, never married.

7   Even these two local insurance companies, whose offices had been destroyed by Portland's conflagration, made partial payments.

8   Cornelia Metz was Edith's close friend from Basin, which lies thirty miles north of Worland. Cornelia and Edith were both active in Girl Scouts leadership. Mrs. Metz served as chair of the regional Girl Scouts Board while Edith was on the National Board of Directors. The last chapters of the book include letters to Cornelia Metz.

9   Pioneering Utahans' determination to populate their state can be seen in the obituary of Mary Fife Patterson, Alec's grandmother. When Mary died in 1908, the Ogden *Standard* noted that nine of the eighty-one-year-old widow's ten surviving children were with her when she passed away, including Mary Ann Healy (Alec's mother). Noting that Mrs. Patterson had seventy-eight grandchildren and sixty great-grandchildren, the *Standard* praised her, saying, "She had been a useful woman in her long years of life."

10   Maytor and Eleanor Healy arrived in Hancock, Michigan, with six children: Mary Bridget, 18, Patsy, 15, Ellen, 10, Julia, 8, Belinda (Bella), 7, and Daniel, 3. Their last child, Maytor, was born in 1865, three years after they arrived in Hancock.

11   On May 10, 1869, Patsy Healy witnessed the golden spike hammered into place at Promontory Point, Utah, thirty miles west of Ogden. The celebration marked the joining of the Union Pacific and Central Pacific Railroads. With the golden spike set, the United States was connected from ocean to ocean.

12   Alec Healy was the source of that story. He wrote about his father and uncle to Edward N. Wentworth, author of *America's Sheep Trails: History, Personalities*. The original letter is in the University of Wyoming Archives at its American Heritage Center.

13   Support for the camp counselor theory comes from certain dates, her age at the time and the fact that Edith has the 1907 copyright in her name as composer and lyricist to a song called *Wyonegonic* held at the Library of Congress. However, perhaps she simply enjoyed spending vacation time at the camp. According to the journal kept by Holden Furber's aunt, Edith had gone to a camp in July 1902.

14   CW Holden told colleagues at a surprise welcome home party that the trip to California was his first vacation since he started in the insurance business thirty-five years before.

15 Henry Sampson's youngest son, Caleb, married into the Pilgrims' famous love triangle, as relayed in *The Courtship of Miles Standish* by Portland native Henry W. Longfellow. In the epic poem, the widowed Captain Miles Standish felt too shy to press his courtship with Priscilla Mullen, so he sent his aide, John Alden. "Speak for yourself, John," said Priscilla. They married and Miles Standish later married another woman. The Standish's son and the Alden's daughter later wed. It was their daughter, Mercy Standish, who joined the Sampsons, according to the meticulous *Ancestral Tablets* that CW and Elizabeth made for each of their daughters (see also, John Adams Vinton, *The Sampson Family in America*, 1864).

16 CW's mother, Elizabeth Sampson Holden, died a few weeks after *Stag Hound* set sail. George's exploits would have continued to impress her children given that Elizabeth's younger sister, Ann Sampson, carried on living with the Holdens and helped raise her nephews and niece after their mother's death. Several years later, after Charles Holden remarried, his sister-in-law moved to the home of his oldest son, George Holden, to help care for his children. Coincidentally, the Holden's youngest, Ann Holden, also never married, like her Aunt Ann Sampson.

17 Dan's family inherited George Sampson's leather, wood, and brass trunk. Inside, a note written by Aunt Georgie Sampson in January 1911 explains that this is one of five trunks brought by George R. Sampson from China filled with silks for his fiancée in 1836. An additional note from Edith said the trunk was a gift for her to transport her wedding linens.

18 Jennie Furber, Mabel Holden's sister-in-law, was a Wellesley College graduate.

19 Although, Alec traveled many places, he never visited Europe.

20 Dan Healy said that his father never again was in touch with Douglas Fairbanks; that Alec felt their lives had gone separate ways and was comfortable with that.

21 An ongoing difference of opinion never resolved has resulted in different spellings of Big Horn versus Bighorn. Old-timers refer to the river, basin, mountains, and county as Big Horn. The U.S. Geological Survey says on its website that "Bighorn Basin is classified as a Basin in Big Horn County, Wyoming." As an old-timer, I chose to use the Big Horn in all geological instances (except book and film titles), as I was taught.

22 Patsy, Jr. and Mary's oldest child, Patricia, graduated from Miss Mills School in New York, followed by earning an associate degree from Mount Vernon College in Washington DC. Patrick, III, and Stuart both graduated from Loomis School in Windsor, Connecticut, and attended Amherst College in Amherst, Massachusetts. After graduating from Amherst, Patrick, III, attended graduate school in public administration from Syracuse University. Both Amherst and Syracuse awarded him honorary doctorates to mark his work as head of the National League of Cities/U.S. Conference of Mayors, which included strong efforts in the War on Poverty in the 1960s.

23 Wyoming audiences responded with great enthusiasm to nineteenth-century Romanticism's songlike melodies and technical flourishes. Schubert's *Ave Maria* always delighted Edith's audiences, including her grandson, Tim, who remembers playing on the Healys' porch when he was about three and stopping still in amazement to listen to his grandmother playing *Ave Maria*, accompanied by her player piano. Tim went on to graduate with a master's in classical guitar from the New England Conservatory of Music in Boston.

24   Patsy Healy, Sr., invited the first Basque immigrants into the Buffalo area in 1902 to work for him herding sheep. The story goes that Patsy ran into a lonely Joanes (John) Esponda on a train to California. John was on his way to meet his older brother, Jean, a sheepman. Patsy successfully persuaded John to come work for him in Buffalo, and before long, Jean moved there, too. Although Jean returned to France, John remained. He hired many countrymen, often partnering with them to start their own businesses. In time, he was the largest sheep raiser in the region. Today's Basque descendents stage an annual festival in Crazy Woman Square in downtown Buffalo.

25   Percy Metz, the husband of Edith's friend, Cornelia, was appointed a judge at the early age of twenty-nine, in part because of his skill in winning the convictions of the cowmen.

26   W. Harry Furber, an usher, was the widowed husband of Edith's sister.

27   Now called the Organization of American States (OAS).

28   Frank Wheeler Mondell, congressman from Wyoming.

29   The train candy boy sold newspapers, periodicals, and candy. Sometimes called a candy butch.

30   Perhaps the candy boy was referring to Lizzie Borden, who was acquitted of killing her father and step-mother with an ax in 1892 in Falls River, Massachusetts. The trial was one of the most highly publicized in U.S. history and generations later, even in my childhood, girls still skipped rope to this verse: Lizzie Borden took an axe—And gave her mother forty whacks. —When she saw what she had done—She gave her father forty-one.

31   Aunt Georgie is the widow of CW's cousin, Augustus N. Sampson.

32   Troops suffered the second-highest losses of the war at Chickamauga, with 1,657 Union soldiers killed and 2,312 Confederates dead. Only at the Battle at Gettysburg did the armies suffer higher casualties.

33   William Jennings Bryan (1860–1925) was the Democratic candidate for president three times, 1896, 1900, and 1908.

34   The Holdens had traveled by train across Utah on their 1892 winter vacation to California. Remarkably, Edith's grandmother, Harriet Harmon from Portland, Maine, had already ridden the rails to San Francisco four years before.

35   Some people get groggy for the first few days after traveling to a higher altitude. Some discount this claim as folklore, and others consider it a reaction to the thinner air. Buffalo, with an elevation about five thousand feet above sea level—so nearly a mile high—was a much higher altitude than Edith experienced in Boston, whose official elevation is nineteen feet.

36   Emma was a friend of the family close enough to be called "Aunt." The *Dinah* may have been another name for a *housewife* or small, handy sewing kit.

37   Edith's cousin, Lillian Harmon Stone, was the daughter of Mrs. Holden's brother, George Harmon, a jeweler in Portland, Maine. Lillian evidently made it a habit to visit Edith and Alec every year, causing much merriment and a sharing of stories after her departure. Lillian was a hefty woman who collapsed on the sofa causing the springs to rock, the pillows to rise, and her audience to fear for the sofa legs. When she played bridge, she flashed her diamond ring to signal her partner about her card suit strength. Lillian and her husband had no children.

38   Chow chow, a southern relish, consists of chopped vegetables preserved by being pickled in mustard and vinegar. Edith's daughter, Helen, says chow chow is the only thing that Edith knew how to cook when she got married.

39   Edith is referring to their Beacon Street, Boston address.

40   Edith is referring to the bed.

41   Uneeda biscuits were like large, puffy, unsalted saltines. They were the first biscuit made by Nabisco and sold in packages, rather than scooped as bulk items from loosely packed barrels.

42   Known as the Powder River Basin, this region of northeast Wyoming and southeast Montana supplies 40 percent of the U.S. coal today and contains one of the largest low-sulfur coal deposits in the world.

43   Sedgwick, Maine, is a small coastal town about 150 miles north of Portland near what is now the Acadia National Park.

44   Sheep are sheared in late spring when their wool is thickest after the winter. At that point in the nomadic cycle, they are in the lower elevations where they have wintered on range grasses, supplemented when necessary by hay from the irrigated fields along the creeks. Lambs are born a few weeks later, and the herds begin to slowly trail up to the thick grass on the high mountain pastures.

45   These moving pictures were silent films. The usually chatty Buffalo *Bulletin* does not say in the ad for the "Theotorium" what "photoplay" will be shown, only that it will be a good print and will be changed every couple of days. By the way, the first commercial showing of talkies wasn't until 1923 and only for short movies; the first talking feature film, *The Jazz Singer*, wasn't released until 1927.

46   Unitarians believe in the unity (God), not the trinity (Father, Son, and Holy Ghost/Spirit). The New England Unitarian beliefs evolved from the Pilgrims' Congregational parishes.

47   We ended up with Edith's copy of *Molly Make-Believe* (1910) by Eleanor Hallowell Abbott. It's about a man who exchanges letters with an unknown letter writer through an advertisement to relieve his boredom while recovering from an illness. He begins falling in love, which is complicated by not knowing the letter writer and already having a fiancée. My sister, Debbie, and I both loved it. One Christmas Debbie gave me a soft knitted throw blanket, like the one that Molly gave the hero in the book. I still snuggle into it on snowy afternoons.

48   Water boils at a lower temperature in higher elevations because the atmospheric pressure is less than at sea level. In Boston, water boils at 212° F. Up in the sheep camps, water boils at 197° F so it takes longer to cook food.

49   The begats: Edith's grandmother, Harriett Harmon (1815–1894) was the daughter of Harriet Studley Harmon, who named another of her daughters Sarah, a Studley family name. Since Elizabeth Holden was seventy-four when Edith wrote these letters to her, the "Sarah" she is referring to must be a Studley cousin of Elizabeth's or Edith's generation.

50   My father, Dan, and I assumed this was for women's right to vote. Nine more years passed before the Nineteenth Amendment to the U.S. Constitution was passed. In Wyoming Territory, women had already gained the right to vote in 1869.

51   Patsy, Jr., and Alec's heirs who inherited Patsy, Sr.'s mountain property, including Billy's Flat, eventually sold it to Arnaud Auzqui, a Basque American from Buffalo. After Auzqui's two sons, Frank and Paul, inherited the acreage, they dissolved the partnership. Frank sold the western portion, and Paul held on to the eastern portion, toward Buffalo.

52   Crazy Woman Canyon is now one of the scenic drives promoted by the Buffalo Chamber of Commerce. The thrilling drive squeezes through narrow sandstone walls en route to the forests and meadows above. Magnificent!

53   Mount Washington, New Hampshire, is the highest peak in the northeastern United States at 6,288 feet (1,917 meters) and famous for unexpected, dangerous storms, especially in the winter months when winds hit hurricane strength.

54   Mrs. Furber was the mother-in-law of Edith's sister, Maria Louisa Ames Furber.

55   A spider pan is a three-footed, cast iron frying pan.

56   Edith's riding habit made of *crash,* refers to a fabric that was probably stiffened linen.

57   Alec's surveying instrument would cost $8,100 in 2012 dollars.

58   Dan Healy said that out-of-season venison was called *government mutton.*

59   Apparently the Holdens sometimes enjoyed Independence Day celebrations in Gloucester with fireworks, organized picnics, ballgames, and a band concert on July 3. Gloucester, a picturesque deepwater harbor, lies about 40 miles north of Boston. By the time Edith was growing up, Gloucester not only boasted the oldest seaport in the United States, which dominated cod and halibut fishing in the area, but also its oldest art colony. Winslow Homer, the most famous Gloucester artist, first painted the seaport in 1873, six years before Edith was born.

60   Jannette Mercer Webb, the daughter of Wyoming notable Asa Mercer, was raised on the Mercer ranch in Hyattville on the western side of the Big Horns. Asa Mercer, a founder and first president of the University of Washington, became a cause célèbre, when the book he wrote about the Johnson County War, *The Banditti of the Plains, Or the Cattlemen's Invasion of Wyoming in 1892 (The Crowning Infamy of the Ages),* was ordered destroyed by the courts after the Wyoming cattlemen sued and won their case. Later, Mercer's book, which sympathized with the homesteaders, was proven accurate. The book was reprinted in the 1950s by the University of Nebraska Press.

61   The Webb Ranch annual Fourth of July events got their start in 1902.

62   According to family lore, Edith sat first chair in the violin section. We don't know which symphony orchestra, only that it was not the Boston Symphony Orchestra, whose history included only four women players through 1947. The first female violinist, Ikuko Mizuno, joined the orchestra in 1969.

63   Edith obviously used her notes to write this letter, so information and phrases are duplicated.

64   Rest of letter is missing.

65   Letter is missing two pages here.

66   In the 1940s, Edith compared the famous Boston store, Filene's, to Neiman Marcus so that her Western friends understood the fashionable importance of Filene's in the East. One of Edith's classmates at Boston Girls Latin School was the granddaughter of Filene's founder, William Filene.

67   John (known as Jack) was a year younger than his cousin, Patricia. Helen Healy Lynch, Alec's older sister, had traveled from Ogden with her parents to attend Edith and Alec's wedding. By then, her husband, John Connor Lynch, was the manager of the New Healy Hotel, which had been totally gutted, remodelled and reopened that same year, 1911.

68   *Rarebit* is a savory cheese sauce on toast.

69   Five Hundred, a popular card game in the early 1900s, was somewhat like bridge.

70   From Sheridan, they would have taken the train to Ogden. The roads were "terrible, rutted dirt or mud, poor bridges," recalled my father, Dan. He remembered how in 1925, when the family drove to New Mexico on a trip, his mother complained about Alec's heavy foot on the pedal. "Father you're going over thirty-five miles an hour and I can't see anything."

71   Edith is referring to the telephone operator.

72   The town of Buffalo supplied the troops at Fort McKinney on Clear Creek, which was one of several forts built in reaction to the defeat of Custer at the Battle of the Little Big Horn in 1876.

73   *Prairie chickens* are short-tailed birds in the grouse family that average a little over two and a half pounds.

74   The online archives of the Wyoming Newspaper Project are a user-friendly and informative source of information.

75   The Willys-Overland Motors, which ranked second in sales to Ford in the early 20th century, became best known for its military Jeeps during World War II.

76   With this timeline, Edith would have just missed the flood that devastated downtown Buffalo in the early evening of June 11, 1912. Triggered by a cloudburst between the old Fort and the Big Horns to the West, Clear Creek frothed into rapids that rose ten feet above the sidewalks and tore out the bridge over Main Street. The flood killed one person, left about a half million dollars in damages, and required a tremendous community effort to clean up.

77   Daniel Healy, Patsy, Sr.'s brother, owned the most lavish boarding house in Leadville, Colorado, which he lived in with his companion Nellie Healy. The couple couldn't marry in the Catholic church because they were first cousins. Today the former boarding house is the Healy House Museum.

78   Waban is one of the thirteen villages of Newton, Massachusetts, a suburb to the west of Brookline.

79   Mrs. Chase was Edith and Alec's live-in housekeeper.

80   *The Tale of Terrible Towser* as Told by Himself (1914) is the story of a dog's adventures in the country. The illustrator is A. E. Kennedy, but the author remains anonymous.

81   "Boxing darkies" were part of a family of highly successful "talking machine toys" developed and manufactured by National Company out of Boston. They were loosely strung 4 -inch wooden dolls that were attached to the Victrola turntable in a way that caused them to "dance" with the music.

82   The Johnson County Library's stellar local history collection has copies of both the first and second editions of *Buffalo Cookery*.

83   The name was changed by the federal government to Medicine Wheel/Medicine Mountain National Historic Landmark in 2011, in recognition of increased archaeological knowledge about seven thousand years of artifacts showing human habitation in the Big Horn Mountains.

84   It should be noted that the same "of course," reaction reflected Wyoming's expectation about federal response to their proposals.

85   Dr. Grace Raymond Hebard, state regent of the Wyoming DAR, was professor of Political Economy at the University of Wyoming.

86   Current measurements say the Medicine Wheel has an eighty-foot diameter.

87   According to the official history of the flag from Netstate.com, Verna Keays from Buffalo was a recent graduate of the Art Institute of Chicago. Her original design had the bison facing away from the flagstaff, symbolizing the freedom with which the buffalo once roamed Wyoming. Dr. Hebard thought the design "would be more balanced" if the buffalo faced the flagstaff. This version became the state flag.
        The Fourteenth State Legislature adopted the flag design reportedly after teasing one another about changing the buffalo to a donkey or elephant or a moose to represent the political parties. (The moose was the symbol of former President Theodore Roosevelt's independent Bull Moose Party.)

88   Homesteaders received free federal land if they were twenty-one or the head of a family, and lived on the property for at least five years and improved it. Eventually 1.6 million homesteads were granted between 1862 and 1934, a total of 10 percent of all lands in the United States, according to *Wikipedia*.

89   Per Jim Magagna, the shortage of American herders resolved after the war as men returned, particularly Hispanic Americans, and found other jobs not available. Jim, a third-generation sheep rancher out of Rock Springs with a Stanford law degree, also is the executive vice president (director) of the Wyoming Stock Growers Association.

90   During World War I, civilian clothes and some military uniforms were made of *shoddy* wool, that is, old wool or sometimes cotton rags rather than virgin fleeces. Sometimes as much as 50 percent of the "wool" came from rags. Wool was so essential to the war effort that by 1916, the U.S. government ordered that all civilian clothing be made from shoddy wool.

91   Despite the distance—a hundred miles over the mountains—the Healys continued their Buffalo friendships. In fact, Dan's best friend in Buffalo, George Knepper, joined him eight years later at the University of Pennsylvania's Wharton School of Business, where they both were members of the Alpha Tau Omega fraternity.

92   About 150 years earlier, German beet-growing prowess had inspired the German-born Russian Empress Catherine the Great to invite German beet growers to settle a desolate area by the Volga River near the city of Saratov. The settlers were able to keep their own language and live in their own villages and towns. Old-timer Volga Germans in Worland said their lives were again disrupted by the Bolshevik Revolution.

93   The weekly Worland *Grit* on October 9, 1924, recommended "that the voters should give him their loyal support at the polls. Mr. Healy . . . is a businessman with a wide experience and has a level head; he knows the needs of this section better than any other person . . ." Alec won the election on Tuesday, November 4 with 651 votes against his opponent, H. L. Clark.

94   Eileen's and Helen's sister, Jean, raised by a University of Wyoming professor and his wife, was sent to Vassar, but she wanted to major in geology so returned home to complete her studies at one of the top geology schools in the country. Not long after graduation, Jean married her boyfriend from the East, Bill Coolidge, an engineer who worked for General Electric in Schenectady, where they settled.

      Robert's mother, Helen, married her former beau, Mr. Bates, an attorney who became head lawyer for the Metropolitan Life Insurance Company. The Bates's had three more sons. Robert, called Bob, prepped at Choate and graduated from Cornell. He raised his family in Connecticut, where he worked for Sikorsky Aircraft, a global helicopter company.

      In their seventies, all four siblings met again for the first time since they were separated at Eileen and her husband Jim Horn's cabin in the Big Horn Mountains. Eileen and Helen invited my father and mother to join them. Since my sister Debbie and I were home at the time, we were included in this extraordinary experience—in fact, I didn't know my aunts weren't born into my family until then. When we met, Bob was a stranger to me, but Jean looked like Eileen and sounded like Helen. During that first reunion, the blood-related siblings slowly reconnected. For the next seventeen years, the siblings got together annually for a reunion, usually in Wyoming, until Eileen died in 2010 and Jean in 2011.

95   Edith told the girls that she wouldn't give them middle names because when they married, Healy would be their middle name. She explained that having four names was a bother. Edith herself later dropped "Holden" from her name, thereby keeping the ESH initials she always had.

96   Daniels & Fisher Department Store in Denver was located on 16th Street and founded in 1910. The store has been demolished, but the distinctive clock tower still stands and is on the National Register of Historic Places, per *Wikipedia*. The tower used to rise above the city and when driving to Denver from Worland, Wyoming (five hundred miles north), catching sight of the D & F tower signaled you were nearly there.

97   *Little Orphan Annie*, a popular newspaper comic strip, was the favorite of Alec's mother, Mary Ann Healy.

98   The Healys owned a player piano with rolls of classical music that could be inserted and played while Edith practiced her violin.

99   Edith and Alec would have been deeply pleased in 1968 when the Girl Scouts opened their National Center West in the familiar red canyons and pine forests of the Big Horns above Ten Sleep. The purchase totaled 15,400 acres, 640 donated by the U.S. government. Unfortunately, costs to maintain the center became prohibitive and the Girl Scouts sold the land in 1991. In honor of Patrick III, his widow, Martha Ann Dumke Healy, facilitated the purchase of 9,851 acres during the sale for the creation of the Nature Conservancy's Ten Sleep Preserve.

100   Also by luck and foresight, in January 1929, Alec's older brother, Patsy, Jr., sold out his interest in the Commercial Security Bank, which consisted of his Commercial National Bank and the Security State Bank, a consolidation that he had helped oversee in 1925.

101   Dr. Furber's research resulted in a monograph, *The Private Record of an Indian Governor-Generalship: The Correspondence of Sir John Shore, Governor-General, with Henry Dundas, President of the Board of Control,* published by Harvard University Press in 1933.

102   The Dickie was my all-time favorite childhood place. In the 1950s, my best friend, Eleanor Dent (Frank and Dorothy's youngest), and I galloped to the magpie trap, trotted to Dave Dickie's imported marble mausoleum on a high rocky ridge overlooking his domain, and walked, trotted, and loped the long, dusty road for nine miles up Enos Creek to the Dipper, with its fresh spring water and fields of wild iris. I don't think it had changed a bit since 1936.

103   Edith clearly loved music. Edith once told Alec, Jr., that she didn't care for care for jazz. "I remember my father saying that in later years she admitted to an appreciation for jazz," said Tim. "Any reservations might have resulted from a concern about the "wild" life that jazz musicians were reputed to live. I suspect this was more of a concern that my father not get mixed up in a lot of drinking and carousing."

104   Eventually Jack Lynch moved to Honolulu, where he married a Hawaiian. Jack Howell, a Worland friend, was stationed briefly in Honolulu during the war so went to find Jack Lynch. It was easy, Jack Howell said. He asked the headwaiter at a Polynesian-themed restaurant, like Trader Vic's, and the man nodded toward a table. "That's his table. Mr. Lynch will be here in about an hour."

105   Sometime after his divorce, Jack sailed his boat to Papeete, where he married Suzanne Faugerat, a Tahitian pharmacist with Polynesian, English, and French ancestry, who was the daughter of a prominent judge. Jack, 62, died from cancer and is buried with Suzanne and her family in the Faugerat tomb in the Papeete cemetery, an above-ground, open air collection of vaults. The only larger tomb in the cemetery is that of the Tahitian kings Pomare I through IV.

106   Jack's step-son, Narii, took me to the cemetery years ago, along with his wife and their daughter who are direct descendents of Fletcher Christian, famous for leading the mutiny on the *HMS Bounty.* I looked at Narii who learned to love cars from Jack and owned the Honda dealership in Tahiti, and I looked at the small drawer with Jack's name on it and thought: "Jack, you really lived your life!"

107   And, by the way, Jack's step-daughter and Narii's sister, Aiu, had Jack's saddle gleaming with polish on a pedestal by the front door of her elegant home which in the back, featured a dock and a yacht. Alex, Jr., had found the saddle in an LU warehouse and shipped it to his cousin as a relic of good times together.

108 Dr. Holden Furber, a professor of history at the University of Pennsylvania from 1949 to 1973, was widely regarded as a leading published authority on colonial history in South Asia, in particular the trading companies. He published five books: *Henry Dundas, First Viscount Melville*; *The Correspondence of Sir John Shore, Governor General, with Henry Dundas, President of the Board of Control, 1793-1798*; *John Company at Work*; *The Bombay Presidency in the Mid-18th Century*; *Rival Empires of Trade in the Orient 1600-1800*, and co-edited *The Correspondence of Edmund Burke*.

109 The Costa Rican Revolution of 1948 was the last revolution in that country and resulted in a new constitution, which disbanded the military. Although about two thousand people died in the forty-day civil war, the end of the conflict saw no firing squads nor calls for "justice" reprisals.

110 Mrs. Alan H. Means was president of the National Board of Girl Scouts from 1941 to 1945.

111 Lloyd C. Douglas's *The Robe* (1942) is a historical novel about how the robe worn by Jesus during his crucifixion affects the centurion who won it while throwing dice. It was a best seller in the 1940s.

112 Capt. Baird McClellan was killed by a sniper in Germany on April 1, 1945, five weeks before the final surrender. Baird was exceptionally handsome and popular. A University of Wyoming graduate, Dan used to joke that Baird majored in girls. He fell in love with and married a British girl during the war. As far as Edith knew, Dan was still in danger in Italy when the McClellan's received the news about Baird. His British wife delivered a healthy son and, after a brief sojourn in Worland, returned to England where they remained.

113 Rowena Montgomery Coons and her husband, Jerry, were close friends of Edith and Alec. When the children were young, the Healys sometimes drove to Basin for Thanksgiving with Rowena and her husband. The Coons eventually moved to Tulsa.

114 Although Helen can't remember for sure, she thinks that she, Buren, and their children, Kay and Dick, probably were home for Christmas in 1945. Both families usually came back to Worland from the ranch in Montana for a few days over the holidays.

115 *Little houses* were built specifically for Girl Scout troop meetings. Alec completed the fundraising and built the Little House in Worland to honor Edith when she died. It still is called the Edith S. Healy Little House.

116 Name redacted because this is an unsubstantiated, alleged criminal act in a private letter.

117 Glenn Nielson founded the Husky Refining Company in Cody in 1938. Today Husky Energy is a publicly traded Canadian company with extensive petroleum and natural gas reserves in Canada, China, and Indonesia.

118 Every year three generations of families came together from Buffalo, Worland, and other nearby towns to celebrate the Fourth at the Healy cabin near Deer Haven, which the Healys finished building in 1929. The men tossed horseshoes, drank beer, and fished for trout. The women set tables loaded with food and the children sat on a mossy creek inlet and dangled our feet in the icy water. We looked for tiny wild strawberries and spit watermelon seeds at each other.

119 Elk Basin is an oil town in Park County in northern Wyoming. Cody is the county seat.

120 Probably the 1947 film noir classic, *Dead Reckoning*, with Lizabeth Scott.

121 Mildred Mudd (Mrs. Harvey S. Mudd) was president of the National Girl Scout Board from 1939 to 1941. She later supported the founding of Harvey Mudd College, an engineering and science school that is one of the Claremont (CA) Colleges, and one of the most competitive schools in the West. Mudd made his fortune in copper mining in Cyprus.

122 Georgia Gray St. Clair's instincts were right about needing to travel overseas while she could—this was the only time that Georgia ventured out of the United States.

123 From a 2012 interview with Georgia St. Clair. They spent the night in New Orleans before flying south.

124 Dan must have been longing for freedom. He wanted his itinerary for the Latin America trip open, so he and his bachelor buddy, Jim Kelly, could travel when and where they wanted. Edith would have none of that for her son's wife and two young children. One day she marched down from her house on Culbertson Avenue to Dan and Martha's house a block-and-a-half away, and ordered Dan to sit down and write out his itinerary. Without a word, she handed it to my mother and left.

      My mother said this was the only time that Edith interfered in their marriage, which Mother thought remarkable since Edith was "such an organizer."

125 Georgia St. Clair probably was talking to the wife of Teodoro Picado Michalski, who at least officially was president until May 8, 1948.

126 *One Night of Love* (1934) starred Grace Moore, known as the "Tennessee Nightingale" in a bow to Jenny Lind, as a small-town girl trying to break into the world of opera. It won or was nominated for four Academy Awards, including a best actress nomination for Grace Moore.

127 Helen Brome was a prominent woman in Basin.

128 Edith's daughter, Helen, and her daughter Kay, have all been members of PEO, which emphasizes educational opportunities for female students. Kay graduated from Cottey College, a two-year women's college in Nevada, Missouri, which is a one of PEO's major projects.

129 Dr. John H. Tilden (1851–1940), a graduate of the Eclectic Medical Institute, Cincinnati, Ohio, opened his practice in Denver in 1890. Tilden's research led to a new theory of disease as caused by the increase of toxins in the blood. His cleansing diet is not dissimilar to some modern diets. Harvey and Marilyn Diamond, for example, claim Tilden as an inspiration for their best-selling book *Fit for Life*, first published in 1985. To follow Tilden's diet, one ate starches and vegetables or meat and vegetables, but no pairing of meat and starches at the same meal. The Healys each had a serving dish of salad as well as al dente vegetables for dinner every night. Butter was allowed on the vegetables, but no cream or cheese sauces.

130 Dorothy Dent, a retired nurse, was the wife of a sheep broker who shared an office with Alec, and a close friend of Edith's. Her youngest daughter, Eleanor Gaye, was my best friend, even though she was a year older. I briefly was married to her husband, Don Kuester's younger brother David.

131 During World War II, when my father was overseas in Italy, my mother and I lived with my grandmother, Catherine Omenson, at the Plaza Hotel in Hot Springs State Park in Thermopolis, with my grandfather, Bill Omenson, easily available at his hotel, the Carter, across the street.

132 Maxine Knoefel was Lorraine and Alec, Jr.'s next door neighbor.

133 Elizabeth Furber also was an historian; her doctorate was in medieval French history.

134 In Edith's letters she sometimes spells Alec, Jr.'s name Alec, with a "c" and sometimes Alex, with an "x."

135 The Beaver Block, in what now is the revitalized Old Port district in Portland, Maine, was part of the Holden family inheritance dating back to 1835, their half of the property split equally between Edith and Holden, her deceased sister's son. The Beaver Block was a four-story department store on Congress Street and had a view of the harbor from the top floors. It was built on the site of a farm, supposedly over the spring that nourished the farmhouse.

136 Deborah Sampson Healy Hammons was born on November 27, 1950, in Worland, where she and her husband, Greg Hammons, continue to live.

137 Edith is referring to young Lochinvar in Sir Walter Scott's epic poem, *Marmion.*

138 Full quote from Ralph Waldo Emerson is, "Spiritual force is stronger than material force; thoughts rule the world."

139 Terrell's book about life with a younger sister with the mind and emotions of a three-year-old was published in 2009 by Hyperion to four-star reviews on Amazon.

140 I don't remember what software program my dad and I were using, but the first set of typed letters is on faint dot-matrix printer paper. The computer and printer were courtesy of my father. Dad wanted so badly to achieve a better analysis of the LU Ranch data that he created a data-processing business in Worland with the then three-area banks so as to afford the rental on an IBM computer in the mid-1960s. IBM told Dad he was the first rancher to computerize, meaning the LU was the first ranch in the world to computerize.

141 Dan Healy and my late sister-in-law, Jean Bailey Healy, were founders of the Washakie Museum and Cultural Center. Two others who helped me in my research, Georgia Gray St. Clair and the late Dorothy Froyd, were also founders. Dorothy's daughter, Sarah Froyd Healy, has served as president of the museum's board and is married to my brother, Mike.

142 One time when I was complaining about this to my step-cousin, Terrell Harris Dougan, she just laughed. She is calling the current book she's writing about her Mormon great-grandfather and his three wives historical fiction. As Terrell pointed out to me, "I have more than 120 first cousins, second cousins, and second cousins once-removed, and they all believe that they have the true story . . . but of course, I have it." Terrell is known for her humor.

INDEX

Cathy Healy, fourth-generation Wyoming advocate, crossed the mountains to see the world as journalist, novelist, magazine editor, and online producer and always returns home.

Cathy is a former editor of Organization of American States' *Américas* magazine and National Geographic's award-winning intranet. She is currently vice president of LU Ranch (Worland, Wyoming) and advisory board member of the International Education and Resource Network (iEARN)-USA, University of Wyoming College of Agriculture and Natural Resources, and World Comes to Wyoming Fund, of which she is the founder.

After Geographic, her life-changing Reuters Digital Vision Fellowship at Stanford University has led to many new adventures, including working with Cèsar Chavez Preparatory Charter School in DC on international outreach, lecturing to worldwide audiences about opening borders with digital storytelling, and TEDx presentations. Her current emphasis is on how students can use video stories to gain deeper understanding of others and other cultures.

Cathy has traveled for work and pleasure to fifty-two countries and savors hosting friends and family in her Washington DC home. *An Improbable Pioneer* is the culmination of her and her father's vision while working together to transcribe his mother's letters some years ago. This is Cathy's third published book.

Photo: David Evans

The Washakie Museum and Cultural Center brings the past to life through exhibits that portray the relationship between the historical people of the Big Horn Basin and their environment. The unique geography of the Big Horn Basin and its world-class archaeological sites allow the Museum to offer one of the finest interpretive centers for local human history, from ancient mammoth hunters through early settlers, as well as the geology, archaeology, and paleontology of the area.

The Museum is creating a series of books under a proposed Legacy Collection to foster preservation of family archives. *An Improbable Pioneer* is the first book in the series and should serve as an encouragement to other families to record their histories.

Washakie Museum & Cultural Center
Legacy Collection

WORLAND, WYOMING

www.washakiemuseum.org

www.ingramcontent.com/pod-product-compliance
Lightning Source LLC
Chambersburg PA
CBHW030909090426
42737CB00007B/139